Writers of Italy Series

General Editor
C.P. Brand
Professor of Italian
University of
Edinburgh

5

UNGARETTI

© Frederic J. Jones 1977
Edinburgh University Press
22 George Square, Edinburgh

ISBN 85224 299 9

Printed in Great Britain by
W & J Mackay Limited, Chatham

*

Edinburgh University Press

Giuseppe
UNGARETTI

Poet and Critic

FREDERIC J. JONES

*

Contents

Preface

Ungaretti's poetry has not so far attracted a great deal of attention in Anglo-Saxon countries and, apart from a short study by Glauco Cambon in 1967 (almost a prelude to his more recent and more extensive one in Italian), no large-scale examination of his work has yet been undertaken in English. Oddly enough, he has also suffered from a dearth of translators, and so it was not until 1958 that the first significant translation of his poems, Mandelbaum's *Life of a Man*, appeared simultaneously in London, New York and Milan. This was followed by P. Creagh's *Giuseppe Ungaretti: Selected Poems* in the Penguin edition in 1969; but neither of these works claims to be complete, and the same can be said of Mandelbaum's enlarged reprint of his original edition in 1975. Ungaretti's apparent neglect, however, is not very surprising for two particularly cogent reasons: first, because he is a hermetic poet who works by allusion rather than by direct statement and for that very reason proves to be a difficult author to translate; and second, because his lyrical ethos is more closely attuned to the French than to the Anglo-Saxon muse. Indeed, whereas his lyrics can often be turned quite neatly into French, the English language seems to possess the wrong type of keyboard to reflect adequately the allusive overtones and cultural resonances implicit in his melodic line. In this respect he differs widely from his well-known contemporary Montale whose work is, if anything, orientated in the opposite direction and who has found a number of translators willing to undertake the considerable risk of putting him into English. By contrast, even the critic feels himself at a loss at times when trying to render in acceptable English the subtleties of Ungaretti's aesthetic theories, so that it is hardly surprising that the task of the translator seems to border on the impossible.

The translations given in this book will consequently be literal rather than ambitiously poetic in style, because Ungaretti's substance is at least as important as his form and there is a danger that content will be unduly sacrificed in the pursuit of any too exacting lyrical resonances. Yet, in fact, even a literal translation is not always possible with a poet who is constantly straining to extend the bounds of expressibility in his own language. Moreover, since his prosody does not usually conform to fixed classical patterns but aims to reproduce, in the first place, a Leopardian 'ritmo analogo ai sentimenti' [rhythm analogous to feeling], and, in the second, Baudelaire's 'soubresauts de la conscience' [pangs of conscience], I have felt it necessary to indicate the varying lengths of his lines by introducing oblique bars in the appropriate places in the English translations. The device does not, admittedly, always convey the same rhythm as that to be found in the original Italian, but it does suggest an approximation to the same formal structures; and on the whole this has been achieved without doing too much violence to English syntax. Probably the reason why it has proved possible at all is that Ungaretti's rhythmical effects (except in a few early poems) normally tend to follow syntagmatic patterns, a fact which also makes the task of the translator much easier, except on the rare occasions when a violent baroque inversion of Italian syntax demands radical readjustments in word order.

Although the scholarship of this book has inevitably leaned heavily on previous Italian sources, an attempt has been made to provide for Ungaretti a new and coherent lyrical perspective, through the close analysis of symbolic patterns both within and between his collections of verse. Furthermore, his aesthetics has been examined in the second chapter against the background of his critical views, as a prelude to a consideration of his poetic texts. This was an extremely difficult task to undertake before the publication of his collected essays in 1974, and even now the important lectures he gave during his University career are still not available.

Footnotes in the body of the work have been reduced to a minimum, but references to authors and works can quickly be tracked down in the bibliography. All quotations, except where otherwise indicated, are taken from the Mondadori editions of Ungaretti's collected works but, since the various reprints of these works differ slightly among themselves, page references will be made to the sixth edition (1972) of *Tutte le poesie* and to the first edition (1974) of *Saggi e interventi*.

My thanks are due to my two colleagues, Mr B.J. Morse and Dr S. Gamberini, at University College, Cardiff for reading the typescript and offering many valuable suggestions. Likewise I am indebted to Professor Piero Bigongiari for information concerning one of Ungaretti's poems, and to the general editor, Professor C.P. Brand, for his considerable efforts in helping me to express the subtleties of hermetic criticism in acceptable English. I need hardly add, however, that all errors of fact or interpretation are my own responsibility.

Much of the research on which this book is based has been financed by travel grants provided over the years by University College, Cardiff, while certain last-minute corrections of perspective and the updating of information have been made possible by the award of a Leverhulme Fellowship permitting me to undertake a prolonged stay in Florence.

F.J.J. *Florence, April 1976.*

ACKNOWLEDGMENT
The Edinburgh University Press is grateful to Arnoldo Mondadori for permission to reproduce extracts from Ungaretti's works.

1. Ungaretti's Life and Cultural Background

Giuseppe Ungaretti was born in Alexandria in Egypt on 8 February 1888. At that period the town had not yet been europeanized by the English and still possessed the fabulous tones and garish colours of an oriental city. But, as time passed and the atmosphere changed, the poet's Alexandrian childhood seemed to him to have receded into a distant, suspended dreamworld, though one which he continued to recapture sporadically throughout his entire life. Indeed, its magical impact can still be detected in a poem written as late as 1932, following a short visit he made to the city in the previous year:

> Ti vidi, Alessandria,
> Friabile sulle tue basi spettrali
> Diventarmi ricordo
> In un abbraccio sospeso di lumi. (*Tutte le poesie*, 161)
> [I saw you, Alexandria, / crumbling on your spectral foundations / becoming for me a memory / in a suspended embrace of lights.]

This skeletal, but persuasively oriental, perspective was soon destined to serve as an important undertone in much of his lyricism. Admittedly, it always remained an undertone subservient to his otherwise European tastes and themes; yet it appears on occasion to have provoked almost visceral effects. So much so that it offered to his senses and imagination the promise of a terrestrial paradise by way of a mysterious regression through the blood to the primitive innocence of a perennial childhood, a vision which was by no means entirely lost even in the verse of his maturity.

As a counterweight to this suspended dreamworld and the instinctive pull of the East we also find in Ungaretti's early lyrical attitudes an atavistic attraction for Italian culture, as he gazes out over the sea from the Egyptian port to his, as yet, unvisited nativeland across the Mediterranean. Consequently, when he first caught sight of the Italian coast in 1912, he describes the experience in highly emotional terms:

> Mi destavi nel sangue ogni tua età,

M'apparivi tenace, umana, libera
E sulla terra il vivere piú bello; (*Poesie*, 162)
[You awakened in my blood all your ages, / you appeared to
me tenacious, human, free / and on earth the finest form of
living]

so, in view of these two counterbalancing tendencies, we are eventually forced to conclude that the subtle combination of their clearly
superimposed and elemental inscapes was mainly responsible for the
fashioning of his sensitivity as a poet.

Ungaretti was the younger son of Antonio Ungaretti and Maria
Lunardini, both of whom were natives of Lucca. At his birth they
had already had a first child, Costantino, born some eight years
previously. The boys' father had originally emigrated to Egypt to
seek employment with the contractors digging the Suez Canal and,
by the eighties, an accident at work, together with the very harsh
nature of his employment, had so undermined his health that he died
an agonizing death of dropsy and gangrene when Giuseppe was
only two years old. Still, even after his death his widow and her
children continued to live in the same distant suburb (Moharrem
Bey) of Alexandria on the edge of the desert as they did during his
lifetime, and the poet describes their house graphically in *Il deserto
e dopo* [The desert and after] (1961) as 'una baracca con la corte e le
galline, l'orto e tre piante di fichi fatte venire dalla campagna di
Lucca' (66) [a shack with a courtyard and chickens, and a garden
with three fig-trees brought there from the Lucchese countryside].
As a baby, Ungaretti was wet-nursed by a Sudanese woman called
Bahita or Jasmina, whom he recalls briefly in a poem entitled 'Le
suppliche' [Entreaties] published in *Lacerba* in 1915. In this lyric we
again note the very intensity of his feelings for the oriental life of his
infancy and its violent sensations. These were instilled into him, or so
he claims, through his very nurse's milk:

Balia sudanese che m'ha allevato
il sole che l'aveva bruciata le ho succhiato.
[The Sudanese wet-nurse who weaned me / the sun which had
burned her I sucked from her.]

In his later childhood, however, he was brought up by his mother's
maid and companion, Anna, who was a Croatian woman from the
Bocche di Cattaro. She apparently possessed a very vivid imagination and a gift for story-telling, and from her he says he soon received 'molte idee favolose' [many fabulous ideas], drawn both
from European and from Arab folk-lore. Her influence seems to have

been a predominant one on his mind until his schooldays, and so perhaps it is to her that we owe that subtle intrusion of oriental imagery which, in his early poetry especially, Ungaretti freely intersperses with his more overt European perspectives.

The school which the poet attended until 1905 was the École Suisse Jacot, one of the best known in the town. Instruction was given in French and from this period we can date the poet's close familiarity with the French language which he both spoke and wrote fluently up to the time of his death. During his school career he tells us that he made his first literary discoveries, reading Leopardi and Baudelaire, Mallarmé and Nietzsche. From 1906 on he also acquired his first literary acquaintances, among whom were his schoolfriend Moammed Sceab, the Thuile brothers, and more especially the novelist Enrico Pea who in his book *Vita in Egitto* [Life in Egypt] (1949) has also written extensively of the Alexandrian middle-class life at the time and of his friendship with Ungaretti.

Despite the poet's slightly disparaging description of his mother's house, we soon discover that she was by no means a poor woman. She owned an important bakery in the district which was much frequented by the European population and she also proved over the years to be an excellent business woman. Although she was herself pious and strictly orthodox in religious matters, she nevertheless showed tolerance and understanding towards her children's guests. Indeed, this tolerance must have been stretched almost to breaking point at times, especially after Giuseppe had struck up his friendship with Enrico Pea. The latter lived in a two-storied wooden house known as 'la baracca rossa' [the red shack]. This house served not only as a dwelling-place but also as a warehouse for storing wood and marble and as a meeting-place for anarchists, atheists and refugees, all friends of the young Pea. Needless to say, these dubious characters quickly invaded the Ungaretti household as well, appearing there in the company of one or the other of the sons, both of whom at the time were undergoing a period of rebellion against the somewhat oppressive and inward-looking atmosphere of their home.

In his youth, therefore, the poet was considered as something of a freethinker, and Piccioni (*Vita di un poeta*, 15) tells us that when his mother called upon the services of a capuchin monk in the hope of reconverting him, he put an abrupt end to his endeavours by trying to set fire to his beard. Even so, his early life was involved much more with the rich variety of oriental myths and sensations than

with religious problems, and these lively impressions no doubt
stimulated his frequent excursions to the desert around the town.
Desert scenes were soon to become one of the favourite backgrounds
to his poetry, and later on he claims that even his baroque cast of
mind was largely the result of the accident of his Egyptian birth. In
an interview on the subject with Denis Roche in 1965 he reflects
that the 'illusion continuelle' which the desert tended to inspire was
the inevitable product of

> le hasard qui m'a fait naître à Alexandrie, c'est-à-dire en
> Egypte ... L'Egypte est un oasis. En somme l'Egypte appartient
> au désert ... puis enfin c'est le désert ... Eh bien le désert donne
> un sentiment du néant, le sentiment de l'infini ... et en même
> temps le sentiment du mirage, n'est-ce pas ? Il vous donne des
> mirages qui sortent pour ainsi dire du néant, qui est en même
> temps l'infini ... Ce qui n'existe plus ... le mirage ... l'illusion sort
> de là, l'illusion comme une sorte de réalité sans matière, plus pure.
> Cette présence des fantômes dans ma poésie est sans doute due
> à mon origine dans la vie.
>
> [the pure chance which caused me to be born in Alexandria,
> that is, in Egypt. Egypt is an oasis. Egypt belongs to the desert ...
> indeed, in the end, it is the desert ... Well then, the desert gives
> one the sense of nothingness, the sense of the infinite ... and, at
> the same time, a feeling for mirages, does it not ? It provides one
> with mirages which arise as it were out of the void, which is
> simultaneously the infinite ... What no longer exists ... the
> mirage ... that is where the illusion springs from, the illusion
> as a kind of dematerialized reality, a purer form. This presence
> of phantoms in my poetry is doubtless due to my origins in
> life.][1]

By way of descriptions of this type the poet slowly imparts to
desert scenes a kind of strange mythological status: they almost
become perennially suspended landscapes in his memory, which
even in his childhood he had already evolved into a dream-reality,
into a series of hallucinatory presences, resulting from a truly orphic
'dédoublement de la conscience'. We can clearly see the process at
work in the following evocation dealing with his early excursions
to visit the Thuile family at Mecs:

> Qui e lí, nella sabbia, pozze d'acqua salmastra, tonde, occhi
> senza luce, non piú larghe d'una bracciata, d'un colore verde
> bottiglia bianchiccio. E ogni tanto spuntavano ancora dalla
> sabbia mulini a vento, con le ali disfatte piene di pipistrelli.

C'era, e c'è, da quelle parti, un'antica necropoli; l'archeologia
non c'era andata ancora a frugare; e qualche volta potevo
vedere i ragazzini indigeni tirarsi, invece di sassi, tibie e teschi.
(*Il deserto*, 71-2)
[Here and there, in the sand, pools of salt water, circular, like
eyes without light, no broader than an arm's length, of a whitish,
bottle-green hue. And every so often wind-mills still sprang up
from the sand, with their sails broken-down and full of bats.
There was, and still is, in those parts, an ancient necropolis;
the archeologists had not yet gone to rummage there; and
sometimes I could see the native children pelting each other not
with stones but with tibias and skulls.]
   To this type of effect are to be added his graphic pictures of the
bedouin, with 'l'occhio esorbitato, la lingua di fuori secca, (che) non
sapevano come salvarsi dalla loro condizione di rantolanti' (*Poesie*, 502)
[protruding eyes, their tongues dry and hanging out (who) did not
know how to save themselves from their condition as death-
rattlers]; or, even more forcefully, the wider hallucinatory effects
he himself experienced in the open desert, where the shimmering of
the sand reduced the landscape to nothing more than the merest
contours of external reality, and where he, too, could feel himself
sinking into a state of suspended, memorial existence and timeless
mystery:
Il sole già cade a piombo; tutto ora è sospeso e turbato; ogni
moto è coperto, ogni rumore soffocato. Non è un'ora d'ombra,
né un'ora di luce. È l'ora della monotonia estrema. Questa è
l'ora cieca; questa è l'ora di notte del deserto. Non si distinguono
piú le rocce tarlate, tigna biancastra fra la sabbia. Le fini ondu-
lazioni della sabbia anch'esse sono naufragate nella fitta trama
dei raggi che battono uguali da tutte le parti. Non c'è piú né
cielo, né terra. Tutto ha un rovente ed eguale colore giallo grigio,
nel quale vi muovete a stento, ma come dentro a una nube. Ah!
se non fosse quella frustata che dalla pianta dei piedi vi scioglie
il sangue in una canzone, rauca, malinconica, maledetta, direste
che questo è il nulla. Essa entra nel sangue come l'esperienza di
questa luce assoluta che si logora sull'aridità. (*Il deserto*, 84)
[The sun was already plummeting down; everything was now
suspended and disturbed; every movement was covert, every
sound stifled. It was neither an hour of shadow nor of light. It
was a moment of extreme listlessness. This is indeed the blind
hour, this is the nocturnal hour in the desert. One can no longer

make out the moth-eaten rocks, whitish ringworms among the
sand. The fine undulations of the sand-dunes themselves are
drowned in the dense pattern of rays which beat down equally
in all directions. There is no longer a heaven or an earth. Everything has a burning and similar yellowish-grey colour, in which
one moves with difficulty, but as though within a cloud. Ah!
were it not for that whiplash which from the soles of the feet
dissolves your blood into a raucous, melancholy and accursed
singing, you would say that this is the void. It invades the blood
like the experience of an overwhelming light that wears itself
away within these wastes.]

Such phantomatic scenes (even though recaptured, as they are
here, at a much later date) remind us of the orphic poet Campana
who delighted in presenting to his readers what he called his 'panorama scheletrico del mondo' [skeletal panorama of the world]. His
aim was much the same as Ungaretti's was to be later, to delineate
the rhythm behind the flux of life by depicting essential contours
rather than substantive forms; and, this being so, it shows that
Ungaretti's lyrical manner was already beginning to crystallize
spiritually and imaginatively, if not yet perhaps intellectually or
conceptually, long before he left Egypt in 1912 to complete his
education in France. Unlike his brother Costantino who married an
Englishwoman and settled down in Alexandria, Giuseppe constantly
felt the urge to commune more closely with his distantly perceived
European culture. So, although some of his deepest metaphysical
experiences had already been acquired in the desert, his lyrical
themes tend, as previously indicated, to be preponderantly European
in origin. Nevertheless the haunting, yet slowly receding, myths of
the East were to remain with him throughout his entire life as part
and parcel of his inner personality; and they emerge and re-emerge
in his verse, as if from the haze of a dream, like the outlines of an
innocent, half-forgotten, though richly endowed, paradise of the
senses. What is more, their constant epiphanies are closely associated
with the figure of the bedouin who symbolizes for Ungaretti the
modern Everyman in his quest for spiritual fulfilment, yet who
always carries around with him the stiflingly sensuous atmosphere of
the desert wherever he goes.

As he set out for France in 1912 Ungaretti must have felt that he
too was a carefree wanderer, very much like the bedouin tribesmen
he had seen at home in the desert around Alexandria. But his description in 'Levante' [The East] in *Allegria* of his journey to Europe,

when he sits aloof in the bow of the ship while others are dancing in the stern, clearly shows that he also retained the bedouin's sense of detachment and wariness. Like him he cherished his freedom above all else and constantly asserted his sense of liberty and space, while at the same time he felt himself to be the secret repository of a time-hallowed tradition. His sea-voyage took him first to Brindisi; then he travelled briefly to Florence where he had promised to deposit Pea's book *Spaventacchio* [Scarecrow] with his publisher, and finally on to Paris. Only after the first World War did he take up permanent residence in Italy and he did not return to Egypt again until 1931. In 1929, however, his mother – then in her eightieth year – came to see him in Rome during the Jubilee of Pope Pius XI, and no doubt this visit rekindled once more in his mind the distant pageantry of the East and eventually inspired him with a longing to re-immerse himself in its magical atmospheres.

Ungaretti's deep interest in European culture, by contrast, derives from his friendship with Pea and his group which dated from his early youth in Alexandria in 1906. Even before setting out for Paris he had corresponded with various Italian literary figures, including Giuseppe Prezzolini, while he claimed equally to be an avid reader of *Le Mercure de France* and of *La Voce*. There are reasons for believing that he also read Marinetti's periodical *La poesia* at that time; but, although Marinetti was a fellow-Alexandrian by birth, Ungaretti was not destined to meet him until he arrived in Europe. Nevertheless, his connection with the ferment surrounding the birth of futurism is partially indicated by his request to Prezzolini for a copy of Gian Pietro Lucini's book, *Il verso libero* (1908). It is also known that he wrote a review of Lucini's *Revolverate* in *Il Messaggero Egiziano*, while Giuseppe Palermo has recently referred to various contributions in Egyptian-based periodicals, indicating quite a copious output and including reviews of Pea's early writings.[2] Moreover, to these largely Italian influences must be added his particular enthusiasm for modern French culture which he had first acquired at school and which was to reach its climax during his University days in Paris.

When Ungaretti finally reached the French capital, he already had a number of friends there. Among these was Moammed Sceab whose subsequent suicide prompted one of his most touching early poems, 'In memoria' [In memoriam]. Sceab may perhaps be regarded as the complete foil to the young Ungaretti at this stage, since his inability to adapt to French customs, his apparent lack of 'disponibilità' or receptiveness to life, contrasts with the poet's own continual hunger for new experiences and his undoubted ability to absorb them into his already consolidated Arabo-Italian sensibility. So, whereas Sceab only manifests one aspect of the bedouin's character, his atavistic yearning for his racial culture without which he feels himself lost, Ungaretti reveals all his main features in a state of equilibrium, especially his intense desire to live accompanied by an equally powerful ability to assimilate new experiences into the fabric of traditional values.

In view of this precocious maturity of his literary sensibility, it is perhaps surprising to learn that the poet first registered in the Sorbonne as a law student, no doubt with an eye to the possibilities of future employment. But almost from the outset he preferred to attend lectures on literature and philosophy, and his acknowledged masters were Henri Bergson, Joseph Bédier, Gustave Lanson and Fortunat Strowski. Under Strowski he apparently wrote a short thesis on Maurice de Guérin's prose poem 'Le centaure', and it is perhaps from this somewhat minor nineteenth-century poet that he drew his orphic cult of night and his conception of the reconditioning of ancient myth. Even so, Bergson represented his most particular interest, because his intuitionalism helped to resolve a problem which had already vexed Ungaretti's rapidly developing sensibility: the problem of how to revivify the outworn poetic word in the Italian tradition and make it again flesh of the poet's flesh. Indeed, in an article written on the French philosopher as early as 1924,[3] he tells us that what attracted him above all was Bergson's ability 'd'infonder vita alla parola profferita' [to instil life into the spoken word], thereby 'lasciando al termine del discorso il lettore, avido di certezza, pieno di sgomento' [leaving the reader at the end of his discourse avid for certainty and full of awe].

Probably, as Rebay among others has pointed out, Charles Baudelaire, Arthur Rimbaud and Stéphane Mallarmé (and to a lesser extent Guillaume Apollinaire whom Ungaretti knew personally) are the most important French influences in the lyrical field, although he was also acquainted with the works of Blaise Cendrars, Max Jacob, Pierre Reverdy, Philippe Soupault and André Salmon, to mention only a few among contemporary poets; while among the avant-garde painters of the period he counted as his friends such figures as Fernand Léger, Robert Delaunay, Pablo Picasso and Georges Braque, together with the Italians, Giorgio De Chirico,

Carlo Carrà and Amedeo Modigliani. At this point, indeed, it is necessary to make a short digression from a strictly factual account of his life because we find that his whole outlook comprised a subtle blending of his dreams and sensations of childhood in Egypt with the purely literary impressions he acquired from the French symbolist and decadent poets. These can be brought fully into focus as a form of 'simultaneità delle sensazioni' [simultaneity of sensations] by reference to some of his early lyrics.

From Baudelaire he may have acquired a certain intense sensuality of tone and, more significantly, a baroque 'culte du laid' [cult of the ugly] which produces the grotesque distortions of some of his war poetry. The lyric 'Veglia' [Vigil] (1915), which was not afterwards subjected to any of Ungaretti's periodic revisions, is an authentic example of this type of early writing:

Un'intera nottata
buttato vicino
a un compagno
massacrato
con la sua bocca
digrignata
volta al plenilunio
con la congestione
delle sue mani
penetrata
nel mio silenzio
ho scritto
lettere piene d'amore
[A whole night / flung beside / a slaughtered / friend / with his mouth / clenched / turned to the new moon / with the congestion / of his hands / penetrating deep / in my silence / I have written / letters full of love.]

Even so, the mainstream of Ungaretti's inspiration relies neither on the element of 'bas romantisme' in Baudelaire's work nor on the visionary fragmentation of the real world implicit in Rimbaud's 'dérèglement de tous les sens' [dislocation of all the senses]; although the kind of orphic climate which these two writers and later Mallarmé were to create in their writings seems to have been integrated by him at an early stage into the shimmering ethereality of his own sun-drenched desert landscapes. However, whereas the symbolists saw the real and the ideal worlds *sequentially* and aspired to pass from the one to the other through a cult of dazzling analogies,

Ungaretti saw the real and the historical worlds *simultaneously*, as a modern 'bifocal' orphic perspective. What we mean by orphic perspective in this context is not quite the kind of vision advocated by the ancient orphic adepts. They believed that the human soul was recycled through a series of reincarnations until it was sufficiently purified to become god-like or omniscient in a memorial sense, after which it could perceive the whole human tradition spread out panoramically before it. In modern orphism this process is applied to the image rather than the soul: the image is universalized and purified by being recycled within the poet's sensibility. The kind of perspective which results is already hinted at in one of Baudelaire's *Tableaux parisiens* where a 'bifocal' world of immediate and historical dimensions is clearly adumbrated:

> Fourmillante cité, cité pleine de rêves,
> où le spectre en plein jour raccroche le passant!
>
> [Teeming city, city full of dreams, / where the spectre in broad daylight seizes the passer-by!]

Ungaretti broadens this perspective in a historico-aesthetic sense by saying in 'Risvegli' [Reawakenings]:

> Ogni mio momento
> io l'ho vissuto
> un'altra volta
> in un'epoca fonda
> fuori di me
>
> Sono lontano colla mia memoria
> dietro a quelle vite perse
>
> [Every moment of mine / I have lived / some other time / in a faraway epoch / outside myself / / I am far away with my memory / following those lost lives.]

But the frightening immediacy with which he brings about these twofold perspectives of present and past existence within his hallucinatory wasteland settings is to be seen in another poem, where he finds himself – though still at heart a bedouin – stranded in the snowy wastes of the Carso in wartime:

> Questo nomade
> adunco
> morbido di neve
> si lascia
> come una foglia
> accartocciata (*Dolina notturna*)

[This nomad / hook-nosed / softened by snow / abandons himself / like a withered / leaf. *Nocturnal gully*]

To accomplish such compression of time and space the poet tells us in 'Sogno' [Dream] that the dream and the reality it represents must converge in a flash:

Da sonno a veglia fu

Il sogno in un baleno, (*Poesie*, 143)

[From sleep to wakefulness the dream / came in a flash]

and this type of compression is taken to extremes in 'Vanità' [Vanity] where symbolically the individual wakes up to find himself a shade as he shakes himself out of a Narcissistic dream:

E l'uomo

curvato

sull'acqua

sorpresa

dal sole

si rinviene

un'ombra

[And the man / bending / over the water / surprised / by the sun / rediscovers himself / a shade.]

Since, moreover, the process is almost instantaneous, one can truly talk of the 'bifocality' of his modern orphic vision, which amounts to a kind of hallucinatory *reductio ad essentiam* of moods, feelings, desert landscapes and displacements in time, for the purpose of providing a historico-aesthetic perspective on life. In this sense Ungaretti is akin to another French poet, Pierre Reverdy, who once observed that the poet is 'a kiln for the burning of the real'.[4]

Nevertheless, we cannot press French sources too far in determining the peculiar realist-literary quality of Ungaretti's early sensibility, since he also underwent another powerful, and this time indigenous, influence at that period – the influence of the Leopardian moonlight scene. In fact, Ungaretti always regarded Leopardi's evocations of sharp metaphysical contours as prefiguring his own orphic dreams, and they clearly have a definite connection with the infinite spaces and formless wastes of the Egyptian desert or the shattered landscapes of the Carso. The result is that art and life are subtly intermingled in his work from the very beginning, and his early atmospheres in the desert and his literary interests as a schoolboy and a young man have a twofold influence upon his tonal qualities.

At the outbreak of the First World War Ungaretti returned to an Italy which was for the moment neutral, with the intention of preparing his 'abilitazione' (teaching diploma) under Professor Arturo Farinelli of Turin. But, before he did so, he had the opportunity to visit in Paris the Futurist Exhibition of 1914 where he happened to meet Giovanni Papini, Ardengo Soffici and Aldo Palazzeschi who jointly invited him to participate in the periodical *Lacerba*. This periodical was then the mouth-piece of futurist aesthetics and, although he was not openly an adherent of the futurist movement, his first poems were published in it on 7 February 1915. In the same year, as a result of Italy's entry into the war, he joined the armed forces and fought on the Carso with the nineteenth infantry regiment. During this period he wrote a large number of the poems destined to be included in his first collection of verse. By chance he also met at Udine the critic Ettore Serra and it was largely due to his good offices that *Il porto sepolto* [The sunken harbour] was first published in December 1916. On the Carso too he appears to have developed that sense of solitude and solidarity with his fellowmen which he describes many years later in *Il Carso non è più un inferno* [The Carso is no longer an inferno] and which lingers as an authentic echo in his poetry throughout his literary career.

Later, in 1918, his regiment was transferred to the Champagne front in France, and on demobilization he decided to take up residence in the French capital, in the Rue Campagne Première. While living in Paris he published a short collection of poems in French, *La guerre* (1919), and obtained a post as Paris correspondent to the Italian newspaper *Popolo d'Italia*. At the end of 1919 his second Italian collection *Allegria di naufragi* [Joy of Shipwrecks] also appeared in print, published in Florence by Vallecchi.

In the following year he gave up his post with the *Popolo d'Italia* to work at the Italian Embassy in Paris reviewing the foreign press. Then, on 3 June 1920, he married a young Frenchwoman, Jeanne Dupoix. The next year, in 1921, the young couple finally moved to Rome where the poet was destined to live for over a decade. He was employed by the Foreign Ministry in the same capacity as in his previous post in Paris, although he now seized the opportunity of contributing to a number of Italian and foreign periodicals and newspapers. This was a period of steady maturation in his personal aesthetics and cultural pursuits and also in his family life. On 17 February 1925 his daughter Anna Maria (Ninon) was born in Rome, and on 9 February 1930 his son Antonietto in the small town of

Marino just outside the city where the family for reasons of economy had then taken up residence. It was the tragic death of Ungaretti's only son which many years afterwards formed one of the main themes of the collection *Il dolore* [Grief] published in 1947.

It was also in the twenties that the poet's so-called flirtation with Fascism took place, although it may seem a strange kind of political creed for a man to adopt who had always dedicated himself, body and soul, to a cult of the freedom of the individual. But Ungaretti, in fact, had no head for politics and mistook his cultural conscience for a social one, without realizing that Fascism was then using cultural arguments as a cloak to attract men of good will, especially those with a broad historical perspective, to far less worthy causes. Hence in his essay *Originalità del Fascismo* (1927) we find him exalting a curious form of national socialism in which he identifies Mussolini with the will of the people:

> Ma per la prima volta dopo tanti secoli, dando un'armonia militare e religiosa alla comunità italiana, un capo sente il carattere soprannaturale dell'impeto che la Provvidenza gli ha dettato di imprimere alla storia. È ricomparso nella storia il torrente, il popolo. (*Saggi e interventi*, 153)
>
> [But for the first time after so many centuries, by offering a military and religious harmony to the Italian nation, a leader feels the supernatural nature of the impulse which Providence has decreed he should impress upon history. The people, the torrent, has reappeared in history.]

What then was the real reason behind such enthusiasm? Simply the fact that Ungaretti was convinced that Mussolini was about to restore through the Fascist Party the magnificence of the Roman tradition. Culture was consequently for the poet the guiding force behind the movement, and he puts the point in the following way:

> Se una cosa è originale nel fascismo, se una cosa è intesa male fuori d'Italia, o appena sospettata, o non voluta capire, è la *magnificentia*, proprio come l'intendeva San Tommaso, è la magnificenza che lievita in questo nostro movimento. (*Saggi*, 153)
>
> [If there is one thing which is original in Fascism, if there is one thing badly understood outside Italy or hardly suspected, or wilfully misunderstood, it is *magnificentia*, precisely as St Thomas understood the term, it is the magnificence which ferments in this movement of ours.]

Later it was probably his dawning realization of Fascism's cultural

poverty in the thirties which caused Ungaretti to drift away from
the movement and to try to replace its stifling and chauvinistic
atmosphere with something more broadly European. Significantly,
in 1933, he undertook a series of international lecturing engagements
and discoursed on Italian literature in many countries, including
Spain, France, Belgium, Holland, Switzerland and Czechoslovakia.
These lectures were accompanied and reinforced by a great deal of
translating work, including Russian, English, French and Spanish
authors. During the whole period from 1931 to 1935, in fact, the
poet acted as the special envoy of the *Gazzetta del popolo* of Turin,
and this appointment not only required him to travel widely within
Italy itself but to take frequent trips abroad. Among the important
ones was a trip to Egypt (which he had not seen since 1912) and
another to Corsica where he appears to have found certain elements
of that primitive 'paese innocente' [land of innocence] which he had
always yearned for in his poetry. Incidentally it was also during this
period that his literary merit was first rewarded, when in 1932 he won
the Gonfaloniere Prize in Venice.

The following year he published his second major volume of
poetry *Sentimento del tempo* [Feeling for time] which immediately
revealed how much progress he had made in the literary field since
the appearance of the fragile lyrics of *Allegria*. Whereas the symbolic
background of the first volume had been the desert and the shattered
landscapes of the war zone, the present one takes as its more fertile
setting the countryside around Rome, no doubt intended by Ungaretti to mirror the now mature state of his richly endowed
sensibility. The most concrete force working upon his imagination
at that time was the city of Rome itself whose baroque 'fastosità'
[sumptuousness] and overwhelming artistic inheritance filled him
with an admiration mingled with awe, even perhaps with a feeling
of terror. Of this period he wrote:

> Una città come Roma, negli anni durante i quali scrivevo il
> *Sentimento*, era città dove si aveva ancora il sentimento del-
> l'eterno e nell'animo nemmeno oggi scompare davanti a certi
> ruderi. (*Poesie*, 533)
> [A city like Rome, in the years when I was writing the *Senti-
> mento*, was a city where one still had a feeling for eternity, which
> in the mind does not disappear even today when one is con-
> fronted by certain ruins.]

What it evokes in his mind is not so much the image of a time-
hallowed historical repository as a kind of sonorous void:

A Roma si ha il sentimento del vuoto. È naturale, avendo il sentimento del vuoto, uno non può non avere anche l'orrore del vuoto. Quegli elementi ammucchiati, venuti da ogni dove, per non lasciare un briciolo di spazio, di spazio libero, per tutto riempire, per non lasciare nulla, nulla di libero. Quell'orrore del vuoto, si può sentirlo a Roma infinitamente di più, e nemmeno nel deserto, che in qualsiasi altra parte della terra. (*Poesie*, 533–4) [In Rome one has a feeling of emptiness. It is natural, when one has a feeling for the void, that one cannot help equally possessing a horror of the void. These piled-up ruins brought from everywhere, in order not to leave the tiniest fragment of space, of free space, to fill everything up, to leave nothing, nothing free. This horror of the void one can feel infinitely more in Rome than in the desert even, or in any other part of the world.] Such a sensation results, in Ungaretti's opinion, from a baroque frenzy which springs from the juxtaposition of the bric-à-brac of the past with Rome's own seventeenth-century architecture. Its decorative non-functionality inspires in the poet a sense of gratuitousness, of purposelessness; yet it is a purposelessness accompanied by a dynamic and distorted sense of human drama, of humanity's metaphysical anguish. Moreover, in his view

dall'orrore del vuoto nasce, non la necessità della riempitura dello spazio con non importa quale elemento, ma tutto il dramma dell'arte di Michelangelo. (*Poesie*, 534) [from a horror of the void arises the necessity not for filling space with any kind of fragmentary ruins, but the whole drama of the art of Michelangelo.]

For Ungaretti Michelangelo is accordingly the only begetter of the baroque mode of invention; and, since it is representative, or so he claims, 'di un mondo privo di Dio' (535) [of a world deprived of God], he envisages it as a curiously modern way of perceiving the universe. So much so that his own poetry in this collection amounts to a form of harmony, of classical maturity, refracted through a deliberately distorting baroque lens.

To fill the void that the spiritual sphere in which he moves appears to open up, the poet constantly tries, especially in the second part of *Sentimento del tempo*, to rejuvenate the classical myths whose phantomatic presences still seem to him to live on and haunt the Roman countryside in his own age, despite – or even perhaps because of – the hallucinatory light of its blinding sun. Also at this point he allows certain Christian values to exert an influence on his sensibility, through a subtle combination of the ancient and Christian ideas of 'pietas'. Basically a sense of piety is for him a cult of ancestor-worship through tradition and a feeling for one's fellow-men; but at times it is also suffused with an authentic Christian aura of pity and sympathy for individual suffering, as may be seen from his note to the poem 'La pietà romana' [Roman piety] (*Poesie*, 540). From this new merging of the Christian and pagan traditions there arises a clearer vision of his 'paese innocente', which he described at one stage as a condition 'di innocenza preadamitica, quella dell'universo prima dell'uomo' (*Poesie*, 536) [of preadamite innocence, that of the universe before man] but which now acquires a much broader and more mature connotation. This kind of yearning may appear at first sight to be very close to Rimbaud's 'élan vers la perfection', but the problem for Ungaretti is not primarily a metaphysical one; it is instead an attempt to recapture orphically and aesthetically, at times even ethically, a primeval innocence of the senses. The Italian poet does not in other words opt out of literature like Rimbaud so as to 'posséder la vérité dans une âme et un corps', he chooses rather to refine his primitivism into a kind of new-born and allusive beauty, one which at times parallels the orphic aesthetic independently adumbrated by Campana in the *Canti orfici* [Orphic Songs] (1914).

It was while he was undergoing these curious metaphysical experiences and was steeping his mind in the waters of the Tiber (just as he tells us he had previously steeped it in those of the Nile, Serchio, Seine and other rivers) that he received an invitation from the Argentinian government to participate in the Congress of the Pen Club at Buenos Aires. During his visit there he was offered the Chair of Italian Literature at the University of São Paulo by the Brazilian government, which after some initial hesitation he accepted. He remained in Brazil for six years in all, returning to Italy only in 1942. During this period, as we have already mentioned, he suffered a tragic loss: the death in 1939 of his nine-year-old son, Antonietto, from a badly diagnosed appendicitis. The literary outcome of this personal tragedy and of the overwhelming disasters suffered by his native Italy during the war years was the collection *Il dolore* (1947), in which the previous tonal background of Latium in *Sentimento del tempo* was transformed into the gigantic and inhuman landscapes of Brazil. These landscapes are described in a peculiarly primitive type of baroque Petrarchism, as may be seen from the dramatic accumulation of adjectives and violent actions in the opening lines of 'Tu ti spezzasti' [You were broken]:

I molti, immani, sparsi, grigi sassi
Frementi ancora alle segrete fionde
Di originarie fiamme soffocate ...
[The myriad, immense, scattered, grey stones / quivering still
from out of secret slings / of primeval flames suppressed.]

This is indeed the apocalyptic mood which dominates Ungaretti's
mind during his entire stay in South America; it is a mood of almost
superhuman emotion and tension which, towards the end of the
volume, is reinforced by the despair he encounters in a shattered
Italy on his return home in 1942. At that time, we recall, Italy was
about to undergo the Anglo-American invasion which led to its
final capitulation to the Allies a year later in 1943.

Even so, the poet himself re-entered Rome covered in glory and
was immediately appointed Professor of Modern Italian Literature at
the university 'per chiara fama' [through great renown]. At the end
of the same year Mondadori undertook to publish his complete
works under the title of *Vita d' un uomo* [Life of a man]; and a little
later, in 1944, he published a number of his translations from Shakespeare's sonnets. From this point onwards nearly all the criticism
which deals with his work recognizes his importance as one of the
major lyricists of the twentieth century, and consequently the
polemics now largely ceased in favour of a juster appreciation of his
literary contribution. In 1945 *Questi giorni*, a Milanese periodical,
dedicated its entire December number to his work, and in 1949 he
received the 'Premio Roma', having in the interval published his
third volume of verse *Il dolore* (1947), together with further translations from Góngora and Mallarmé in 1948. In 1949 he also produced
a first collection of prose writings, *Il povero nella città* [The poor in
the city], which was followed by a translation of Racine's *Fedra* and
by his fourth collection of verse *La terra promessa* [The promised
land] in 1950. This volume and a subsequent one entitled *Un grido
e paesaggi* [A cry and landscapes] (1952) added a further dimension
to his lyricism, although from 1952 onwards the poet normally
strove to consolidate his previous poetic achievements rather than
make any attempt to strike out in fresh, experimental directions.

Ungaretti's old age is, in fact, largely dominated by a single mythological figure with whom he appears virtually to identify himself.
The figure in question is Aeneas as he is depicted in all his 'pietas'
by Virgil; and the poet seems to regard the Trojan hero as the
exemplar of the complete existential man. He symbolizes on the one
hand the empire-builder, the maker of civilization, and on the other

the self-fulfilling sensitive human being, deeply involved in his social
and cultural commitments towards his family and race. Indeed,
Ungaretti now acts towards the cultural heritage of twentieth-
century Italy in much the same way as Aeneas acted by cherishing
his father Anchises and the whole tradition of the Trojan people.
He even tries, in a sense, to lead the Italian people towards a modern
promised land, a wholly spiritual region of cultural serenity and
lyrical fulfilment. To Aeneas's ethical attitudes he tends under-
standably to add a strand of Christian pity and idealism, of redemptive faith even, although he never loses control of his religious
fervour and never allows dogmatic attitudes to destroy his intimate
sense of life's essential contingency. His faith is thus not a question of
theological goals but one of spiritual fulfilment through participation in life; and it is the struggle for this type of personal completion
together with a recognition of the fragility of human existence and
the inevitability of death which above all else colours his perspective
of old age.

In this period of the early fifties, Ungaretti's reputation was
growing very rapidly in France; so that in 1954 a translation of his
poetry into French, undertaken in collaboration with Jean Lescure
under the title of *Les cinq livres*, appeared just one year after an
enlarged reprint of an earlier one by Jean Chuzeville published in
Switzerland in 1953. His fame required more time, perhaps, to
reach the Anglo-Saxon countries, and it was 1958 before a selection
of his poetry translated by Allen Mandelbaum appeared under the
title of *Life of a Man*. Despite his advancing years, Ungaretti's own
cultural activities still continued to be particularly intense at this
time, and his purview ranged over the fine arts, music and architecture as well as literature. But during the fifties the health of his wife
Jeanne gradually declined and on more than one occasion she was
taken to hospital for observation, where she was diagnosed as suffering from a distressing hepatic complaint. Her condition worsened
in 1958 and Ungaretti was called to her bedside from the Venice
Biennale which he had been visiting with his friends Bona De
Pisis, Ottone Rosai and others. In September her condition became
critical, but before she passed away the civil marriage which had
taken place in France after the first World War (between the non-
believer Jeanne and the frankly atheist Ungaretti, as Piccioni puts it
(183)) was solemnized by a religious ceremony, and Jeanne even
received extreme unction before she died. This act of religious piety
clearly indicates how their attitudes to religion had changed and

mellowed over the years. Moreover, 1958 was not entirely a period of gloom. In that year Ungaretti reached his seventieth birthday, and this was a time when the critics found it appropriate to celebrate his continually growing fame by publishing a whole number of *Letteratura* (no. 35-6) dedicated to his work.

After Jeanne's death the poet travelled a great deal, no doubt in the hope of alleviating his sense of loss by indulging once more in almost feverish literary activity. He visited Spain with Carlo Emilio Gadda, and Sardinia (where he was apparently always on the lookout for a meeting with bandits) with Carlo Bo, Giovanni Battista Angioletti, Piero Bigongiari and others. At about the same time he became an intimate friend of Jean Fautrier whose paintings he much admired. Later, in 1959, he was invited by Leonardo Sinisgalli to accompany him on a trip to Egypt; and, not to be outdone, Fautrier and Jean Paulhan proposed in 1960 an even longer trip around the world. At this point Ungaretti became acquainted with jet-travel and wrote a short description of his journey from Japan to Beirut in one of the *Ultimi cori per la terra promessa* [Last choruses for the promised land]. In the next year he published a further volume of prose, *Il deserto e dopo* (1961), which re-evokes many of the hallucinatory desert landscapes closely associated with his early verse. Likewise, a little earlier, another volume of his poetry had appeared, *Il taccuino del vecchio* [The old man's notebook] (1960), which not only contained additional verse but also a large number of 'testimonianze' to the poet by many of the most famous writers of Europe and America.

In 1962 Ungaretti was elected president of the European Writers Union and this office ultimately led him to undertake a visit to Russia where he was granted an interview with Kruschev. Later, in 1964, he travelled to the United States, where he agreed to give a series of lecture courses at Columbia University. He actually stayed in New York for three or four months and was housed in a flat on the campus, where his charm and *joie de vivre* won over both staff and students alike. Piccioni tells us that all the prettiest girls queued up to do his cooking for him, and on one occasion when a particularly charming young lady asked him his age, he replied that it all depended on her reasons for asking. In the same year, however, he was deeply saddened by the death of his friend, the painter Jean Fautrier, which occurred on 21st July.

In 1965 a further proof of his intense literary activity came to light, his translations of the poetry of William Blake, whose visionary attitudes had fascinated him since the early thirties. Then suddenly, in the spring of 1966, he decided to revisit Brazil to make a pilgrimage to Antonietto's grave, which he had not seen since he had left the country in 1942. While in São Paulo he met a young Brazilian poetess, Bruna Bianco, who became deeply attracted to the poet. A largely platonic love-affair ensued which nevertheless, at times, displayed on Ungaretti's part all the fire of a youthful passion. When the poet returned to Italy in the autumn, Piccioni noted that he had thrown away his walking-stick and wore, in place of his normal, rather old-fashioned clothes, coloured shirts and roll-neck pullovers. In short, he seemed virtually rejuvenated and all of this was undoubtedly, in Piccioni's view, Bruna's doing. Later on, she even came over to Italy to attend Ungaretti's eightieth birthday celebrations and the poems he addressed to her, together with her replies, were published in the collection *Dialogo* [Dialogue]. During this period, too, the poet worked hard to establish (or to re-establish) the literary reputations of certain of his friends, especially Gadda, whose candidature he was responsible for pressing when the latter won the Montefeltro Prize in 1967. This honour had already been bestowed on Ungaretti himself some time earlier, in 1960.

In February 1967, just after Gadda had received his award, Ungaretti set off on his travels once again. This time he accompanied his biographer, Piccioni, to Israel. He visited all the main tourist centres and Christian monuments in the Promised Land and wrote at length to Bruna about them. One thing he did not particularly appreciate during this otherwise enjoyable visit, however, was kosher food, especially the oil in which it was cooked; so much so that he ended up eating little or nothing at all.

Before the appearance of *Dialogo* in 1968 the publisher Fógola had also brought out the collected verse of Ungaretti's old age under the title of *Morte delle stagioni* [Death of the seasons] (1967), and Manzú provided an 'acquaforte' for the edition. The result of all this literary activity was a further series of invitations to the poet to visit various countries during his eightieth-year celebrations. For a man of his age he again undertook an incredible number of journeys – to France, Germany, Sweden and Switzerland, not to mention a fresh lecturing assignment in America, at Harvard. In February 1968, moreover, an official reception was held for him in the Palazzo Chigi at Rome by Prime Minister Moro which was also attended by Montale and Quasimodo making up the 'santa trinità' (the holy trinity), as Montale amusingly put it at the time. In the same period he was also granted among other acknowledgements a private audience with Pope Paul VI; so that, despite his still tremendous energy, he had to admit in the end that all these festivities had utterly exhausted him. Piccioni was thereby moved to promise him that for his ninetieth birthday the celebrations would be much less hectic. But at the time Ungaretti did, indeed, become rather seriously ill with circulatory trouble and was nursed through his illness by his daughter Ninon.

When he had recovered, he was visited in Rome by the poet Vinicius de Moraes whom he had known years before in Brazil, and he was also seen often in the company of a young Croatian girl, Dunja, who not only helped him in his work but was to prove the object of his last sentimental relationship. He wrote several poems about her in which he tells us that she reminded him somewhat of Anna, the old Croatian servant of his childhood, whom his mother had employed in their house in Alexandria and whom, we recall, possessed a really fabulous gift for story-telling. He even visited Dunja's native Croatia in 1969, where once again he was fêted by a circle of Yugoslav writers and poets.

In 1970 he undertook his final journey to the United States to receive an international prize at Oklahoma University. When, on his return, he reached New York, he found the city in the middle of a very cold snap and he contracted bronchitis. After a brief convalescence he appeared to have fully recovered and made his way back to Italy. At the end of May, however, he still felt unwell and decided to go to Milan to see a specialist. Unfortunately, before any positive treatment could be given him he died suddenly during the night of 1–2 June. His funeral took place in Rome at the church of San Lorenzo fuori le Mura on 4 June, and he was buried beside his wife Jeanne at Verano, where his friend, the critic Carlo Bo, pronounced a touching funeral oration.

Ungaretti's final period of life was clearly marked, as we have seen, by an almost Herculean series of literary and social activities, and his zest for life appears to have remained undiminished till the end. Equally this tremendous energy of his is reflected in his poetry throughout his career, a poetry which represents the authentic life of a man, not in any mere diaristic or anecdotal sense, but insofar as it is the essence and true measure of his experiential joys and sorrows and of that ultimate feeling of aesthetico-moral fulfilment which breathes through all his writings. His sense of fulfilment is thus not that of the egocentric or solipsist poet but that of the completely committed human being. It involves, above all, as Ungaretti himself always wished, the re-emergence from within his infinitely receptive sensibility of the essential values of the whole Italian tradition, and it produces a lyricism which is at once original and a re-articulation in a modern key of the most profound harmonics of the culture of the past.

2. Personal Aesthetics and Cultural Perspectives

Any attempt to examine Ungaretti's aesthetics is bound to pose a large number of problems, partly because of the complexity of his lyrical vision and partly because his poetic manner is overlaid by an equally complex network of borrowed literary features drawn mainly from Petrarchan sources. It will not be possible to deal with all these difficulties in the space available at present, except perhaps in the broadest outlines; but by adopting a cumulative technique we hope to add more flesh and connective tissue later, when we come to an analysis of his actual poetic texts. Since Ungaretti's critical views, moreover, tend at times to determine his aesthetic interests, his consideration of other poets' work will also throw a greater light on the way in which his lyrical attitudes deepen progressively with the passage of time.

Poetry as re-creation

The foundation on which the poet's aesthetic ideas are based is the concept of creativity. Oddly enough, his first vital step in the process of poetic creation is a paradoxical act of destruction: a process which amounts to the reduction of the real world outside himself to a state of nothingness, or at least to a mere shadowy state of skeletal subsistence. This act of reduction then becomes a prelude to another, purely mental act of regeneration, one which is intended to endow the phenomena of the senses with an anthropocentric emotional charge, transforming things and situations into a thoroughly inward-looking and human, rather than an outward or cosmic perspective. The poet put his doctrine succinctly to Denis Roche towards the end of his life when he noted that 'cette poétique est née du sentiment qu'on ne peut se représenter les choses poétiquement, c'est-à-dire qu'on ne peut les saisir dans leur réalité la plus profonde que quand elles n'existent pas; et c'est à ce moment-là seulement qu'elles sont à nous, et cela par notre inspiration' (Sanavio, 249) [this poetic arises from a feeling that one cannot present things lyrically to oneself, one cannot, that is to say, seize them in their deeper reality, except when they no longer exist; and it is only at that moment that they belong to us, and then through our own inspiration]. Clearly, what he is expounding here is the view that poetry is never a *creative* process at all, but a *re-creative one*: a process which annuls contingent elements (those which Mallarmé would describe as belonging to the realm of 'le hasard') while substituting for them an absolute sphere of emotion peopled by imaginative forms. Indeed, the phenomenologist Paci argues that by adopting this attitude towards reality Ungaretti was himself behaving as a phenomenologist *avant la lettre* and the poet seems to have agreed with him (See *Lettere a un fenomenologo*, 10). Paci considered, in fact, that Ungaretti had invented an aesthetic equivalent to image-suspension or *epoché* as early as 1916 and he attempts to define exactly what this process consists of in phenomenologist philosophy. According to him it amounts to a 'liberation from the circumstances of the world' through a process of 'phenomenological reduction' of things to their bare essentials; then, after the annulling of the worldly (the *Weltvernichtung*), the procedure is reversed and a new grade of reality is established, one which is a return to life, to authentic life (ibid., 17). Fortunately Ungaretti's aesthetic equivalent of a state of *epoché* is somewhat clearer than the original process itself; it consists of endowing external reality with that inward-looking or anthropocentric charge which we mentioned above, and in *Allegria* he uses the symbol of a flower to illustrate the point. He explains that between the 'plucking' of the real flower and its subsequent recreation as a meditative 'offering' in his poetry there lies an 'inexpressible void':

>   Tra un fiore colto e l'altro donato
>   L'inesprimibile nulla (*Eterno*)
>   [Between a flower plucked and the other proffered / the inexpressible void.]

This brief hiatus lying between the inner vision and the outer reality is, he believes, the one thing which allows the poem to transcend the objective situation on which it is based and to become an interpretation of a mood rather than the reproduction of a scene.

Memorial insight

What does this somewhat strange doctrine imply? Although the poet only works out its full implications over a period of time, his pure state of nothingness is an essentialized and emotive form of image-suspension and the process gives rise to a reconditioning of reality in which ordinary phenomena become charged with mysterious powers. They can then be used by the poet as instruments of mediation for the acquisition of certain flashing or 'fulminatory' insights into the nature of things. The insights acquired, however, are not mere mystifications, since they always subsist in a sphere of racial memory in which elements specific to a particular culture are stored and endlessly recycled by successive generations of poets. They may be identified as lyrical resonances in a state of dynamic suspension in order to distinguish them from the more static, Platonic Ideals; and they amount to the voices of the dead continually reawakened for us in the poetic 'word' over the aeons of time. Poetry is, in fact, for Ungaretti a form of communication with the dead, and in lyrics like 'Terra' [Land] he describes their intimations as being an infinitely more powerful force than any to be found in physical phenomena:

Il vento continui a scrosciare,
Da palme ad abeti lo strepito
Per sempre desoli, silente
Il grido dei morti è piú forte.
[Let the wind continue to squall, / let the din for ever lay waste / between palm and fir, silent / the cry of the dead is stronger.]

Such lyrical intimations are clearly cultural memories, and in Husserl's phenomenology the sum of our acquisitions from the past crystallizes at any given time into a balanced state of society which he calls the *Lebenswelt*, a concept which can be defined as a suspended condition of the spirit implicit in the mass-psychology of a society at any particular moment in its unfolding. In similar fashion we find that Ungaretti's aesthetics is a remodulation of the tastes implicit in the *Lebenswelt*, which is an area of feeling governed not by normal logic but by a logic of associations; and so the end-product of his lyrical meditations is not a conceptual statement about the condition of society but an emotive recrystallization of its time-hallowed sensations. The idea implies that within the sphere of taste and aesthetic harmony the Aristotelian pattern of logical unfolding no longer holds. In its place there emerges an analogical or impressionistic form of logic, of verbal and imaginative associations, based on a Bergsonian type of intuition. This particular mode of poetic logic does not deal directly with the real world, nor does it try to transcend it intellectually by cognitive acts of greater and greater generalization: *it simply transfigures it emotionally from within*. A lyrical flash spiralling towards this type of instinctively determined and largely precognitive insight is to be found in 'Fase d'oriente' [Oriental phase]:

> Nel molle giro di un sorriso
> ci sentiamo legare da un turbine
> di germogli di desiderio
>
> Ci vendemmia il sole
>
> Chiudiamo gli occhi
> per vedere nuotare in un lago
> infinite promesse

[In the gentle spiral of a smile / we find ourselves bound by a whirlwind / of budding desires / / The sun harvests us / / We close our eyes / to see swimming in a lake / infinite promises.]

Now this kind of analogical approach to feeling no doubt has its origin in decadent sources, although it is certainly not decadent itself. Instead it serves to distinguish modern Italian poetry from French symbolist verse, since the present poet, although admitting in the same spirit as Mallarmé the necessity to detach poetry from the contingent world, nevertheless detaches it in a very different way. Normally he seizes on the psycho-sensuous essence of an experience and suspends it in the detached sphere of *epoché*, whereas the French poet tended to isolate only its metaphysical constants. As a result, Ungaretti does not undergo the type of metaphysical *échec* which Mallarmé experienced, since he does not try to soar towards the other-worldly, but merely uses the concrete elements of existence as a means of representing 'questo mondo terreno considerato come continua invenzione dell'uomo' (*Poesie*, lxix) [this earthly existence conceived as the continual invention of man]. His method of image-suspension aims, in short, at a series of immanent transfigurations of the real cast into a recollective mould; it never attempts, as did symbolist aesthetics, to eternalize the real by reconstituting it as a metaphysical structure.

Lyricism and myth

Such an outlook means that Ungaretti puts much greater emphasis on the intimations of cultural history than on philosophy or religion. So we must not be misled by his definition of poetry as a 'divinazione metafisica' [a metaphysical divining], because he immediately qualifies this apparently speculative process by asking us if these forms of 'illuminazione favolosa, fantasmi e miti, divinazioni metafisiche, non sono forse illusioni di tempo domato, o meglio di tempo abolito' (*Poesie*, lxxix) [fabulous insight, phantoms and myths, metaphysical divining, are not perhaps illusions of 'tamed' time, or rather of 'abolished' time]? No doubt he means by 'tamed' or 'abolished' time here that re-created and mythical temporality which emerges after the 'plucked' flower of experience has been annulled in accordance with the process established in the first poem of *Allegria*. Its lyrical manifestation then becomes a poetic 'offering' which is essentially an illusion or a fiction moving in a very different time-sphere from that of ordinary reality; and the sum of these mythical recalls actually makes up the poet's inner unfolding or 'durata' [duration].

The idea is also closely linked with the concept of memory and amounts to the secret rhythm evolving in his own sensibility which the poet imposes upon that sphere of memory we regard as the cultural tradition. The subduing of time is in other words the re-invention of reality by man, and this re-created reality offers us lyrical insights far more powerful than any we could hope to garner from our normal, everyday time-sphere. In this area, indeed, Ungaretti adopts Bergson's own definition of 'durée', saying: 'Il tempo reale è uno solo: il tempo psicologico, quello di cui potrebbe, a suo modo, averne ogni anima rivelazione' (*Saggi*, 89) [There is only one real time: psychological time, one from which each soul can, in its own way, obtain awareness]. For him art becomes temporality transformed into the magic of a racially matured myth, combining in an intimate fashion both personal and atavistic experiences. So in the last resort the function of the poet is, as Ungaretti puts it himself, to provide 'una sua bella biografia' [a fine biography of his own], because in so doing he will allow his personality to interact with the *Lebenswelt* and modify its tastes and lyrical resonances in accordance with a modern scale of values.

For the purpose of attuning his personal mythology to the historically evolving myth of his nation or cultural group, each poet has to steep himself in his lyrical inheritance. In an interview with Camon, Ungaretti once described the result of this immersion, saying: 'Naturalmente ogni giorno le cose sono diverse e nuove, ma in ogni giorno è contenuto tutto il passato e tutto il futuro. Credo che la mia lingua poetica, continuamente rinnovandosi e rimanendo antica, non l'abbia dimenticato mai.' (Camon, 30) [Naturally things are varied and diversified each day, but in every day the whole of the past and the future is contained. I believe that my poetic language continually renewing itself and yet remaining time-hallowed, has

never forgotten the fact]. By listening carefully to the 'voices' of
the past – which he once referred to in his poetry as the 'buia veglia
dei padri' [the dark vigil of the fathers] – he hoped to be able to
harmonize his poetry on a double string, with present sensations
appearing in the forefront of his melodic line and the whispering of
the tradition playing a mysterious and allusive form of counterpoint
in the wings. Such a process would in his opinion allow him to
'accordare in chiave d'oggi un antico strumento musicale' (*Poesie*,
lxxii) [reattune in a contemporary key an ancient musical instrument]
that is to say, the art of poetry itself. But in order to realize this
ambition, he soon found that he had to evolve novel views about
time, space and memory.

Space

With regard to Ungaretti's sense of space, Camon once suggested
that it results from the sort of optic which makes objects seem solitary
and distant; and in reply to this observation the poet pointed out
that what Sapegno had once called his 'tecnica sillabata' [syllable-
isolating technique] amounted to a description of his lyrico-spatial
dispositions in the contourless wastes of the desert:

> L'immagine della desolazione mi si è fatta ossessiva sino dalle
> mie prime poesie. A precisarla in me, fu il deserto: da esso
> nascevano, nel lontano mio tempo dell'infanzia e dell'adoles-
> cenza, la nozione e il sentimento dell'infinito, del primitivo, del
> decadimento fino al nulla. (Camon, 26)
> [The image of desolation became obsessive with me even in my
> early poetry. To focus it within me, there was the desert: from
> it there sprang in the faraway time of my childhood and
> adolescence a notion and a feeling for the infinite, for the
> primitive, for a fading away to nothingness.]

Even so, it is more probable that his actual ability to change physical
scenes into wholly mental perspectives by way of their reduction to
arabesques of bold contours and muted colours came originally
from Leopardi, especially the Leopardi of the mature idylls, because
in those particular lyrics moonlight scenes take on precisely this
metaphysical dimension. Again, the same process reappears later in
Ungaretti's sense of the void, especially as the idea was first inculcated
into him by the art of Michelangelo, in the Rome of the twenties.
But, despite its apparently eclectic origin, he nevertheless uses the
vastness of space *analogically* in his own particular way: to highlight
the various relations between the major features of his own spiritual

universe by linking them together unexpectedly through a process of revelationary juxtapositions.

This explains his definition of the analogy, which in his hands becomes an aesthetic and ethical device rather than the theological probe into which the *correspondance* had evolved with the symbolists. The technique, we recall, was originally invented by Baudelaire and consisted of the yoking together of a series of very disparate images for the purpose of breaking through from the world of the senses into a higher ideal world, as may be seen in the following *correspondance* taken from 'Le voyage':

> Mon âme est un trois-mâts cherchant son Icarie ...
>
> [My soul is a three-master seeking its paradise.]

But, instead of attempting to link together the real and the ideal worlds as it did for Baudelaire, and indeed even for Mallarmé, with Ungaretti the analogy simply aims at fusing into imagery the most significant moments of the poet's contingent experience. Gradually his version of the technique transfigures the world in such a way that it leads to a state of innocence through the winding back of memory: 'il poeta d'oggi cercherà ... di mettere a contatto immagini lontane, senza fili. Dalla memoria all'innocenza, quale lontananza da varcare; ma in un baleno' (*Poesie*, lxxx) [The poet of today will seek ... to bring into contact far distant images, without connecting links. From memory to innocence, what a great expanse to cross; but in a flash]. The analogy thus becomes for him an instrument of spatial and emotional compression, not a form of platonic escapism.

Time

With respect to time Ungaretti similarly appears to have understood from the outset a distinction which was only later to be formalized in Italy by Montanari[1] and others, to the effect that there are two kinds of temporal flow: the one cosmic, to be indicated by the Latin word *tempus*, and the other human, to be described as *aevum*. It is not under the aegis of the former, which can be represented by the mechanical and therefore humanly insignificant ticking of the clock, but rather under the latter that Ungaretti considers poetry to function. By its very nature the *aevum* amounts to a 'humanly imprinted' sense of time operating within the sphere of myth, and its imaginative and historical perspectives offer the present-day writer a range of tastes and moods stretching back to the very dawn of existence. The authentic poet consequently broods over the latent state of mystery lying in suspension in the language and literary tradition of his native land and draws from it those harmonics which are useful to him in the modulating of his own inspiration. The intended product of this attitude is a reflective lyricism in which cosmic time or *tempus* is underscored by a vein of 'aeval' or psychological time, while deep within psychological time itself a dialectic of memory tends to operate in which, as the poet explains in a note to 'Ti svelerà' [It will unveil you], the temporal flow often becomes reversible:

> La durata interna è composta di tempo e di spazio, fuori del tempo cronologico; l'universo interno è un mondo dove la reversibilità è di regola. Quel tempo non scorre mai in un'unica direzione, non s'orienta mai nel medesimo modo; si può risalirne il corso, non si sa a quale fonte inaccessibile, ma tuttavia è immediatamente presente in noi. La memoria trae dall'abisso il ricordo per restituirgli presenza, per rivelare al poeta se stesso. (*Poesie*, 537)
>
> [Internal duration is composed of time and space beyond chronological time; the internal universe is a world where reversibility is the rule. This time never flows in a single direction, never orientates itself in the selfsame manner; one can trace back its course to one knows not what inaccessible source, yet it is at the same time immediately present within us. Memory draws out of the abyss each remembrance and reconstitutes it as a presence, to reveal the poet to himself.]

What art succeeds in doing, in short, is to bring about the temporal *co-existence* of chronologically separate experiences, by creating a perspective which is not contained within the original situations described but which instead emanates from the 'reconstructed' mental world of the poet. Poetry, in consequence, always evokes a personal perspective, it is not confined to a mechanical regurgitation of present or past situations and sensations – although, even the factual, historical past forms a valuable concrete background for depicting the subtle interplay between the individual's 'personal' tensions and the *Lebenswelt's* 'communal' responses. Hence in the last resort we can regard Ungaretti's poetic manner as a type of deliberate mental regression to the void, followed by a 'timeless' orphic return or memorial reincarnation of the image out of nothingness. Such a dialectic he tells us perfects

> un linguaggio poetico dove, nella ricerca del vero che è il sacro, la memoria s'abolisca nel sogno e dal sogno rifluisca agli oggetti, e viceversa, incessantemente. (*Fedra di Jean Racine*, 11)

[a poetic language in which, in the search for the truth which is
sacred, memory dissolves itself into a dream and from the
dream flows back to objects, and vice versa, incessantly.]
The outcome – if the process has been a successful one – is a lyric
which appears to be a 'miracolo d'equilibrio' (*Poesie*, lxx) [miracle
of equilibrium] of truly classical proportions. Not only does it lead
one to the confines of life's mystery without becoming in itself uselessly mystifying, but it also offsets reality and the dream in such a
way as to produce a balance of lyrical resonances, merging personal
with traditional melodic effects.

What is the mainspring behind such a miraculous interplay of
poetic tensions? According to Ungaretti it is a sense of classical
measure: not a measure of the mysterious, of the unknowable
mystery surrounding life, but rather a measure of the human perspectives within it. This attitude again indicates that he is philo-
sophically a disciple of Bergson, because his transformations of
situations are what he calls 'un sognare ad occhi aperti' [a dreaming
with eyes open] and they rely for their effects on an intuitive sense
of scale rather than rational analysis. But although he is a believer in
this kind of associative, as opposed to any strictly logical or conceptual
type of lyricism, Ungaretti never, on the other hand, adopts the
futurist 'parola in libertà' [word-in-liberty] with its gratuitous associations (which Pound once referred to as 'accelerated impressionism'); nor does he use the technique which Marcel Raymond called
a 'pêche miraculeuse' [miraculous fishing] into the unconscious, as
advocated by the surrealists in France.[2] Both of these manners of
lyrical speculation he regards as being dominated in the last resort by
chronological or cosmic time-sequences. They are therefore once
again identifiable with the untransformed condition of Mallarmé's
realm of 'le hasard', whereas his own art – as we have already noted –
is made up of elements of time both 'subdued' and 'mythified'. In
this sense his poetry is, like Petrarch's, consolatory instead of being
speculative in quality. By reordering or repatterning the chance-
effects of experience it offers a justification for one's inner life which
is highly comforting to the poet: and it also tends to resolve each
emotive, moral and aesthetic problem within society itself rather
than to hypostasize it metaphysically in a sphere of theological
speculation, as the symbolists were inclined to do.

Modern baroque and 'meraviglia'

If we had asked Ungaretti what elements caused the stratified aeons

of time encapsulated in the modern human consciousness to differ
from each other aesthetically, he would probably have been unwilling to supply a direct answer. He preferred to regard the evolving
of aesthetic taste as part of the mystery surrounding the process of
human destiny, and perhaps in his later years would have associated
it with providence. Where he felt himself to be on somewhat firmer
ground was in the analysis of the tastes of his own age which he
asserted were fundamentally baroque in temper. Hence the void
created by the contemporary poet as a result of his *reductio ad nullum*
of the natural world (a precondition, we recall, of the very act of
aesthetic creativeness for Ungaretti) had in his view to be con-
strained in a baroque direction if it were to be satisfactorily attuned
to the ethos of his age. In his opinion the peculiar characteristic of
the modern baroque mode was a certain dramatic tension, an anxiety
which leads to a sense of anguish or 'dolore' [grief] and to its artistic
concomitant, a compensatory overfullness of forms. As this singular
baroque vision develops, it gradually distorts his underlying feeling
for classical balance in an oblique, sometimes even a slightly grotesque direction, although at the same time it also establishes its own
fresh mode of harmony. Nevertheless it is an art of fantastic, almost
superhuman, proportions,

> spinta a sorprendere, spinta a darsi per fine "la maraviglia", e
> che tuttavia riesce ad avere accenti, nella meravigliosa sua
> stranezza scopritrice di verità, caldi di promessa umana.
> (*Poesie*, lxxxix)
> [driven to cultivate surprise, driven to establish 'wonder' as its
> goal, yet one which still manages to acquire, in its wondrous
> strangeness revelationary of truth, accents burning with human
> promise.]

This definition, of course, reminds us at once of Marino's description of the baroque in the *Seicento*:

> È del poeta il fin la maraviglia;
> [The poet's aim is the marvellous]

but the crucial difference between Ungaretti and Marino is the
difference between an internalized and an externalized or merely
decorative form of the baroque. So, whereas the following conceit
drawn from one of Marino's sonnets (*Amori*, 111) describes the
charms of a black slave-girl in what amounts to a form of externalized wit:

> Là 've piú ardi, o Sol, sol per tuo scorno
> un sole è nato; un sol, che nel bel volto

porta la notte, ed ha negli occhi il giorno,
[There where you most burn, o Sun, solely to your shame / a
sun is born; a sun, which in her lovely face / bears night, and
has in her eyes the day]

the intention behind the following lines from 'Malinconia' [Melan-
choly] in Ungaretti's *Allegria* is a kind of existential self-surprise,
which finally becomes thoroughly transfigured when it is confronted by death:

Mondo

Attonimento
in una gita folle
di pupille amorose

In una gita che se ne va in fumo
col sonno
e se incontra la morte
è il dormire piú vero

[World // Astonishment / in a wild flight / of loving eyes // In a
flight that melts in smoke / with sleep / and if it meets with
death / is the truest slumber.]

The aim here, in other words, is no longer one of creating far-fetched
analogies to mesmerize the reader: the first to be amazed and overwhelmed by the very depth of his sense-impressions and imagery is
the poet himself; and he constantly remains dumbfounded that his
perception of sensations can retain such vividness even when they
flash unexpectedly upon his inward eye from deep within the
oubliettes of memory. The point is also made conceptually in 'Casa
mia' [My home] where he revisits his childhood home, and notes:

Sorpresa
dopo tanto
d'un amore

Credevo di averlo sparpagliato
per il mondo

[Surprise / after so long / of a love // I thought I had scattered
it / about the world.]

This type of self-surprise is clearly an internal feature of Ungaretti's re-created baroque universe, and its spiritual manifestations are
characterized by a series of imaginative *implosions* into the deeper
reaches of his spirit which contrast with the often aimless *explosive*
displays of imagery to be seen in Marino and his followers in the
Seicento. But, although it provides a new dimension for the baroque

Muse in Italy, the same form of oblique, imaginative writing is already familiar to us in some of the 'metaphysical' poets in England, and it is perhaps even more closely akin to the production of the Gongorists in Spain. This explains why Ungaretti later regards the members of both schools as his masters.

Memory and 'la parola'

The baroque mode raises nevertheless a peculiar difficulty for Ungaretti since it is a poetry of foreshortened memory: a poetry in which memory has virtually been annulled by a cult of immediate sensations and which adheres so closely to present realities as almost to exclude perspective altogether. His own verse, on the other hand, being largely a reconstituted reality, must by definition be one of deep memorial penetration. The full extent of this problem will only become apparent later, but the way in which he resolves it is to replace the foreshortened, baroque memory in his work by an aura of nostalgia derived cumulatively from the past, while at the same time he tones down the movement's bizarre and rarified sensations until they become fused with the time-hallowed lyrical textures that form his own cultural hinterland. This is not to say, however, that the way in which Ungaretti recaptures the resonances of the tradition and incorporates them into his poetry is by the simple device of interlarding his verse with literary reminiscences. He prefers to work through a more refined technique which may be described as 'lo scavo della parola' [the excavating of the word] and which has as its aim the liberating of personal inflections through the exploration in depth of the hidden cultural and sensory resonances implicit in words. In this sense the poetic image is no longer to be considered as being magically linked with spells or on a religious plane with the utterances of God; instead it resembles a sponge saturated with the quicksilver of the emotions of the past. Accordingly, Ungaretti's immediate lyrical problem was how to supersaturate it with his own immediate emotive impressions while still maintaining as a series of echoing harmonics the elements of its previous cultural charge. When grappling with this difficulty he noted in 'Commiato' [Envoi], as early as 1916:

> Quando trovo
> in questo mio silenzio
> una parola
> scavata è nella mia vita
> come un abisso

[When I find / in this silence of mine / a word / it is dug into my
life / like an abyss.]
Such an approach is clearly a necessary extension of his overall
aesthetic manner and links his lyrical prescriptions to the technical
sphere of word-combinations and their phonic implications. But its
solutions are by no means confined to technical matters: they are
often broadly philological and cultural in the Leopardian sense, and
they aim at plumbing the depths of memory so as to bring forth the
monolithic radiance of an essentialized poetic image, redolent with
the lingering resonances of its historical and lyrical usage. In *Allegria*
such images form the timeless exultation of the poet's 'gridi' [cries
of joy], while in *Sentimento del tempo* they become, as we shall see
later, temporally prolonged so as to weave the connective tissue
between the poet's own emotions and those of the poetic tradition.
In both cases what Ungaretti is striving to create is a 'tempo del-
l'anima' [time of the spirit] which will simultaneously reflect the
consolidated lyricism of the past and graft on to it the contingent
experience of his own inner life. The product is an almost visceral
interaction between racial and personal feelings, whose atavism is
especially stressed in poems like 'Lucca'.

The simultaneity of sensations

In the process of creating tremulous, yet monolithic, images in
Allegria we note a tendency on Ungaretti's part to borrow and adapt
the futurist doctrine of the 'simultaneità delle sensazioni' [simul-
taneity of sensations] in art. This doctrine – which even stimulated
Apollinaire's imagination – is probably an offshoot of the futurists'
aesthetic of speed. When speed becomes infinite, they argued, then
all sensations coincide, and the dynamic or kinematic trend in
modern imagery should try to approximate in its effects to an ideal
of impressionistic synchronism of all the senses. Mostly with the
futurists the 'parola in libertà' amounts to a display of synesthesia,
but with Ungaretti it goes beyond this process to evoke a suggestively modern baroque continuum of momentary effects, replacing
concrete reality, almost as it were weight for weight, with a series
of lyrical inscapes, as may be seen in 'Rose in fiamme' [Roses in
flames]:

Su un oceano
di scampanellii
repentina
galleggia un'altra mattina

[On an ocean / of tinkling bells / suddenly / there floats another morning.]

This poem actually deals with the awakening of a village to the realities of the morning, but it is to be noted that allusive, secondary effects are evoked in place of the original concrete scene. This use of the second elements of analogical landscapes and the suppression of their first terms or actual physical outlines is a favourite device with all the hermetic poets. It might be regarded as a perfect form of *epoché*, since it essentializes and focuses emotive tensions without overt reference to initial circumstances, and its effectiveness consists in the raising of the analogical flash of remembrance instantaneously, without proceeding to intermediate conceptual generalizations, 'dall'inferno all'infinito d'una certezza divina' (*Poesie*, lxxvii) [from an infernal state to the infinite of a divine certainty]. With Ungaretti the leap is from the real world into one of transfigured emotion, not into a metaphysical realm of the kind proposed by Mallarmé; but, like the symbolists, he too may have derived the idea from Schopenhauer, since for the German philosopher all recollections amount to recalls of existential situations in the past shorn of their original emotional clashes and contradictions. As such, they must necessarily appear as lost paradises of serenity and are used by the imagination for purposes of lyrical consolation.

Death

What emerges from the process for Ungaretti is not so much an unreal form of consolatory escapism, however, as a third type of temporality: one which synthesizes both the concepts of *tempus* and *aevum* while still remaining realistic. We might call it a condition of orphic *co-temporality* which makes present existence seem nothing more than the tip of an iceberg, almost completely submerged in that greater ocean of memorial transformation or becoming which is death. This view of life and death's co-existence in the sphere of the *aevum* sometimes leads the poet to invert the two concepts, since death is the more clear-sighted. Thus in his poetry the idea of 'luce' [light] is often associated with the process of extinction and the idea of 'ombra' [shadow] or 'notte' [night] with man's purely contingent sensations. One apocalyptic example of this kind of inversion is to be seen in 'Ombra' written in 1927:

Uomo che speri senza pace,
Stanca ombra nella luce polverosa,
L'ultimo caldo se ne andrà a momenti

E vagherai indistinto ...

[O man who hopes restlessly, / a weary shadow in the dusty
light, / its final warmth will depart soon / and you will wander
dimly perceived.]

Although the poem appears to be a literal description of sunset, its
deeper implication is that true insight has died with the sun and all
that is left behind is the darkness of our sensory contingency. In
contrast with this, the poet uses light as an intense foil to emphasize
the opaqueness of the mysteries of death in 'Canto primo' of the
section *La morte meditata* [Death meditated], and throughout the
sequence, quite contrary to traditional representations of death,
images invoking light are predominant:

O sorella dell'ombra,
Notturna quanto piú la luce ha forza,
M'insegui, morte.
[O sister of shadows, / the fiercer the light the more nocturnal, /
you pursue me, death.]

However artificial this inversion may seem at first sight, it leads
to a fully developed, yet very different, outlook from that of the
traditional neoplatonic poets. For the conception which Ungaretti
holds of the lyric tradition is not the usual static one which considers
past and present to be in separate, watertight compartments; instead
he regards the one as overflowing into the other and vice versa, and
their osmotic interaction allows the modern poet to commune
intimately in the very act of composition with his dead ancestors.
They are, as he says, 'the shadows which give weight to our names',
while his own contingent existence is the flame which carries the
power of lyricism into the future. Yet as a torchbearer in the void of
time, he carries forward paradoxically not only his own light but
theirs too, so that death is not an unmitigated tragedy for him. On
the one hand it will render him an immortal – even if immobile –
memory in the consciousness of the race and provide him with the
consolation of an 'innocence regained':

Morte, arido fiume ...

Immemore sorella, morte,
L'uguale mi farai del sogno
Baciandomi.

Avrò il tuo passo,
Andrò senza lasciare impronta.

Mi darai il cuore immobile

D'un iddio, sarò innocente,
Non avrò piú pensieri né bontà. (Inno alla morte, *Poesie*, 117)

[Death, arid river ... / / Immemorial sister, death, / the equal
you will make me of a dream / by kissing me. / / I shall have your
step, / I shall walk without leaving a trace. / / You will give me
the motionless heart / of a god, I shall be innocent, / and shall
no longer have thoughts or goodness. *Hymn to death*]

While, on the other, he will then stand as a beacon-light to others:

Cogli occhi caduti in oblio,
Farò da guida alla felicità. (ibid., 118)

[With my eyes fallen into oblivion, / I shall act as a guide to
happiness.]

Orphism

What we can probably detect here are the two principal aspects of
orphism, the ancient and the modern. As we have previously indicated (p. 10), ancient orphism was a religious cult in which the adept
raised himself to an immortal, statuesque state of memorial omniscience by way of a ritual of purification in this life. This process of
purification could even continue through the successive lives of the
same individual by means of the 'eternal return' (or metempsychosis)
until such time as the adept was sufficiently purified to associate with
the Gods. In modern orphism on the other hand such recycling
through the 'great Wheel of Being' has been transferred from the
individual soul to the poetic image and this element of his lyricism is
successively refined or clarified within the poet's mind until it expresses the exact configuration of his mood. In our first quotation
from 'Inno alla morte' we thus sense the hypostasis of the ancient
orphic adept wholly immersed in his detached memorial dream of
omniscience, while in the second we detect the presence of the active
orphic poet who whispers the secret harmonies of his art to posterity
and thereby ensures the continuation of the hallowed 'voice' of the
Italian lyric through time. The latter concept is indeed not very
different from Petrarch's belief in the possibility of literary immortality within the Halls of Fame, while in English the same
doctrine has convincingly been advocated by Eliot in 'Tradition and
the individual talent' (1919), where he writes: 'No poet, no artist of
any art has his complete meaning alone. His significance, his appreciation is the appreciation of his relation to the dead poets and
artists. You cannot value him alone; you must set him, for contrast
and comparison, among the dead. I mean this as a principle of

aesthetic, not merely historical, criticism. The necessity that he shall conform, that he shall cohere, is not one-sided; what happens when a new work of art is created is something that happens to all the works of art which preceded it. The existing monuments form an ideal order among themselves, which is modified by the introduction of the new (the really new) work of art among them. The existing order is complete before the new work arrives; for order to persist after the supervention of novelty, the *whole* existing order must be, if ever so slightly, altered; and so the relations, proportions, values of each work of art toward the whole are readjusted; and this is conformity between the old and the new'.[3] We can regard this statement as a critical counterpart to Ungaretti's doctrine of lyrical resonance, which is essentially a cohering and simultaneously a breaking with the past through the supervention of novelty. He puts it as follows:

> Volevo suggerire che il poeta è difatti, quando riesca ad esprimersi, radicato nella storia, non potendo, se è poeta, non accorgersi della sofferenza umana che lo circonda; ma volevo soprattutto suggerire che al poeta, e per le vie che gli sono proprie e non possono essergli dettate, è impossibile, se riesca ad esprimersi, non sentirsi naturalmente portato a dare alle proprie parole un significato di rottura dei limiti della storia. (Spagnoletti, *Poesia italiana contemporanea*, 304)
> [I wished to suggest that the poet is indeed, whenever he succeeds in expressing himself, rooted in history, and is unable, if truly a poet, not to notice the human suffering around him; but I wished especially to suggest that it is impossible for the poet, except through the avenues which are his own and cannot be dictated to him – if he does manage to express himself – not to feel himself naturally driven to implying a sense of breakdown of the limits of history.]

Disintegration followed by reintegration is in other words Ungaretti's view of the authentic art-process. Through it he hopes to establish a new order of lyrical values, not in any ideal sense but rather as a constant revaluation of man's inner temporality. Hence, even if he depicts at one stage the very contingency of his artistic attitudes as a kind of eternalized transfiguration of the human world in a heavenly setting, the paradox is still more apparent than real, because he believes that a disembodied, theological heaven is unknowable to man, whereas a heaven of eternalized humanity with corporeal, life-like gestures is a readily understandable ideal. True,

such an ideal does not wholly transcend our human purview and
reveal the substance of God, but it does emphasize and reflect
human solidarity over the ages within the unfolding of the cultural
tradition. Hence in 'Dove la luce' [Where the light] we find him
hypostasizing his dead mother, and by extension himself and the
whole of humanity, in an eternal – yet still highly touching – gesture
of intimate, human slumber, no doubt representative of a vigilant
emotional subsisting after death:

> L'ora costante, liberi d'età,
> Nel suo perduto nimbo
> Sarà nostro lenzuolo.
> [Freed from time, the unchanging hour / in its lost halo / will
> be our bed-sheet.]

Here death appears to him as a sleep of endless human maturation in
a thoroughly existentialized, orphic dream-world; and, through the
previously mentioned 'buia veglia dei padri' [dark vigil of the
fathers], its secrets are constantly handed down from generation to
generation.

Literary influences

If we were to enquire of Ungaretti the origin of his aesthetic outlook, he would no doubt have claimed that he derived it pragmati-
cally from the European tradition, except perhaps for that single
process which we have already called the *reductio ad nullum* of the
world. This baroque device probably sprang from his childhood
impressions, especially those he encountered in the desert landscapes
around Alexandria, but also from his shattering wartime experiences
on the Carso. Mingled with his direct experiences, moreover, we
have to remember his indirect literary ones, since even when he was
still at school he tells us he had read Petrarch and Leopardi and had
even become involved in the literary appreciation of Mallarmé:

> Mi gettai su Mallarmé, lo lessi con passione ed, è probabile, alla
> lettera non lo dovevo capire; ma conta poco capire alla lettera
> la poesia: la sentivo. (*Poesie*, 506)
> [I threw myself at Mallarmé, I read him with passion and,
> probably, I did not understand him literally; but it counts for
> little to understand poetry to the letter: I felt it.]

At the same time he was deeply interested in Baudelaire and Nietzsche, but unlike his close friend Moammed Sceab who worshipped
at the shrine of these two authors, he tells us that he preferred
Mallarmé and Leopardi, and it may even have been from the Mal-

larmé of 'Igitur' that he drew his idea of 'il nulla'. In later years he
also acknowledges the influence of Góngora, Shakespeare, Donne,
Blake, Apollinaire and many others; but nevertheless his sheet-
anchor in the lyrical field is always the type of hermetic Petrarchism
practised by Mallarmé, which he closely associates with that peculiar
lucidity and historico-aesthetic understanding of the unfolding of
the poetic tradition which, as we shall see later, he considered implicit in Leopardi's outlook.

Petrarch

In trying to assess his debt to the lyric tradition, we have in the first
place to turn our attention to his earliest readings, and on this subject
he tells us that in his youth he opted decisively for Petrarch rather
than Dante. The reason for such a preference is no doubt to be found
in the respective styles of the two poets. In Ungaretti's view Dante's
poetic line is drawn from nature and is plastic and impressionistic in
quality, relying less on literary refraction than on direct perception
of the outside world. Petrarch, on the other hand, is in his opinion
largely dominated by his literary reminiscences and their concomitant musical inflections, and these often overwhelm Nature and its
immediate sense-impressions in his art. So in his essay on Petrarch –
significantly entitled *Il poeta dell'oblio* [The poet of oblivion] – he
links together Virgil, Tasso and Petrarch himself as poets of hushed
existential suspension, who work within a continuum of orphic
darkness which they allow to become the stable backcloth to their
imagery. To illustrate the point he quotes typical lines from each,
starting with Virgil:

> Quum medio volvuntur sidera lapsu
> Quum tacet omnis ager pecudesque pictaeque volucres.
>   (*Aeneid* IV, 524–5)
> [When the stars have rolled half their course / when the fields,
> flocks and gay-plumaged birds all are silent.]

He contrasts this peaceful scene of pastoral darkness with an equally
evocative and resonant one from Tasso:

> Era la notte allor ch'alto riposo
> han l'onde e i venti, e pare muto il mondo ...
>   (*Gerusalemme liberata*, II, 96)
> [It was the night when the waves and the winds / felt deep re-
> pose, and the world seemed hushed.]

Finally, he quotes Petrarch's own adaptation of the same Virgilian
lines:

> Or che 'l ciel e la terra e 'l vento tace
> e le fere e gli augelli il sonno affrena,
> Notte il carro stellato in giro mena,
> e nel suo letto il mar senz'onda giace ... (*Le Rime*, CLXIV)
> [Now that the heavens and earth and wind are silent / and the
> birds and wild beasts are tamed by sleep, / night wheels her
> starry chariot around, / and in its bed the sea lies waveless.]

Afterwards he tries to assess the varying poetic weight of these three
evocations and shows that by the time Tasso was writing, Italian –
thanks largely to Petrarch's elegiac cast of mind – had become a
mature language, relying more on its own keyboard of literary
reminiscences, on a return to its own origins and traditions, than on
the naturalistic effects on which Dante – through the lack of a
mature tradition – had been compelled to base his style. Petrarch's
revolution was consequently that of an intimate mellowing of
language, after which Italian could be classed – and indeed was
classed by foreigners such as Du Bellay – as the equal of the ancient
languages of Latin and Greek.

As a result of Petrarch's inventiveness, the continuum within
which the European lyric operates has never in Ungaretti's view
been the same again. From that time on it has acquired an orphic
dimension, because it has attempted a clarification and a reinterpretation of the past not against the intellectual backgrounds of theology
and philosophy, but against its own evolving emotions and its
temporally-ordained fluctuations in taste. Petrarch's ethical and
aesthetic goal was indeed for Ungaretti an ascent through the
memorial re-evocation of refracted literary impressions towards a
distant, even an unattainable, perspective of lyrical fulfilment and
plenitude. As he himself explains:

> Il Petrarca dilata il suo io nell'universo notturno, e vi si specchia
> coll'aiuto dei suoi ricordi, e si prova a decifrarvi il passato.
> (*Saggi*, 405)
> [Petrarch dilates his ego in a nocturnal universe, and mirrors
> himself there with the aid of his memories, and strives to deci-
> pher therein the past.]

Now inasfar as this strange new poetic continuum was based on the
orphic symbol of night used to represent pure, though as yet unformed, existence, it opened up a void to be filled; and it is precisely
because of this void in his work that Ungaretti refers to Petrarch as
the poet of oblivion. So, although the modern poet's own sense of
the void tended to arise instinctively at first from his experiences in

the desert, it is all too clear that his personal feelings were soon re-inforced by his early readings of the *Rime*.

For him Petrarch's closed circle of experiences has as its two polarities reality and the dream, and an endless dialectic results from their interaction which is to be equated with acts of recollection and forgetting. In his view recollection is a Petrarchan-like infusion into each poet's present sensations of an aura of past tradition as he tries to regenerate in a contemporary key the imagery and the lyrical resonances of the dead. Oblivion or forgetting, by contrast, is the means whereby we unburden ourselves of the lumber of past memories, although even this lumber still remains in the racial consciousness in a state of suspension until it can next be revivified. Ungaretti notes by way of definition that it amounts to 'esperienza nostra oscuratasi in noi, è la nostra interna notte' (*Saggi*, 408) [our experience grown dark within us, it is our internal night]. Like Petrarch himself, he considers that he reigns over a 'universo di fantasmi' [universe of phantoms], so that it is precisely the rekindling of memories in the present which gives rise to his peculiar type of humanism born at the intersection between tradition and immediate sensory perception. It is, as he again points out, the product of a 'fede quasi esclusiva, nell'immortalità dell'opera umana, nell'immortale momento di perfezione d'una civiltà, d'una lingua' (*Saggi*, 409) [almost exclusive faith in the immortality of human works, in the immortal moment of perfection of a civilization, of a language]. Petrarch's constant re-evocations of Laura, his virtual obsession with the passing of time and her hallucinatory absence, are similarly in Ungaretti's opinion the 'principio d' un disperato restauro nell'oblio da chiarire' (*Saggi*, 410) [basis of a desperate re-creation within the oblivion that is to be clarified], and all such desperate re-creations derive from an inaccessible orphic vision which he believes to be both Petrarch's lyrical faith and his own. He makes the point in the follow-ing way:

> Se noi potessimo ricordare tutto, e non dimenticassimo invece quasi tutto per l'enorme ignoranza che rare particole di cose lascia intravedere al ricordo, e male, noi sapremmo tutto, e non ci sarebbe più morte nel mondo. (*Saggi*, 410)
> [If we could remember everything, and did not instead forget nearly everything through the enormous ignorance which only allows us to glimpse scattered particles of things, and those but dimly, we would be all-knowing, and there would no longer be death in this world.]

Here the poet is simply contrasting as starkly as possible the perfect modes of recollection of the god-like orphic heroes of antiquity who have escaped from the constant reprocessing of the 'great Wheel of Being' and the fragmentary recalls of our own contingent minds. This attitude proves to be the guiding light for his interpretation of cultural history and also, as we shall see, for our comprehension of his poetry.

It is in Ungaretti's view only when we understand the deep ethical piety behind Petrarch's conception of recall that we can also understand Laura's true function. She is simultaneously a refraction of the literary past and a living beauty adhering closely to the poet's meditated, rather than immediate, sense-impressions. Petrarch is constantly desirous of restoring her to her pristine beauty despite the ravages of time, and his art is subsumed in this ritual of restoration, as Ungaretti explains when contrasting his manner with Shakespeare's:

> S'indugia l'amore del Petrarca a riparare le rovine minuto per minuto, quasi insensibile alla fuga del tempo, e dando al tempo gradualmente spazio d'infinita profondità storica, suscitando una forma, forma terrena, bellezza nell' incorruttibilità delle idee: Laura. (*40 Sonetti di Shakespeare*, 13)
>
> [Petrarch's love lingers over restoring its ruins minute by minute, almost insensible to the passage of time, and giving gradually to time the spaciousness of an infinite historical profundity, evoking a form, a terrestrial form, beauty in the incorruptibility of the idea: Laura.]

Since he cannot restore her beauty in flesh and blood, he tries to restore it in the infinite subtleties of his word-music; and, as her idealized, recollected grace emerges from his poetry, it serves paradoxically as the measure of our own imperfection: the imperfection of our contingent human condition and its powers of lyrical expression, which the fourteenth-century poet constantly tries to extend in his verse.

The inner plenitude of Petrarch's spirit, as opposed to the necessarily fragmentary insights of his actual poetry, emerges therefore in Ungaretti's view not so much from his imagery as from his sense of musicality; from which we can, perhaps, deduce that with him the melodic inflection is more important in the last resort even than the refracted literary reminiscence. But melodiousness is not merely the result of phonic combinations, it also includes lyrical tone and imaginative landscaping; and the result is a clarity and a limpidity of outline which allow the fourteenth-century poet's word-music to act as the power which fuses together memory and attenuated sensations in the *Rime*. For Ungaretti it is in this intimate synthesis that the true weight of Petrarch's lyrical patterning lies: his poetic line is a chord surrounded by an infinite memorial silence, both visionary and hermetic in its overtones and resonances.

Baroque poetry

We have already associated the infinite silence of the void with the baroque in Ungaretti's aesthetics; but, when we try to discover the origins of the baroque mode itself, again Petrarch proves to be its major source. In his 'astruserie' [word-plays] he attempts in Ungaretti's view to reanimate ancient mythology through 'concetti' [conceits] which remind us constantly of the art of the *Seicentisti*. In fact, Ungaretti quotes the bizarre ending of Sonnet XXXIV as an example of evocativeness taken to the highest possible degree; yet the conceitedness of the illustration also reveals his own baroque tastes, for the imagery deployed describes the lady as being simultaneously a woman and a laurel-tree, protecting herself with her own shade from the sun as she sits on the grass:

> Sí vedrem poi per meraviglia inseme
> seder la Donna nostra sopra l'erba
> e far de le sue braccia a se stessa ombra.

> [Thus shall we see through a miracle together / our Lady seated on the grass / and making with her arms a shade for herself.]

However, although Ungaretti acknowledges that many images like this one appear in Petrarch's poetry, in the last analysis he still does not count him as inventing, but simply as prefiguring baroque modes. Instead he normally seeks his illustrations of baroque writing from other poets, but not from Tasso whom he also regards as little more than an ambiguous precursor of the movement.

On the one hand Ungaretti clearly acknowledges the latter's classicism, exemplified in the lines previously quoted (p. 41) where he compared Tasso's orphic tendencies with those of Virgil. Yet even while agreeing that he has a fine Virgilian ear, elsewhere he suspects his manner so much that he describes him as 'il vero primo Arcade; un Arcade che pure rimaneva un Barocco, e forse già era un Romantico' (*Saggi*, 454) [the first true Arcadian; an Arcadian who still remained a baroque writer, and who was perhaps already a Romantic].

The authentic baroque poets, by contrast, seem to him to adhere much more closely to the classical norm, even though they become 'gli atleti della regola ricevuta, gli allenati invasati che fanno alle forze, i titani della regola' (*Saggi*, 453) [the athletes of the prescribed rules, the obsessed champions who make a test of strength, the Titans of the rules]. And, he adds forebodingly: 'C'è sempre da essere allarmati quando in arte, e in qualsiasi attività della vita, compaiono gli atleti' [there is always reason to be alarmed when in art, or in any of life's activities, the athletes make their appearance]. Very much like De Sanctis he seems to think that art gradually declined after the Cinquecento into an empty musicality, although for him the baroque period is an interlude in that process: one which foreshortened Petrarch's wide-ranging memorial vistas but did not destroy them completely. What occurred after these temporal perspectives had been compressed was that poets came face to face with the spectre at the end of memory's tunnel, that is, with death. To escape from its starkness and corruption they tended to indulge in a cult of intense sensation; and later it was indeed an escape from this struggle between sensation and death which the Arcadians sought when they allowed poetry to degenerate into a form of pastoral sentimentality.

As we already know, the full impact of the baroque mode did not strike Ungaretti until he took up residence in Rome in the early twenties, since it was there that he was finally confronted with the art of Michelangelo whom he considered to be the inventor of the baroque manner. He states:

> Michelangelo mi ha rivelato, dunque, il segreto del barocco. Non è una nozione astratta che possa definirsi con proposizioni logiche. È un segreto di vita interiore, e la lunga intimità con quel barocco, che mi era poco prima tanto estraneo, mi ha abilitato all'accettazione di tutte le differenze, di tutte le tensioni interne, di tutti quegli apporti che l'uomo può pervenire a fondere nel suo proprio genio, se ne avessi [sic]. (*Poesie*, 530)
>
> [Michelangelo therefore revealed to me the secret of the baroque. It is not an abstract idea which can be defined with logical propositions. It is a secret inner life, and a long intimacy with that type of baroque which was a little earlier so foreign to me, has accustomed me to accept all clashes, all internal tensions, all those additional elements which a man can succeed in merging into his own genius, should he have any.]

Of what then did the baroque secrets of Michelangelo consist? Ungaretti tries to answer the question by reverting once more to Petrarch and Laura. He tells us that whereas Laura represents an

absent universe, 'un universo da ricuperare' [a universe to recapture],
Michelangelo's universe is not one of absence to be redeemed, but
one of forlorn emptiness; so that, in point of fact, 'il vuoto nel-
l'ispirazione poetica appare con Michelangelo' (*Poesie*, 535) [the void
emerges in poetic inspiration with Michelangelo]. In Ungaretti's view
this emptiness amounts virtually to an absence of God, and his whole
ontology of the baroque spirit is summed up in a series of anguished
questions, as follows:

> La sensazione dell'assenza radicale dell'essere è forse, in realtà,
> sensazione dell'assenza divina? Solo Dio può sopprimere il
> vuoto, essendo, Egli, l'Essere, essendo, Egli, la Plenitudine? È il
> sentimento dell'assenza di Dio in noi, rappresentato non sim-
> bolicamente, rappresentato, in realtà, da quell'orrore del vuoto,
> da quella vertigine, da quel terrore? Michelangelo e alcuni
> uomini dalla fine del '400 sino al '700 avevano, in Italia, quel
> sentimento, il sentimento dell'orrore del vuoto, cioè dell'orrore
> di un mondo privo di Dio. (*Poesie*, 535)
>
> [Is the feeling of a radical absence of Being perhaps, in reality, a
> feeling of divine absence? Can only God suppress the void, since
> He is Being, since He is Plenitude? Is the feeling of the absence
> of God within us represented not symbolically, but represented,
> in reality, by that horror of the void, by that sense of vertigo, by
> that terror? Michelangelo and a few men from the end of the
> fifteenth up till the eighteenth century had, in Italy, that feeling,
> a feeling of horror of the void, that is of horror of a world
> deprived of God.]

Now just as Petrarch experienced an overwhelming desire to
restore Laura's presence through recollection, so the baroque artists
of the *Seicento* felt an equal desire to restore that sense of memorial
perspective which they had abolished by their metaphysical obsession
with the void. In order to achieve their aim, they indulged in an
excessive cult of immediate sensations, which did not in fact succeed
in dilating their foreshortened vistas but at least gave them the
impression of filling the void with a superabundance of forms. Hence
their attempts at restoring the past through memory amount to the
superimposing of a multitude of sensory images upon the void, and
although this was clearly not a solution to their artistic problem, it
gave them momentarily the illusion that their faculty of memory
had not been so foreshortened as to reach the point of extinction. In
fact, we can describe their cult of luxuriant and far-fetched imagery
as a kind of instinctive recoil from the reality of their condition, a

compensatory *horror vacui* – a horror, that is, of sheer subsistence devoid of memory.

Still, however impressed Ungaretti was by Michelangelo's apocalyptic vision, his own baroque taste does not fall naturally into the main stream of Italian baroque literature. He tends to avoid Marino's sultry luxuriance in favour of Góngora's 'culteranesimo' or even, at times, for the approach of the English 'metaphysicals', especially Donne. Admittedly, he does not actually take up an entirely negative attitude to Marino and expresses the curious view that the *Adone* had a powerful influence on French classicism, especially Racine; but at the same time he judges the seventeenth-century Italian poet's cult of the marvellous as 'lo spropositato dell'ispirazione' (*Saggi*, 529) [the grotesque in inspiration]. In its place he proposes the 'argutezza' [the wit] of Góngora, which he considers to be a more satisfying way of depicting the strange sensuo-metaphysical drama played out by baroque artists. Later, in addition to Góngora, he not only acknowledged Donne as a master in this field but also Shakespeare, Scève, and even Blake, despite the fact that the latter is, strictly speaking, chronologically outside the baroque canon.

Perhaps what most attracted Ungaretti to the baroque was his belief that it amounted to an exacerbated stage of Petrarchism which still, however, in the last resort clings to the original Petrarchan belief that the profoundest human insights can only be expressed 'per rivelazione di parola memore' (*Saggi*, 528) [by the revelation of the hallowed word]. So, once the cultural tradition of the Renaissance had exhausted both the poetic and technical modes of Petrarchism, the baroque poets could only flounder about in the wasteland which had been left to them; and their new synthesis, their new poetic 'word', amounted to a turning away from Petrarch's memorial resonances towards the sensuous impressionism of the present, which replaced for them the cultural keyboard of the past. As Ungaretti puts it himself, they demanded 'tale parola che anche aderisse, e con estrema immediatezza, al loro esistere carnale' (*Saggi*, 529) [that such a word should even adhere, and with absolute immediacy, to their carnal existence]. Accordingly, they envisaged life as the struggle of the ephemeral, sentient being to maximize his enjoyment before his inevitable decline; and, as living became for them an obsessive cult of sensation, they introduced into art a process of 'trompe-l'œil' [visual illusionism], with the express aim of 'outwitting' death.

The spectre of death, however, constantly lurks in the wings behind the baroque poet's world-picture and creates in his mind a feeling of restlessness and 'caducità' [transiency]. Hence Ungaretti's description of baroque art is one in which

> il decoro del secolo precedente è mandato in frantumi e ricosti-
> tuito in modo che sia armonioso, ma mettendo in risalto una
> violenza di rovina, senza – sebbene sia stato il Barocco a inven-
> tare lo spirito d'evasione insegnando a fare tesoro dell'esotico –
> lasciare, per potersi uno rivolgere ad altri pensieri, la minima
> libertà di spazio. (*Fedra di Jean Racine*, 10)
>
> [the propriety of the preceding century is broken up and re-
> constituted in a way which is harmonious, but which throws
> into relief a ruinous violence, without leaving – although it was
> the baroque which invented the escapist spirit by teaching us to
> cherish the exotic – the slightest spatial freedom, to enable us to
> turn to other thoughts.]

Shakespeare and Góngora

According to Ungaretti there are two main categories of baroque poets who aspire to this new type of harmony: those who recount moment by moment the decline of vigour with age, and those who make an eternity of the vitality of the passing moment. Shakespeare is the prototype of the first category, Góngora of the second. The Shakespeare of the sonnets, he tells us, is essentially confined to one obsessive theme, the evocation of 'la bellezza nella drammaticità della sua gioventú effimera e permanente' (*Saggi*, 567) [beauty in the dramatic force of its transient and yet permanent youth]. With him, in other words, the eternal pattern of the beautiful is framed in the transient world of forms against the background of the destructive-ness of death. The result is a kind of manichaeism in which the perennial indestructibility of youth is offset by its constant fading in the individual. On the other hand, Góngora's formulation of the baroque is his cult of an instantaneous or contingent eternity. As Ungaretti himself explains:

> La novità del Góngora era di sentire il valore ossessivo degli
> oggetti, era di affinare ogni accortezza d'arte affinché gli oggetti
> nei vocaboli ritrovassero e attestassero la verità sensuale della
> realtà. (*Saggi*, 529)
>
> [The novelty of Góngora was his sense of the obsessive value of
> things, it was his refining of every artistic insight so that through
> words objects might rediscover and attest the sensuous truth of
> reality.]

But precisely because of the peculiar sensuo-metaphysical nature of

the baroque mode, Góngora's obsessive and magnified sensations
also tend in the end to dissolve and become swallowed up by the
void. The types of momentary vision he produces are somewhat
intellectualized and abstract, not direct representations of the real
world. Instead they prove to be fundamentally a 'realtà di cultura'
[a cultural reality] and it is wholly in this sense that Ungaretti under-
stands 'culteranesimo'.

He illustrates the point by quoting from Góngora's sonnet 'Mien-
tras por competir' where, true to his desire to present us with a
pageant of pure literary sensations flitting perilously over an ever-
present existential abyss, the Spanish poet urges his lady to enjoy
her physical charms immediately, at the moment of their fruition,
because soon they will fall to dust:

> Goza, cuello, cabello, labio y frente,
> Antes que lo que fué en tu edad dorada,
> Oro, lirio, clavel, cristal luciente,
> No sólo en plata, o víola troncada
> Se vuelva, ma tú, y ello juntamente,
> En tierra, en humo, en polvo, en sombra, en nada.

> [Enjoy, neck, hair, lip and brow, / before what once was in
> your golden age, / gold, lily, carnation, shining crystal, / not
> only to silver, or a plucked violet / be changed, but you and it
> together, / turn to earth, smoke, dust, shadow, nothingness.]

By considering poems of this kind, Ungaretti concludes that
Góngora's style proceeds 'per squilli di tromba' [by trumpet-blasts],
because

> ciascun elemento ha, per quanto fondendosi, piú che non si
> fosse mai visto, negli altri, vita avulsa dagli altri, vita cruda-
> mente indipendente, vita che vale perché manifesta e sollecita
> sensazioni di calore, di splendore, di spasimo fisico: ossessive
> sensazioni visive, tattili. (*Saggi*, 535)

> [each element although blending with the others, has, more
> than had ever been seen before, a life foreign to the others, a life
> crudely independent, a life which is authenticized because it
> displays and stimulates sensations of warmth, of splendour, of
> physical shuddering: obsessive visual, tactile sensations.]

So, while Shakespeare resorts to a form of neoplatonism, or better
to an orphic return of youth, in which he sees the indestructible
image of the Beautiful behind the tragic fading of all instances of
earthly beauty, Góngora tries to consolidate earthly beauty in its
momentary fruition, by weaving a dense web of powerful yet

artistically hypostasized sensations over the abyss of time. Since, in
short, Góngora's aim is to shore up his imagery against its inevitable
ruin, impermanence in his poetry is offset by a new form of per-
manence on a purely mental level, by a phenomenology which sees
all experience in a suspended state of temporal parenthesis, where,
while retaining its sense of transience, it offers us a moment of
perfect maturity.

Blake

Ungaretti's considerations on Blake take this process a stage further,
because he believes that the latter finally welds the baroque aesthetic
into a visionary metaphysic. For him Blake's whole output is a type
of miracle, one which appears to mythify and therefore to unite the
fragments of the earlier baroque Muse into a coherent whole:

> Il miracolo, come facevo a dimenticarmene, è frutto, me l'aveva
> insegnato Mallarmé, di memoria. A furia di memoria si torna,
> o ci si può illudere di tornare, innocenti … E il miracolo è
> parola: per essa il poeta si può arretrare nel tempo sino dove lo
> spirito umano risiedeva nella sua unità e nella sua verità, non
> ancora caduto in frantumi, preda del Male, esule per vanità,
> sbriciolato nelle catene e nel tormento delle infinite fattezze
> materiali del tempo. (*Saggi*, 597)
>
> [The miracle, how did I come to forget it, is the fruit, as Mal-
> larmé taught me, of memory. By dint of memory one returns
> or persuades oneself that one returns to a state of innocence …
> And the miracle is the word: through it the poet can regress in
> time to the point where the human spirit stands unified in its
> truth, not as yet shattered into fragments, a prey to Evil, es-
> tranged by vanity, and crumbling in the fetters and torments of
> the infinite material facets of time.]

It seems, therefore, that Blake's search for a world of innocence
transcends the disintegrating world of the baroque and changes its
artificial cult of surprise into a fresh immediacy of the senses: one
which springs from a feeling of wonder or self-surprise at the vividness of the poet's own sharply experienced sensations. This im-
plosive form of self-surprise, as we have already noted, is at the root
of Ungaretti's own baroque aesthetics.

Leopardi

The next significant stage in Ungaretti's cultural outlook centres on
Leopardi, for whom he expressed a lifelong admiration. He again

places Leopardi firmly within the Petrarchan tradition and assures us that 'memoria e innocenza sono gl'inscindibili termini della poetica del Leopardi' (*Saggi*, 434) [memory and innocence are the inseparable poles of Leopardi's poetics]. On the other hand, in his view Leopardi differs from Petrarch in the sense that he seeks in antiquity not models of wisdom but examples of living, since he felt instinctively obliged to transform knowledge into sentiment before he could make effective use of it in his verse. Leopardi consequently stands for reason tempered with emotion, for wisdom on a human scale, whereas Petrarch was normally inclined to rely more on the atemporal wisdom associated with the medieval conception of 'auctoritas', even though his 'auctores' were decisively those of antiquity rather than the medieval theologians. As a result, even memory for Leopardi

> non è piú tanto intellettiva funzione, mera attività in sede mentale, quanto sofferenza del corpo, sensibile presenza cosí nella storia dei singoli come in quella delle civiltà e financo in quella dell'universo. (*Saggi*, 438)
>
> [is not so much an intellectual function, a mere activity in the mental sphere, as a bodily suffering, a corporeal presence both in the history of individuals and in that of civilizations, even in that of the cosmos.]

The nineteenth-century poet does not operate like Petrarch in a reflective – and thereby detached – artistic sphere, but rather in the sphere of nature itself. Nature represents for him an immutable and eternal beauty, with which man contrasts the transient beauties of his own traditions; and his inner world is peopled by things which Ungaretti defines almost in a 'laric' sense as the 'familiarità degli oggetti' (*Saggi*, 440) [familiarity of objects]. Leopardi's poetry is in other words wholly one of human scale, dealing with everyday life and common humanity; and yet these familiar objects and situations are often framed within a more terrifying structure, the arid expanses of cosmic space.

Since Leopardi was continually aware of the precariousness of his condition, he naturally searches in his turn for some ontological constant on which to base his philosophy, and he eventually realizes that while times and customs undergo continual change, one quality in human life is immutable: its anguish. In Ungaretti's view, this sense of anguish is the outcome of an unconscious Christian conditioning of his mind, but nevertheless Leopardi does not choose to treat his grief as a concomitant of the Christian processes of sin and redemption; he prefers to regard it as a form of modern heroism which resists the buffetings of Fate. This is an attitude which parallels in all essentials the heroism of antiquity and results in a cry of combined hope and despair echoing endlessly down the ages. In his philological studies Ungaretti accordingly sees Leopardi as refracting through the traditional usage of the poetic word the whole course of human history. His theory of stylistic 'elegance' amounts to a natural regeneration of the lyrical voice within the bounds of the tradition, perhaps to be identified with what Cardarelli once called 'una felice infrazione all'uso' (*Opere comp.*, 520) [a happy dislocation of usage]. This idea is closely related to Ungaretti's own views on the sacred in art, because he tells us that 'il linguaggio è sacro, se è legato al mistero della nostra origine, e dell'origine del mondo' (*Saggi*, 471) [language is sacred, if it is linked to the mystery of our origin, and to the origin of the world]. Even so, for Leopardi the substance of this mystery is not religious revelation in the orthodox sense, it is compounded from the very density of sensations and aesthetic responses locked in the human tradition and it is produced whenever 'il ricordo dall'oblio si risusciti, dolcemente vago in un'infinita malinconia di pensieri' (*Saggi*, 488) [a memory is reborn from oblivion, gently lulled in an infinite melancholy of thought].

Since Leopardi's view of the poet's duty was historico-aesthetic, his lyrical practices slowly underwent a further metamorphosis. Afterwards he no longer tended to operate in a baroque sphere of culture but in a transfigured sphere of nature. Natural objects like trees then became for him, in the modern poet's opinion, symbolic expressions of human nature, and this type of anthropomorphism turns out to be a newly-discovered world of pathos and primitivism of feeling, though a far more self-conscious one than ancient primitivism itself ever was. The happy combination of sensation and sentiment which such a lyrical attitude produces leads directly to an understanding of stylistic responsibility, the forerunner, or so it seems, of the hermetic school's equally self-conscious, critical and artistic responsibility. Leopardi reaches this position by adopting a relativistic attitude to art and literature, so that he is always conscious of the mutability of taste as it unfolds throughout the ages and believes that it is the duty of each poet to re-create in a new key the composite song of human anguish for his own generation. Similarly the infinite variety he displays in the expression of pathos and in re-evoking the harmonics associated with the poetic 'word' again

provides in Ungaretti's judgement Leopardi's immense range of
lyrical values, and he asserts:

> Per ritrovare le tradizioni della nostra poesia e proseguirle, per
> rituffare la nostra poesia nella storia, si doveva risalire al Leo-
> pardi, e capirlo. (*Saggi*, 490)
>
> [to rediscover the traditions of our lyricism and continue them,
> to replunge our poetry into history, one had to return to Leo-
> pardi, and understand him.]

Indeed, all the poets of the nineteenth century following him seem
in his view to be anachronistic by Leopardian standards, except perhaps Pascoli.

Baudelaire and Bergson

Leopardi's essentially classical treatment of passion and pathos was
as far as Ungaretti himself was prepared to go in the direction of
romanticism: he was never willing to take the further escapist step
of moving into an area of sentimentality. In this sphere, of course,
sentiment necessarily gives way to the subjective illusion of the
pathetic fallacy, which Ungaretti rejects so completely that he
passes over a whole epoch of European literature and readjusts his
cultural focus deliberately to concentrate on the post-romantics,
especially the 'poètes maudits '[accursed poets] of the French decadent school and the symbolists. His rejection of romanticism may be
illustrated by his view of Hugo, who he says 'porta il dramma nelle
immagini, ma senza intuire propagini complessive' (*Saggi*, 10)
[carries drama into his images, but without perceiving complex
structures]. By contrast, he greatly admires Baudelaire whom he
regards as the real torchbearer of the future in the Romantic age. He
associates him closely with Leopardi's historical and atavistic perspectives and describes him as:

> Poeta di una razza; venuto a risoffrirla e rigoderla in tutte le
> sue epoche, in tutti i suoi palpiti, in tutte le sue fantasime,
> in tutti i suoi inquinamenti, in tutta la sua estrema purità.
> (*Saggi*, 11)
>
> [Poet of a race, come to suffer for it and to enjoy it again in all
> its epochs, in all its pangs, in all its phantoms, in all its states of
> corruption, in all its extremes of purity.]

What Baudelaire achieves above all for Ungaretti is to fuse the
baroque elements of modern life with a new type of classicism, by
rediscovering the hidden memorial connections between objects in
his *analogie universelle* or *correspondance*. The result is that he tends to

stand as the modern poet of the whole Latin race, not merely of the French people. Likewise Bergson complements Baudelaire on a philosophical level, especially in his analysis of the powers of intuition. So much so that Ungaretti says of him that 'rovistando sin dentro la linfa del tempo, egli ha aperto spiragli sin nelle radici dell'essere' (*Saggi*, 86) [groping deep in the lymph of time, he has opened up shafts even into the roots of being]. Thus, since life is often envisaged by the Italian poet as an immense dialectic between being and becoming, between dreaming and wakefulness, the interpretative rôle which he considers these two writers play in the modern age is equally immense. Their ideas are not only crucial to his own art, but also for the development of the whole of modern taste.

Mallarmé and the French tradition

Even more important for Ungaretti than Baudelaire was perhaps Mallarmé. As we have already hinted, he considered the latter to be an involuted Petrarchist who at times showed an excessive faith in the allusive qualities of words. He already knew Mallarmé's poetry – as he knew Baudelaire's and Leopardi's – when he was still in his early youth in Egypt; but he tells us that his understanding of Mallarmé's deeper implications only came to him with time. What enchanted him from the outset was his word-music, although he himself differs essentially from the late nineteenth-century French poet in one vital respect, in that he is an immanentist or realist poet whereas Mallarmé was always a transcendental Platonist. The same thing applies to his relationship with Valéry whose poetry he describes as a 'lirica dell'intelletto' (*Saggi*, 85) [lyricism of the intellect]. Consequently their specific contribution to his own art is mainly in the area of orphic synthesis and his manner of perceiving the world; and, although Mallarmé's traditional orphism is certainly at the root of Ungaretti's more modern form, it is nevertheless filtered beforehand through Campana's *Canti orfici*, or even earlier through Pascoli and certain elements in the crepuscular poets, especially Corazzini.

Other French poets influencing Ungaretti's critical perspectives have been mentioned by Rebay[4] and they include poets like Guérin, Verhaeren, Reverdy and Apollinaire, the latter being no doubt the vehicle through which the lessons of Baudelaire, Rimbaud and Mallarmé were driven home to him. On the other hand, his admiration for surrealism and the surrealists was at best only lukewarm, despite his friendship with Breton; and, as for Dadaism, his opinion may be judged from a disparaging remark he once made about its arch-priest Tristan Tzara, of whom he observed 'je n'ai jamais considéré ça plus que de la farce' (*Saggi*, 38) [I have never considered him as being more than a farce]. He maintained this attitude towards extreme literary movements throughout his life, and indeed neither surrealism nor Dadaism ever caught on in Italy, although certain modern Italian poets use their procedures occasionally to produce specific lyrical effects.

Ungaretti showed an equal interest in the painting of the first decades of the century, particularly in the post-impressionist, cubist, futurist, orphic and metaphysical painters, among others. At one stage he even went so far as to assert that fine art and poetry are the fundamental arts, whereas music and dancing can at best be nothing more than accessories to the other two. But for him poetry is even more important than painting, since poetry works in many di-mensions while 'la pittura fa vedere: questo è il limite, troppo spesso dimenticato, dei suoi mezzi' (*Saggi*, 271) [painting concentrates on the visual: this is the limit, all too often forgotten, of its modes].

Futurism

With regard to those twentieth-century movements indigenous to Italy, he tells us at once that futurism is a by-product of French decadentism and he contrasts it with surrealism by observing that, whereas the former is an imitation of the 'cieco oggettivo' [blind objectiveness], the latter is the result of a 'cieco soggettivo' [blind subjectiveness] (*Saggi*, 361). What differentiates his own art from both, he observes, is that before putting pen to paper he divests his words of all arbitrary elements and ensures that they reach 'una pienezza di contenuto morale' [a fullness of moral content]. The arch-futurist Marinetti, by contrast, sought only in his view an 'impressionabilità fisica' (*Saggi*, 298) [physical impressionism].

The one quality Ungaretti prized in futurism, on the other hand, was its struggle to replace traditional logic with certain associations of ideas, although even in this area he regarded the futurists' cult of mechanical processes instead of the free-ranging activity of the creative memory as a simple, exasperated flexing of the artist's muscles, a kind of gymnastic rather than an authentic creativity. So of all the so-called futurists the one he seems to favour most is the painter-poet Soffici, especially the Soffici of the *Primi principi di una estetica futurista* [First principles of a futurist aesthetic] (1920). In reviewing this book he points out that, like himself, Soffici believes that art tends towards a 'libération suprême' (*Saggi*, 43) [supreme liberation]; and, in complete contrast with this idea of supreme liberation, he sees the telegraphic style of the futurist 'parola in libertà' as a kind of 'cieca fiducia nella materia grezza' (*Saggi*, 172) [blind faith in one's raw impressions], which can only result in a gratuitous display of sensations.

Croce

All in all, therefore, Ungaretti remained steadfastly of the opinion that experimentation in art is only significant if the artist recognizes that it is not an end in itself, but simply a means of heightening emotional tension and presenting it in an appropriate form. In the last resort it is always lyrical substance which is important, not the vehicle of its expression; and here, it is to be emphasized, he tends to differ even from the extremists of the hermetic school whose lyrical views he can be said to have been the first to formulate. In his contempt for the hermetic 'technocrat' it could perhaps be argued that he had learned Croce's lesson that form and substance must be intimately combined to create authentic lyricism; but he also clearly stresses that he differs from Croce in emphasizing that the role of memory in art is as vital as that of imagination. For him, in fact, Croce's doctrines lack a fundamental historico-aesthetic perspective and only deal with the immediacies of intuition. He puts the point in the following way:

> La debolezza del sistema crociano ch'egli stesso ebbe a rilevare applicandolo, dipende da un piccolo errore del Croce, intorno al quale Croce gira e rigira, ma che esita a riconoscere anche ora, dopo che gli è stato indicato da tutta la polemica letteraria svoltasi in Italia e fuori, negli ultimi quindici anni. Vico aveva detto: fantasia e memoria. Il Romanticismo è sorto negando – negando fino ad un certo punto – negando la memoria. Croce, venendo fuori direttamente dalle estetiche romantiche, ha creduto che Vico non avesse parlato se non di fantasia e nel suo spirito, intuizione ed espressione non entrano in funzione se non per virtú di sola fantasia. La verità, la verità che chi ha praticato l'arte dovrebbe conoscere bene, è che non c'è fatto artistico, che non c'è identità fra intuizione e espressione se la fantasia, e la memoria, funzioni necessarie dell'intuizione, non divengono funzioni dell'espressione. (*Saggi*, 344–5).

[The weakness of the Crocean system, which he himself had to

acknowledge in applying it, depends on a small error made by
Croce around which he twists and turns, but hesitates to accept
even now, even after it has been pointed out to him by the whole
literary polemic waged inside and outside Italy, in the last
fifteen years. Vico had said: fantasy and memory. Romanticism
grew up denying – denying to a certain extent – denying
memory. Croce, emerging directly from romantic aesthetics,
thought that Vico had only spoken of fantasy and in his mind
intuition and expression operate by virtue of fantasy alone. The
truth, the truth which those who have practised art should know
well, is that there is no artistic product, that there is no identity
between intuition and expression unless fantasy, and memory,
both necessary functions of intuition, equally become functions
of expression.]

In short, Ungaretti sees Croce as explicitly denying that orphically-
orientated sense of taste and history which he believes began with
Leopardi's aesthetics and subsequently developed into a special
feature of the modern sensibility. In the last resort he even regards
him as misrepresenting Vico's *twin* messages of imagination and
memory; and so in a partial condemnation of his doctrine he points
out that expression too has its own historical hinterland in that it
echoes and re-echoes literary refractions from the past. If then Croce
applies his a-historical doctrine strictly and without modification to
his criticism, he automatically cuts himself off from appreciating
the resonances of most poets' melodic lines.

The emphasis which he places on Croce's lack of historical perspective brings us back to our point of departure, to Ungaretti's
views on Petrarchism and the memorial process through time. As
Diacono explains, all the poet's criticism is in a sense a self-reading
(autolettura) because he specifically picks out for the purposes of
study poets in whom he finds modern elements, and these elements
are then destined to be incorporated into his own art and aesthetic
theories (*Saggi*, lxvi). For preference he chooses to write about those
who accept or at least exemplify some aspect of Petrarch's elegiac
cast of mind, although he also recognizes the major defect of this
type of poetry: its lack of a positive, forward-looking dimension and
its tendency to recoil, as though shell-shocked, from all commerce
with elements in the present which have non-elegiac implications
for the future.

Death is perhaps the only promise for the future that Petrarch's
work in the last resort offers, and the same thing seems to apply for

Ungaretti. But the modern poet elaborates on the Petrarchan idea of death, giving it at least an eternal, if not a future, dimension. What is clear is that he does not see it either as an unknowable absurdity like Cardarelli or as a state of memorial inertia like Montale. Instead it becomes in his eyes a resonance-chamber of the human tradition quivering with the authentic lyrical voices of the past such as Leopardi, Baudelaire, Mallarmé and others. It is indeed this memory-laden song of humanity passed down from age to age that he values most, and he struggles to recapture it in his own verse while constantly attempting to analyse it in his critical writings.

3. *Allegria* and Associated Collections of Early Poetry

Ungaretti's first volume of poetry which in its definitive version is entitled *Allegria* was not originally composed as a single unit; it is instead an amalgam of several distinct components, including *Il porto sepolto* (1916), *Allegria di naufragi* (1919), and various other enlarged re-editions of one or the other of these volumes, spread over a period of some twenty years. The collection, in fact, only takes on its final form in 1942, although its definitive title already appears as early as 1931, in the Preda edition. Because of this somewhat chequered history we find that it acquired its present structure as a result of a steady accumulation of lyrics over the same period of time; but this is perhaps not the most serious of the problems associated with the work: far more intractable is the great profusion of variants between editions, since the definitive text is not only changed considerably in style, imagery and content from the first edition, it also differs in many respects from all the intervening editions, while these too differ significantly among themselves. What we are dealing with, therefore, is a process of organic lyrical growth, and the real reason for the volume's long period of gestation lies in the fact that Ungaretti consciously adopted Petrarch's cult of variants. Since, moreover, he used this procedure as a method of improving his initial lyrical textures and perspectives throughout his entire career, we soon discover that the only stable feature in his endless struggle for self-expression is his sense of approximating more and more closely in successive editions to the 'ideal' mood or pristine essence of the poetic vision he had really been intent on evoking from the very beginning.

Fortunately a number of examinations have already been made of a wide range of variants in the different editions of this and other collections, although none deals with his poetry as a whole. From the various partial analyses available we can deduce that a certain process of involution or 'hermeticizing' of Ungaretti's imagery took place with the passage of time, since, as Genot (36–9) has recently pointed out, there is a tendency towards parataxis, hypo-parataxis and disjunction as we proceed towards the definitive text. Indeed at

times these features are accompanied by other technical and linguistic artifices as well, such as ellipsis, experimentation with pre-
positions, the juxtaposition of nouns and adjectives in a striking
manner, and so on. The continuous process of refinement which
results undoubtedly gives us some confidence in making a choice of
the definitive text as our basic working material, at least from the
aesthetic standpoint, since the line of development towards it seems
to be both artistically progressive and unambiguous. Furthermore,
although his variants seem largely linguistic at first sight, Ungaretti's
patient experimentation with words eventually tends to have an
aesthetic rather than a merely verbal impact, especially when he
succeeds in changing the direction of the allusive resonances in his
poetry. Yet, oddly enough, the process does not radically change
the underlying substance of most compositions, and from this we
soon realize that in the last resort his object was to clarify in an orphic
sense (see p. 38) – not to substitute for – his original lyrical perspectives. For all these reasons, therefore, and despite the fact that from
a purely historical standpoint we cannot avoid a certain distortion
of the literary facts, we are driven to conclude that the use of the
definitive text will be the most satisfactory way of examining the
collection. Even so, our analysis of it will be interspersed with appropriate examples of lyrical forms drawn from earlier variants when
required.

Although Ungaretti's style, as we have indicated already, tends to
become more hermetic with the passage of time, the loss of content
in the definitive edition usually amounts to nothing more serious
than the omission of discursive elements or autobiographical material
in favour of certain compressed 'fulminations' or analogical flashes
of insight. At the same time a deeper involution and a greater complexity can be seen to be evolving in his symbolism; although again,
paradoxically, even while he was developing his linguistic and
symbolic compression, he was simultaneously moving away from
the prosodic dislocation he had inherited from the futurist cult of
the 'parola in libertà' and the Vocian obsession with the 'frammento'
[fragment] towards the creation of a more traditional type of metre.
This included, as De Robertis has shown (see *Intro.* to *Poesie disperse*)
the concealed hendecasyllable. The use of this traditional line and
also of the *settenario* (an equally traditional seven-syllabled metre)
will later be a feature of his second collection, *Sentimento del tempo*;
but even in his early collection the movement towards their use in a
modern key is clearly discernible and tends to enhance the linguistic

as well as the emotive tension of his work. The result is a form of
hermetic classicism, inspired perhaps by the practices foreshadowed
by *La Voce letteraria* (1914–16) and later by *La Ronda* (1919–23),
since the cultural ferment surrounding these periodicals had a crucial
effect on the aesthetic outlook of Ungaretti's entire generation. As
we have already mentioned, the former review was responsible for
the cult of the 'frammento' form, especially fostered in literary circles
after the publication of translations of Rimbaud's *Illuminations* by
Soffici in 1911; while *La Ronda* consolidated the classical element in
twentieth-century Italian lyricism, under the directorship of Cardarelli and Bacchelli. Nevertheless, before we consider further what
influences external literary and aesthetic pressures exerted on Ungaretti's early lyricism, we shall need to deal briefly, through the use
of a typical illustration, with the complicated issue of his variants.

Very few poems, in fact, underwent large-scale transformations
like 'Popolo' [People] as the poet searched for clearer, more subtle
and allusive forms of his original vision. Instead, the vast majority of
Ungaretti's early lyrics tended to be remodelled by slight retouches,
though one should not imagine for a moment that such minor
changes were incapable of redimensioning certain compositions,
especially when the omission of excessive biographical or situational
material was accompanied by a movement towards a finer allusive
grace. The greater effectiveness of the final form of a poem like
'Fratelli' [Brothers] from this point of view may be assessed by
comparing the version of 1916 with that of 1942. The earlier text
reads as follows:

> Di che reggimento siete
> fratelli?
>
> Fratello
> tremante parola
> nella notte
> come una fogliolina
> appena nata
> saluto
> accorato
> nell'aria spasimante
> implorazione
> sussurrata
> di soccorso
> all'uomo presente alla sua

fragilità (*Soldato*)

[Of what regiment are you / brothers? / / Brother / word quivering / in the night / like a tiny leaf / only just born / an anguished / greeting / in the agonizing air / a whispered / imploration / of help / to man confronted with his own / fragility. *Soldier*]

By contrast, the definitive text not only acquires a greater tremulousness and sensitivity but also at the same time an unexpected and incisive form of lyrical toughness:

Di che reggimento siete
fratelli?

Parola tremante
nella notte

Foglia appena nata

Nell'aria spasimante
involontaria rivolta
dell'uomo presente alla sua
fragilità

Fratelli (*Fratelli*)

[Of what regiment are you / brothers? / / Word quivering / in the night / / Leaf scarcely born / / In the agonizing air / the involuntary revolt / of man confronted with his own / fragility / / Brothers. *Brothers*]

If we were to ask ourselves what the differences are between these two texts, we would note at once the following points: first, the reduction of sentimental material by the omission of the greeting and imploration which are both at the second stage implicit rather than explicit; next, the compression of the image of the leaf which, by the omission of 'come' [like], becomes a metaphor not a simile, while losing its effete diminutive form; thirdly, the lessening of the adjectival load, somewhat excessive in the first version, but which in the second enhances the lyrical grace; and, finally, the spatial separation of the stanzas which introduces the sharpness of focus lacking previously, even though this sharpness is still deliberately attenuated by the dying falls of the cadences of the middle stanzas. Through subtle changes of this kind, therefore, Ungaretti significantly intensifies his version of a dramatic encounter between two patrols of soldiers in the no-man's land of war and, by extension, in the no man's land of life. At the same time the considerably higher pitched emotional tension of the final version again stresses the naked existentiality and precariousness of the human condition.

Generally speaking, this is the direction in which most of the variants move. The process almost always involves an orphic clarification of the essence of a mood by the shaping of a deeper, more emotively compressed, perspective; and the resulting lyric is normally more evocative, more delicate in its contours, while being less dispersive in its situational and sentimental features than the corresponding earlier renderings. On the other hand, although such processes of refinement and maturation go far towards justifying our initial choice of definitive texts as a basis for the examination of Ungaretti's lyrical achievements, we should not forget the arduous period of experimentation which many of his early compositions underwent when they were in the process of being perfected. The type of refinement they received was aesthetic and symbolic, not merely linguistic, in quality; but this heightening of their lyrical grace was normally brought about without undermining the authenticity of their original thread of inspiration.

One further task needs to be tackled before we finally proceed to an examination of the lyricism of *Allegria* proper: a brief consideration of a few lyrics pre-dating the 1916 version of the *Porto sepolto* and published by De Robertis in 1945 under the previously mentioned title of *Poesie disperse* [Scattered poems], together with a number of Ungaretti's early French lyrics. Some of these poems reveal his first literary influences, especially his predilection for the poetry of Palazzeschi, as may be seen from the 'gaminerie' expressed in 'Cresima' [Confirmation]:

> Inseguitemi. Correte. Correte.
>
> Pigliatemi.
>
> Marameo!

[Chase me. Run. Run. // Catch me. // Cock a snook!]
Other lyrics, by contrast, like 'Ineffabile' point to the influence of Pascoli in their impressionistic descriptions of phantomatic landscapes and solitary, almost cosmic, wildernesses, where only the home is a secure refuge:

> Casa a tentoni
> da una parte troppo mare
> troppo deserto dall'altra
> troppe stelle visibili

[A groping house / too much sea on one side / on the other too much desert / too many stars visible.]

Even so, this second type of poem also introduces a clearly Ungarettian sense of space and it no doubt recalls either his own house in Alexandria or, more likely, that of the Thuiles at Mecs, caught between the featureless wastelands of desert and sea. Similar scenes, as we know, will later form the background to *Allegria*, and to a large part of the poet's entire lyrical output. Together they symbolize the contourless plains of pure existence – also evoked on occasion by images of night – and it is against these dramatic backgrounds that the poet plays out the many vicissitudes of his personal destiny.

The other poems making up the early period of Ungaretti's inspiration are those published in the French collection *La guerre* (1919). The volume consisted of eighteen poems in all, eleven of which had already appeared in Italian while the remainder were, it seems, composed directly in French. Although these lyrics are mainly impressionistic in tone and are written in a type of free verse which borders at times on prose, one or two compositions already contain elements, especially in the field of symbolism, which will prove important for the future. One apt example is Ungaretti's tendency towards cultural atavism, in the form of a lyrical ancestor-worship, as may be seen in a line from 'Conclusion':

partout me guette un réveil de regrets d'ancêtres

[everywhere an awakening of ancestral regrets stalks me.]

Another is the symbol of the 'agneauloup' [the lamb-wolf] in 'Calumet'[1] [Pipe of peace] which Seroni (*Ragioni critiche, passim*) sees as a prefiguration of the bedouin-poet's temperament:

seul là s'est endormi
     cet agneauloup

seul ne serait étranger
     au climat
     de la mort
          cet agneauloup
               en exil
               partout

[only there slept / this lamb-wolf / / he alone would not be a stranger / to the realm / of death / this lamb-wolf / in exile / everywhere.]

Between them, therefore, these two poems already strike a main chord in Ungaretti's symbolism and philosophy of life: the first

indicates the halo of shadowy racial sensations which create traditional resonances within his melodic line, while the second marks the
poet's continual 'disponibilità' [receptivity]. In the bedouin this
sense of receptivity manifests itself as a hunger for the widest range
of experience possible, which he hopes will stretch the absorptive
powers of his personality to the limit, thereby fulfilling it through a
form of self-surpassing (dépassement de soi).

Even so, despite the presence of these suggestive themes, the first
major collection which Ungaretti produces undoubtedly remains
Allegria, under one or other of its varying titles. It is made up essentially of a nucleus of poems first published as *Il porto sepolto* in
1916, to which he later added those of *Allegria di naufragi* appearing
in 1919, and subsequently others as well. The work is divided into
sections which aim at giving it a coherent structure. It starts with the
section *Ultime* [Final poems] in which there appears the previously
quoted lyric 'Eterno' indicating that 'inesprimibile nulla' [inex-
pressible nothingness] which is the basis of the poet's aesthetics. The
poems of *Il porto sepolto* come next, and they explore the furthermost
reaches of the poet's sensibility, trying to depict his secret truths;
then we pass on to *Naufragi* describing certain vivid personal experiences and rebuffs which apparently take their title from the
Leopardian idea of the shipwreck in 'L'infinito'. From there we
proceed to 'Girovago' [Wanderer], which stresses the poet's hunger
for experience, and finally end with *Prime* [First Poems], composed
mostly of occasional poetry, though once again even these compositions still tend to have a clear bearing on the poet's wider themes.

Portinari (31-3) associates *Allegria di naufragi* with background
imagery drawn from Baudelaire, Rimbaud and Mallarmé, together
with the deeper metaphysical attitudes implicit in Leopardi's well-
known line from 'L'infinito':

E il naufragar m'è dolce in questo mare
[And to be shipwrecked in this sea is sweet to me.]

Ungaretti himself acknowledges this Leopardian influence on many
occasions, and he describes his own particular 'shipwrecks' as
moments of exultancy, of liberation, snatched from the whirlpool
of time:

Il primitivo titolo, strano, dicono, era *Allegria di Naufragi*. Strano
se tutto non fosse naufragio, se tutto non fosse travolto, soffocato,
consumato dal tempo. Esultanza che l'attimo, avvenendo, dà
perché fuggitivo, attimo che soltanto amore può strappare al
tempo, l'amore piú forte che non possa essere la morte. È il

punto dal quale scatta quell'esultanza d'un attimo, quell'allegria
che, quale fonte, non avrà mai se non il sentimento della
presenza della morte da scongiurare. (*Poesie*, 517)
[The first, somewhat strange title, they say, was *Allegria di
Naufragi*. It would be strange if everything were indeed not a
shipwreck, if everything were not overwhelmed, stifled, con-
sumed by time. An exultancy which the moment, as it happens,
provides because it is fleeting, a moment which only love can
tear away from time, a love stronger than death. It is the point
from which there bursts forth that exultancy of a moment, that
rapture which may have only as its source a feeling for the presence of death, of death to be exorcised.]

The poetic process which develops from these 'shipwrecks' buried
deep in the shadows of time is one of lyrically re-created memory,
of recollective orphic insight penetrating into the mysteries surrounding human experience. At one point the poet defines this sense
of mystery as man's continual inventiveness as he works out his
endless imaginative transfigurations of events and situations. For
him the very aim of poetry is to evoke this mystery within the framework of a sense of human measure, to make it specific and fruitful
in the life of the individual, through its intense emotive delineation.
By such expedients he believes one often succeeds in evoking 'l'in-
visibile nel visibile' (*Poesie*, lxxx) [the invisible within the visible],
and this 'bifocal' perspective has the consoling effect of allowing
man a momentary 'liberation' from the non-historical and solipsist
blindness of the self.

What Ungaretti proposes as his vision of life is accordingly a social
and cultural area outside direct experience, consisting of a greater
orphic pattern constantly returning and dissolving again as each
generation succeeds in bringing about its own salvation. It is this
perspective which saves the individual as well as society as a whole
from their own opaque forms of egocentricity, from being entirely
dominated by the flux of their immediate sense-impressions; and in
a personal context he explains the point lyrically in 'Sereno' [Clear
sky] where the orphic pattern behind the flux is clearly delineated:

Mi riconosco
immagine
passeggera

Presa in un giro
immortale

[I recognize myself / as a fleeting / image / / caught up in an immortal / spiral.]

His grasping of this sense of eternity within life's changeability naturally involves him in constant transfigurations of earthly situations, and very frequently he tends to achieve them by partially dematerializing a scene or an encounter. The doctrine appears in its stark cosmic setting in poems like 'Vanità', where, as we have seen, man rediscovers himself as a shadow; but his intimate personal settings are perhaps more important, as Ungaretti has illustrated in 'Nostalgia', where he describes an encounter with a girl loved both by him and by Apollinaire in Paris before the first war. Her very fragility gives the impression of a dematerialized state of grace and beauty, while the secret behind this grace is the poet's ability to conflate the ephemeral world of this life with the eternal, orphic pattern. Here both states are emergent in a composite form from the specific instance of experience in a way which Ungaretti would consider akin (as we have already seen) to the artistic practices that Shakespeare used in order to evoke the eternal grace of youth behind its transitory representations in his sonnets:

In un canto
di ponte
contemplo
l'illimitato silenzio
di una ragazza
tenue

Le nostre
malattie
si fondono

E come portati via
si rimane

[In an angle / of a bridge / I contemplate / the limitless silence / of a slender / girl / / Our / sicknesses / merge / / And as if borne off / we linger.]

Not only is a situation dematerialized in poems of this kind, but very often the objects which compose it are 'time-hallowed', made into so many fetishes or 'laric' possessions, through their close attachment to the poet. They are then re-introduced by him with subtle recurrent associations as personal harmonics or inflections into the keyboard of the tradition. Ungaretti draws this technique from

Petrarch and he associates it with a specifically Petrarchan type of 'dolcezza' [sweetness] in 'Risvegli':

Mi desto in un bagno
di care cose consuete
sorpreso
e raddolcito
[I awaken in a bath / of dear customary objects / surprised / and mellowed.]

He even regards such orphic hallowing of reality as a form of ethical maturing, which he explains as follows:

Non ci sono due linee parallele fra le cose e le parole: le cose, quando le guardiamo, non sono già piú esterne, sono già in noi, sono noi: ed esse tornano esterne, colle nostre parole, vi tornano trasformate da cose materiali in cose morali. (*Saggi*, 362)
[There are not two parallel lines between things and words: things, when we look at them, already are no longer external, they are already within us, they are us: and they become externalized again with our words, emerging when transformed from material into moral objects.]

For him, in short, the drama (he says the tragedy) of writing consists 'nel trasformarsi della parola in rivelazione' (*Saggi*, 361) [in changing the word into a revelation]; and it is, of course, the self-surprise of his modern baroque outlook which he regards as being the very hallmark of this miracle of ethical and expressive revitalization. Mystery, human measure, and an orphic perspective thus mingle inextricably in the overtones of his melodic line, and the secret resonances of the past as much as the sensations of the present provide depth and authenticity for his poetry.

Needless to say, this doctrine has a powerful effect on the poet's manner of representation, and it now superimposes on the former impressionistic and discursive tendencies of his *Poesie disperse* or French verse the further complicated lyrical technique of hermetic involution. Hermetic involution is briefly a process whereby the symbolic and the emotive spheres of the poetic image become dynamically unbalanced. So, if we take the classical image as our norm and consider it as containing one hemisphere of symbolic or conceptual matter and another of dark emotional tensions, we would normally expect it to appear to the reader like a half-moon, one quarter radiating the brightness of conceptuality and the other the darkness of emotion. The hermetic image, by contrast, changes these proportions, so that most of the hemisphere turned towards us is dark and emotive in quality, while the white light of its symbolic import only appears as a slender crescent, very much like a new moon.

In *Allegria* entire poetic situations are involuted in this sense and these infolded situations consist either of biographical material reduced to its essential components or else of compressed and allusive examples of *epoché*, that is, of inner suspended landscapes of passing moods or incidents (see p. 24). In the present collection this form of stylistic alternation seems to have persisted right up to the appearance of the definitive edition, and perhaps the final versions of the poems 'In memoria' and 'Levante' will illustrate the point in its most dramatic form. The first is characterized by a dry, laconic style which acquires its cutting-edge from its compression and an extreme succinctness of biographical narration:

> Si chiamava
> Moammed Sceab
>
> Discendente
> di emiri di nomadi
> suicida
> perché non aveva piú
> Patria

[He was called / Moammed Sceab / / Descendant / of emirs of nomads / a suicide / since he no longer had / a Native Land.]
In these lines we find that the essentialized discourse centres around three words – nomad, suicide, native-land – which together reveal the full extent of Sceab's inevitable alienation from his Arab culture once he had moved to France and tried to acquire a French personality. Their incisiveness is further intensified in the final version by the last stanza which has an equally laconic pathos:

> E forse io solo
> so ancora
> che visse,

[and perhaps I alone / still know / that he lived.]
This replaces the conclusion of some earlier versions which tended towards a somewhat slack, sentimental comment, one which applied not to Sceab's fate but to the impact on the poet's own sensibility of his friend's rapid descent into oblivion:

> Saprò
> fino al mio turno

di morire
[I shall know / till it is my turn / to die.]

In 'Levante', by contrast, the infolding process is imaginative and impressionistic rather than laconic or terse in a narrative sense, although here again compression is still uppermost. The scene described is the dancing on the boat bringing Ungaretti to Brindisi on his way to France in 1912, which in the final version is hermetically compressed by parataxis and certain 'fulminatory' or startlingly analogical juxtapositions of words and sensations:

Picchi di tacchi picchi di mani
e il clarino ghirigori striduli
e il mare è cenerino
trema dolce inquieto
come un piccione

[Clicks of heels claps of hands / and the clarinet strident spirals / and the sea is ashen / quivers sweet and restless / like a pigeon.]

From this we deduce that there is a dialectic between discursiveness and allusive essentiality in the whole development of *Allegria*, and the transformation of lyrical effects from version to version tends to derive from a gradual fragmenting of connective links and a simultaneous deepening of the poet's mental perspectives and analogical procedures.

Since many of the lyrics in the collection are tremulously brief, they have often been associated with the *haikai* form of Japanese poetry which was all the rage in Europe at the turn of the century. Enzo Palmieri claimed that Ungaretti's lyrics were imitative of those translated by H. Shimoi and Gherardo Marone (one of the poet's closest friends) and published under the title of *Poesie giapponesi* [Japanese Poems] in 1917.[2] As a result of this accusation there followed an angry exchange of letters between Palmieri and the poet in the *Italia letteraria* (7 and 21 May), but in denouncing the critic's chronology and in attempting to show the undoubted precedence of his own compositions over Marone's translations, Ungaretti himself falls into chronological error. He claims, for instance, that his poems in *Lacerba* date from 1914 instead of 1915 and assures us that it was Marone who was influenced by him and not the other way round. This may well be so in the published volume of Japanese translations but his arguments do not convince us that he was not himself influenced by the *haikai*, especially since we find that he was associated with the publication of these very forms in the periodical *Diana* in 1916, and indeed one of its issues carries next to *haikai* by Akiko

Yosano and S. Maeta a similar short lyric by Ungaretti himself
(May issue, 99–101). Probably the poet would again counter this
charge by pointing out that most of his haikai-like poems in *Il porto
sepolto* precede those found in the *Diana*; but not even they were the
earliest published Japanese lyrics in twentieth-century Italy. For
example, Mario Chini produced translations of *tanke* in *Poesia* (nos
8, 10–11) in 1905–6, and one of these even bears the same title as a
poem by Ungaretti called 'Annientamento'. Moreover, despite the
indifferent quality of these lyrics in general, at least some of them
have a certain haunting Ungarettian atmosphere about them, perhaps even the one mentioned above:

> Sono stanco di penare.
> Nel profondo del mare
> voglio sparir: ma come
> potrò dunque portare
> con me fino il mio nome?
>
> [I am weary of suffering. / In the depths of the sea / I wish to
> disappear: but how / shall I then take / with me even my name?]

Since then we know from his own admission that Ungaretti was an
avid reader of the *Mercure de France* at that time, it seems likely that
he would also have read *Poesia* avidly as well; and, if so, perhaps the
tone of these poems could have remained unconsciously in his
memory and exerted an influence upon his sensibility.

Where Ungaretti scores heavily, on the other hand, over these
earlier translations is in the deeper emotivity of his compositions and
their denser symbolism. For a lyric like 'Tramonto' [Sunset] does
not confine itself in the same way as the average *haikai* to the evocation of a tremulous sense-impression, but tends to evoke vast cultural
resonances linked with his own authentic feelings as a bedouin-poet:

> Il carnato del cielo
> sveglia oasi
> al nomade d'amore
>
> [The rosy flush of the sky / awakens oases / in the nomad of
> love.]

Here a dilation of reality is brought about in two ways: first, by a
subtle personification of the sky (carnato) and, second, by the
evocation of the background scenario of the desert, not through
direct description but through allusive references to its typical
human inhabitant, the nomad, and the slaking of his thirst for fresh
experiences at oases. Indeed, combinations of the desert, nomad and
oasis henceforth appear to become archetypal in Ungaretti's verse,

often with the suppression of the first term in favour of the second or third; and the device develops into something which is much more than a mere technique, proving to be almost a spiritual procedure awakening echoes in the deepest recesses of his conscience. Thus an impulse which at first seems to define an expansion into cosmic visionariness in poems like 'Mattina' [Morning]:

M'illumino
d'immenso
[I illuminate myself / with immensity]

later changes into a form of mental implosion, a penetration into the further reaches of a sphere of atavistic and instinctive insight for the purpose of mingling the resonances of the dead with Ungaretti's own immediate and living sensibility.

These resonances are, of course, memorially recaptured from that 'inexpressible void' which surrounds the poet's lyrical re-creations; and, needless to say, the imagery which the process evokes becomes steeped in the lyrical harmonics emerging from the poetic 'word' as a result of his 'scavo della parola' defined in 'Commiato' (see p. 34–5). In short, Ungaretti now aims to 'decant' the experience of the dead and attempts to revitalize it orphically by means of a process of purification that strips it of all but its relevant nucleus of emotivity. Often the ritual of purification which the imagery undergoes is identical with the orphic one of immersion in water, and we already find it, for instance, in 'Universo' [Universe] written in 1916, where Ungaretti steeps his mind in Lethean urns of freshness and brings back from them a poetic feeling endowed with a deathless sense of complete serenity:

Col mare
mi sono fatto
una bara
di freschezza
[With the sea / I have made for myself / a coffin / of freshness.]

Elsewhere a similar plundering of the emotive resonances of words and images leads to an exhaustive exploration of the perspectives behind the twofold tradition – the Arab and the European – which from a very early age had become fused in his mind. The oriental strain is hermetically sealed in all its richness and splendour in 'Fase' [Phase], where the sensuous serenity of a passionately felt love is set against the background of the myth of the Arabian Nights, alluded to indirectly in 'mill'una notte' [a thousand and one nights] which is the usual Italian title for this collection of stories:

Cammina cammina
ho ritrovato
il pozzo d'amore

Nell'occhio
di mill'una notte
ho riposato

[By walking and walking / I have rediscovered / the well of
love / / In the eye / of a thousand and one nights / I have slept.]
  By contrast, although the Italian tradition is perhaps less elemental
and instinctively felt by Ungaretti, it nevertheless seems to be more
deeply implanted in his mind than even the distant oriental perspectives of his childhood. Normally it is associated with a Leopardian
sereneness, but even when it is at its most emotive it is still linked
with the self-conscious passion of the adult mind for the mysterious
siren voices of the fatherland, as may be seen in the poet's hymn to
his cultural ancestors in 'Popolo'. Here he identifies himself with
their pure harmonies, just as if they represented a hungry singing in
his blood:

O Patria ogni tua età
s'è desta nel mio sangue

Sicura avanzi e canti
Sopra un mare famelico

[O my fatherland all your ages / are awakened in my blood / /
You advance confidently and sing / over a ravenous sea.]
This singing and the vision of the hungry sea of existence not only
evoke the stark contingency of the human condition, but also in
compensation, as the poet tells us himself, 'il riconoscimento della
mia appartenenza a un particolare popolo e al popolo nella sua
totalità storica' (*Poesie*, 519) [his acknowledgement of belonging to a
particular people and to that people in its historical totality].
  What is the nature of Ungaretti's peculiar type of ethico-aesthetic
ancestor-worship? In part, it derives from his reading of Barrès who
tells us that our living bodies are nothing less than 'les prolongements
de nos morts' [extensions of our dead][3]; but it may be likened also
to Virgil's attitude which Ungaretti tries to describe by contrasting
it with Dante's. In his view the latter had from the outset envisaged
the possibility of a *homo optimus* who

avait reconquis la mémoire, il avait retrouvé le savoir; à cette
mémoire ne devait pas manquer la possibilité de s'intensifier, de

s'abolir, de souffrir et de se sublimer dans l'innocence, l'absolu d'une image. L'art de Dante consiste à transformer un système d'idées en une multitude de figures pétries avec un réalisme assez puissant pour en éterniser l'obsession. L'art de Dante consiste à matérialiser des idées, à leur donner à toutes un corps, du sang, un visage, des passions, une douceur, en les tourmentant avec une obstination telle que ces corps finissent par exprimer avec une rigoureuse précision leur âme, c'est-à-dire l'idée qu'ils ont charge de représenter. (*Innocence*, 10–11)

[had reconquered memory, rediscovered knowledge; and this memory was not lacking in the power to intensify, abolish, suffer and sublimate itself in a state of innocence, in the absoluteness of an image. Dante's art consists in transforming a system of ideas into a multitude of figures kneaded together with so powerful a realism as to eternalize his obsession with them. The art of Dante consists in the materialization of ideas, in giving them all flesh, blood, features, passions, and gentleness, in torturing them so obstinately that their very flesh finally succeeds in expressing their souls with rigorous precision, that is to say, the idea they were charged with representing.]

With Virgil, by contrast, it is not so much the *ideas* as the *feelings* of the race which are perpetuated, its inner rhythm. So he insists that it is in 'l'unité spirituelle et la continuité physique de la race, voilà le secret que dévoile à Virgile son voyage d'outre-tombe' (*Innocence*, 15) [the spiritual unity and the physical continuity of the race that the secret lies which unveils his journey beyond the grave to Virgil]. Not only this: Ungaretti adds for good measure that in one sense

l'esprit de Virgile n'est pas mort: ... il vit, en ce moment même où nous en parlons, dans notre esprit; et s'il est vrai qu'il a modifié et imprégné toute notre culture, il reste constamment vivant et présent en nous. (*Innocence*, 12)

[the spirit of Virgil is not dead: ... it lives in this very moment in which we are speaking about it in our spirit; and if it is true that he has modified and suffused our entire culture, he remains constantly alive and present within us.]

In the same way the poet's own atavism is both psycho-sensuous and cultural: it aims at dredging up from the visceral depths of his being a racially hallowed song whose varying modulations will blend with the sense-impressions of his present living sensibility and create a modern – yet traditionally saturated – word-music.

Such a view amounts, once again, to an assertion of mankind's

continual consolidation of the poetic spirit through death, because
Ungaretti firmly believes the present-day poet's immortality is not
ensured by his own efforts alone, he must also be attuned to the
deep-seated ferment of past racial melodies. Hence his aphorism in
'Sono una creatura' [I am a creature] that

> La morte
> si sconta
> vivendo
> [Death / is discounted / by living]

and his constant desire to ascend through atavistic tensions and
resonances to a memorially recaptured 'paese innocente' [innocent
land] imbued with the sweetness and charm that only a time-
hallowed civilization can ensure. Such a process he regards as a repenetration of the past for the purpose of establishing a sense of
human perfection; one which is not an ideal or metaphysical entelechy, but rather a shared state of lyrical communion wrought from
experience over the ages. As he puts it himself,

> la forza di spirito cui aspiravo volgendomi alla poesia, alla
> poesia che è sempre se è poesia, l'atto con il quale un uomo
> tende alla purezza, tende ad amare, anche se la carne rimanga
> debole, ciò che l'oltrepassa: l'Umana Perfezione. (*Saggi*, 791)
> [the power of the spirit to which I aspired by addressing myself
> to poetry – to poetry which is always, if it is really poetry, an
> act through which a man moves towards purity – tends to
> yearn, even if the flesh remains weak, for that which surpasses
> it: Human Perfection.]

When we turn away from Ungaretti's combination of immediate
with traditional imagery and consider the background and the
symbolism which pervade his lyricism, we find that the atmospheres
which evolve in *Allegria* are of a rather distinctive kind. They are
basically constructed from background landscapes with featureless
contours – his wastelands – consisting of desert or wartime mountain
scenes, yet a number of human figures are dramatically highlighted
against their disturbing nocturnal canvases. The result is that it appears as if the poet is secretly creating life's thread out of a pure –
because as yet uninhabited – void of orphic suspension. The descriptions to which we refer are so common that specific examples need
hardly be given at this stage; so instead let us for the moment concentrate our attention on the human figures which actually people
his early *tabula rasa* universe. Of these we soon discover that the most

important is the bedouin or nomad whose ceaseless, compulsive wandering symbolically represents the endless vicissitudes of our journey in this life.

Normally the bedouin has a twofold duty for the poet: he is simultaneously the jealous guardian of his distinctive racial culture and an experience-hungry and receptive wanderer open to all the impressions and situations which life has to offer. As we have already seen, when the bedouin-poet Ungaretti is confronted in 'Dolina notturna' with the traumatic experience of war in the snow-covered Alps, he wilts before its inhumanity and assumes the spectral in-substantiality of an alienated orphic worshipper who has suffered a bewildering *déplacement* in space and time:

Questo nomade
adunco
morbido di neve
si lascia
come una foglia
accartocciata

[This nomad / hook-nosed / softened by snow / abandons him-self / like a withered / leaf.]

The terror experienced in such a situation is, however, gradually internalized so as to become a veritable wasteland of the soul. This implies that it is not simply the terror of war that he feels, but also the terror of human contingency in the sense that it is mirrored in 'San Martino del Carso'. There the shattered wartime landscape evokes the death of all transient creatures, especially the poet's friends:

Di queste case
non è rimasto
che qualche
brandello di muro

Di tanti
che mi corrispondevano
non è rimasto
neppure tanto

Ma nel cuore
nessuna croce manca

È il mio cuore
il paese piú straziato

[Of these houses / there remains / but a few / remnants of wall / /

Of so many / who were linked with me / there remains / not
even so much / / But in my heart / no cross is missing / / My
heart is / the most anguished landscape.]

It is nevertheless from the sheer desolation of such soul-scapes that
the Ungarettian hero is 'liberated' from time to time by the cries of
joy inherent in the very title and conception of the collection. This
joy is clearly the joy of the self-fulfilling bedouin-poet who first
appears, we recall, as the 'agneauloup' in the French poem 'Calumet'.
His stimulation of his own life's experiences by communing with his
age-old traditions is clearly paralleled throughout the volume by the
instinctive experiences of Ungaretti's own infancy, or as the poet
puts it himself, by his brooding over the sunken port of Alexandria
which simultaneously offered him a way of escape from the desert
and a mirage of a mythified Italy beyond the sea:

Il porto è stato quindi un po' per me il miraggio dell'Italia, di
quel luogo impreciso e perdutamente amato per quanta notizia
ne avessi dai racconti in famiglia. Si tratta della mia prima infanzia, di quel momento della vita che rimane nella mente
tuffato nella notte o nel solleone del miraggio. (*Poesie*, 502)

[The port was thus to me something like a mirage of Italy, of
that imprecise place so distractedly loved as a result of the information I had received about it from family tales. It is connected with my early infancy, with that moment of life which
remains buried in the mind in darkness or in the intense heat of
the mirage.]

Later these cross-currents of Eastern and European culture and the
crisis of self-awareness they provoke are completely fused together
in the major lyric of the collection 'I Fiumi' [The rivers]. This poem
illustrates above all others the peculiar state of suspension or *epoché*
which was then the hallmark of Ungaretti's rapidly developing
aesthetic manner. Its subtle harmonies convey to us the true nature
and the spiritual evolution of his early sensibility, and show how his
bedouin mind was slowly made receptive to wider horizons of
thought and more subtle responses by a growing familiarity with
the myths of a variety of different traditions.

Since Ungaretti's lyrical formation was intimately bound up with
echoes from these multiple traditions it is only natural that the opening scene of the poem should also be a composite one, depicting what
Eliot would have called an 'objective correlative' to his mood, that
is to say, a landscape or a set of events or objects which sum up, without superfluous or decorative elements, the exact configuration of

the poet's literary and moral tensions. The scene which is evoked is, in fact, again a wilderness with broad, contourless features, a craggy fastness on the Carso in wartime, suffused with a Leopardian type of moonlight. As Gutia has pointed out (3–18), scenes like this are not abstract visions in *Allegria*, but are immediately made specific by the use of demonstratives; and, indeed, the transitoriness of the setting is further emphasized in this case by the dynamic, contingent effect of the gliding of clouds across the moon:

> Mi tengo a quest'albero mutilato
> abbandonato in questa dolina
> che ha il languore
> di un circo
> prima o dopo lo spettacolo
> e guardo
> il passaggio quieto
> delle nuvole sulla luna
> [I cling to this shattered tree / abandoned in this gully / which has the languor / of a circus / before or after the performance / and I gaze at / the silent passing / of clouds across the moon.]

Not only the initial scene but even the individual symbols in the lyric invoke resonances in minds attuned to twentieth-century hermetic poetry. The tree, for instance, is often used by hermetic poets as a symbol of human anguish (see particularly Quasimodo's early lyricism), while the technical word 'dolina' greatly reinforces the wasteland effect and echoes the harshness of the battles which make the Carso renowned in military history. In a similar way the word 'circo' reminds us of the disorder of a circus and also of the scattered detritus of a theatre of war; while the function of the moonlight is clearly to disembody the whole landscape, to make it spectral, ghoulish and metaphysical, so as to provide a hollow resonance typifying that horror of the void associated by Ungaretti with the human condition itself. Even the rhythmic effects are broken and unequal, following the syntagmatic pattern of the sense-groups rather than any preconceived type of prosody; and this too has the result of highlighting in turn every element of the scene and of gradually producing an inner equilibrium between its various parts.

The opening landscape, therefore, sets the necessary mood for the whole poem, and after describing it the poet passes on to examine his personal activities within the overall situation. But he still evokes his responses allusively and symbolically rather than discursively, by way of a subtle analogical experimentation upon his lyrical keyboard. In this way his morning bathe in the Isonzo is immediately transfigured into a ritual of orphic purification, leading to a sense of death-like subsisting, after the manner of Corazzini – a point which is clearly stressed in the image of the poet as a relic enclosed within the confines of an urn or coffin. In such a state of death-in-life Ungaretti seems to experience a momentary lull in the universal tensions surrounding him:

> Stamani mi sono disteso
> in un'urna d'acqua
> e come una reliquia
> ho riposato
> [This morning / I stretched out / in an urn of water / and like a relic / I rested.]

The surprising resilience he feels as a result of this experience is perhaps to be likened to a feeling of momentary hypostasis, during which he imagines himself as resembling spiritually one of the polished stones lying mellowed by the water at the bottom of the riverbed.

From this point on, however, his hitherto meditative inaction is changed into a compulsive activity and we are presented with the scarecrow figure of a refugee from war. The image may have been complicated by an incipient religious symbolism, despite Ungaretti's claim to have been an atheist at the time of writing it. Thus the figure of the 'quattr'ossa', although a graphically colloquial way of describing the human frame in Italian, could by its overtones of emaciation depict Christ's suffering for humanity, especially since in the final version there is a variant which seems to suggest a symbolic walking of the waters. Likewise, both the idea of the 'four spare bones' and the mention of the 'acrobata' [acrobat] tend to refer back telescopically to the previous images of the mutilated tree and the circus, thereby refocussing and subtly underlining those implications of anguish and irony which suffused the initial scene:

> Ho tirato su
> le mie quattr'ossa
> e me ne sono andato
> come un acrobata
> sull'acqua
> [I gathered up / my four spare bones / and went away / like an acrobat / over the water.]

By contrast, this possible Christianizing trend is in its turn counterbalanced in the next stanza by an allusion to the Islamic religion and

its rituals, and at this point the 'quattr' ossa'are clearly to be identified
with the bedouin sullied by war who turns towards the East to pray:

> Mi sono accoccolato
> vicino ai miei panni
> sudici di guerra
> e come un beduino
> mi sono chinato a ricevere
> il sole

[I squatted / near my clothes / filthy with war / and like a
bedouin / I bowed down to receive / the sun.]

Once again, then, Ungaretti is virtually transformed here into the
bedouin-poet whose duty it is not only to represent but also to
protect the traditions of his race from the onslaughts of the barbarian.

The traumatic effect of his swim in the Isonzo results in an awakening of the poet's mind to his cultural responsibilities. Momentarily
he appears to become identified with his racial destiny, which he
places within the setting of a cosmic harmony with nature. He also
informs us that for him, at least, existential anguish now only makes
itself felt when nature's hidden melodies are disturbed:

> Questo è l'Isonzo
> e qui meglio
> mi sono riconosciuto
> una docile fibra
> dell'universo
>
> Il mio supplizio
> è quando
> non mi credo
> in armonia

[This is the Isonzo / and here I have better / recognized myself /
a docile filament / of the universe / / My anguish / is when /
I do not consider myself / to be in harmony.]

What, we might ask, ensures the continuance of this harmony
throughout the poet's temporal existence? He seems to imply that it
is once more an atavistic ability to merge with past tradition whose
hidden resonances knead him through and ensure his integration as
a lyricist into the pure poetic voice of the race:

> Ma quelle occulte
> mani
> che m'intridono
> mi regalano

       la rara
       felicità
       [But those hidden / hands / which knead me through / grant
       me / a rare / happiness.]
Happiness is perhaps to be equated with a form of ethico-aesthetic
serenity in the present context and is no doubt born of 're-created
experience' within the bounds of his 'paese innocente'. This very
fact at once reveals that Ungaretti no longer yearns for the metaphysical paradise of the symbolists; his absolutes are nothing more
mysterious than moral and poetic feelings of fulfilment, always
accessible on this earth. It also explains why he never suffers like his
predecessors from a sense of metaphysical 'échec'. For, unlike them,
what he seeks is the clearly attainable contentment of aesthetic
harmony brought about by his personal contribution to the enrich-
ment of the fabric of the lyric tradition.
     The last section of the poem amounts to a review of his own past,
of the conditions he considers vital in one's cultural upbringing to
ensure for oneself moments of fulfilment. He mirrors these conditions in the waters of the rivers along whose banks he has successively
matured. Already we have seen the Isonzo acting as the river of his
self-conscious awakening to the breadth of human suffering; the
Serchio appears next with its atavistic implications, since it is the
river of his ancestors whose history stretches viscerally back for two
thousand years in the district around Lucca. The Serchio is then
followed by the Nile which – as the river of his childhood – marks
his early stage of unself-conscious participation. Needless to say, the
laconic or essentialized imagery in which this carefree state is evoked
reminds us once more of his life in Alexandria and the boundless
spaces of the desert:
       Questo è il Nilo
       che mi ha visto
       nascere e crescere
       e ardere d'inconsapevolezza
       nelle estese pianure
       [This is the Nile / which saw me / born and grow up / and burn
       with unself-consciousness / in its extended plains.]
     Finally, there appears the Seine which is the river of his intellectual
formation; and afterwards, on returning momentarily to the initial
scene along the Isonzo, he tells us he can recount all these other
rivers of experience, and even assess their contributions to his sensibility, in the depths of its flowing waters. Together they produce an

integrated perspective on life which is depicted as a whorl of memories, and their simultaneity of impact reminds us of the futurists' (and vorticists') cult of the same artifice, although with Ungaretti it is achieved on a much more effective level:

> Questa è la mia nostalgia
> che in ognuno
> mi traspare
> ora ch'è notte
> che la mia vita mi pare
> una corolla
> di tenebre

> [This is my nostalgia / which in each one / emerges for me / now that it is night / that my life seems to me / a corolla / of shadows.]

Consequently, whereas the poem starts with a disintegrating and hollow kind of landscape revealing the external tensions which racked the collective sensibility of mankind during the first World War, it finishes on an integrated soul-scape which harmonizes the poet's memories and fuses them into a close-knit memorial lyricism. It is therefore his desire to reinsert his sensibility into the Italian tradition despite his birth in exile which is perhaps Ungaretti's major aim in *Allegria*. At length, in the section *Prime* appearing as an epilogue to the work, he claims to have succeeded in this task, and in a poem significantly entitled 'Lucca', the home-town of his parents, he writes:

> Ora lo sento scorrere caldo nelle mie vene, il sangue dei miei
>
> > morti.
> Ho preso anch'io una zappa.
> Nelle cosce fumanti della terra mi scopro a ridere.

> [Now I feel pulsating through my veins, the blood of my dead ones. / I too have taken up the hoe. / In the steaming thighs of the earth I find myself breaking into laughter.]

This lyrical ancestor-worship, this desire to merge with the inner traditions of the Italian race, is accordingly more than a mere intellectualized goal for Ungaretti. It amounts to a fleshly conjunction of his body and soul with the tissue of the racial consciousness. From here on he will always proclaim that it is the poet's duty to make his very words the living flesh of the lyric tradition, although he acknowledges that in his case the Italian tradition must necessarily be contaminated by a sensuous oriental vein springing from his childhood. Even so, he assures us that this foreign infusion provides it with additional strength instead of indicating a weakness, since without a rich flow of instinct as well as reason he doubts whether any lyrical production can in the last resort prove authentic. In this sense *Allegria* is largely a composite work of art in which Italian, oriental, and the wider European traditions of lyricism are all fused together into a delicate orphic perspective of existence; and, although its perspectives are immersed in the present, they are mediated by a shadowy halo of memories arising from the past.

4. *Sentimento del tempo*

The poetry of *Sentimento del tempo* differs from that of *Allegria* in three ways: in its setting, its atmosphere of heightened baroque tension, and, above all, in its attitude to time and rhythm. At first sight the change in setting is the most obvious of these transformations, because the background is not now the Egyptian desert nor the craggy fastnesses of the Carso in wartime: it is the city of Rome and the calm, summery serenity of the Latian countryside. This change of scene, as the poet himself emphasizes, tends to reflect more adequately the controlled intensity of his own maturity and marks a watershed in his lyrical development.

He began to compose the poems belonging to the collection on his return to Italy from France as early as 1921, but a few poems predating that event nevertheless find their definitive place in *Sentimento del tempo* despite the fact that some of them represent a transitional phase between it and *Allegria*. In notes written many years later in collaboration with A. Marianni, Ungaretti tells us that the greatest shock he received after his transfer to Rome was precisely the sight of a totally baroque architecture, one which on the surface at least appeared to lack all sense of cohesion and unity. Later, however, when the city began to represent for him the inner genius of Michelangelo's art, this sense of a lack of cohesion gradually tended to diminish as he learned to understand more intimately the nature of the latter's achievement and the secrets lying behind the aesthetic canon of the baroque movement. Moreover, not only did he associate the baroque at this stage with Michelangelo's highly personal form of mannerism, he also linked its peculiar atmospheres with the season of summer whose shimmering heat predominates in the lyrics making up the first half of the volume. As he himself explains, the reason for this association is that

> il barocco è qualche cosa che è saltato in aria, che s'è sbriciolato in mille briciole: è una cosa nuova, rifatta con quelle briciole, che ritrova integrità, il vero. L'estate fa come il barocco: sbriciola e ricostituisce. (*Poesie*, 530)
> [the baroque is something which has been blown into the air,

which has crumbled into a thousand pieces: it is something new, reshaped from those fragments, which rediscovers wholeness, truth. Summer acts like the baroque: it shatters and reconstitutes.]

Now, since he sees this process taking place both inside Rome and outside it in the Roman countryside in summer, he tries to compound from the sultry violence of the summer's heat and the straining architecture of the city a fresh spiritual climate for the baroque mode, yet one which still aims at representing, though in a modern key, the kind of anguish which once possessed Michelangelo's tortured artistic temperament.

What then does Ungaretti's conception of the baroque really consist of? At first he accepts, as we have already suggested (see p. 46–7), Michelangelo's premonition of a brooding void, a hollow spaciousness, indicative of an absence of God. He claims that because of this deeply felt sense of loss there arises in the traditional baroque artist's mind an equal and opposite longing for *material* plenitude, a desire to act as a god in his own right and fill the void left by the absence of the Divinity in any way he knows how. Eventually the only effective answer the *Seicentisti* discovered to the problem posed by the void was, as we have already seen, a cult of sensations of almost hysterical proportions, and in Ungaretti's opinion this is the major solution favoured by Marino and his followers.

Even so, the poet appears to have recognized from an early stage that the baroque manner in the modern age could not avail itself of such a naive form of self-deception; and therefore his own answer is not the traditional baroque response of intensifying sensations and indulging in all sorts of *trompe-l'œil*, even though the magnification of sensations (or rather of lyrical tensions) is admittedly an important accessory to his art. Instead, his personal manner has a deeper aim: it attempts to 'repeople' the void by evolving in an orphic sense a 'ricupero' [recuperation] of the past, and by fusing together historical tastes and immediate visceral feelings in a new lyrical perspective. In this sense he actually changes the artistic goal of the *Seicentisti*, since he is not so much trying to fill a 'void' as remedy a sense of 'absence', and he makes a sharp distinction between these two words. Whereas the 'void' is for him a metaphysical abyss inherent in the very contingency of the human condition and the individual always runs up against an insurmountable *échec* (as the symbolists did) whenever he tries to fill it, 'absence' (at least as Petrarch conceived it in the case of Laura) is a remediable state of affairs, inasmuch as it can always be transformed into an imaginative 'presence' through our faculty of recollection. In the present age, however, 'absence' can no longer be restored as lyrical 'presence' by mere narrative means; the manifestation of a truly restored 'presence' can only be achieved through the creation of a sense of 'durata', of 'temps vécu', in the Bergsonian sense of the word. Within this profoundly 'lived' and intuitive time-flow the poet hopes that his immediate sense-impressions and the haunting resonances of the past will be recompounded as a new synthesis which will subordinate the decorative baroque features of his melodic line to more authentic tensions, thereby making his lyricism a direct reflection of the inner reaches of his sensibility.

The result of Ungaretti's transformation of the 'metaphysical' baroque of the seventeenth century into the ethical or emotively-directed baroque ethos of the modern age is a change in the very texture of his verse. In particular, the baroque cult of *surprise* which in the *Seicento* was largely a feature external to the poet's vision now becomes completely fused with his lyrical conscience, transforming itself in the process into a form of *self-surprise* closely linked with his personal astonishment at the unexpected freshness and appositeness of his imagery. This interiorized poetry of Ungaretti's modern baroque manner similarly aims at transcending time in its cosmic sense, and the so-called ticking of the universal clock is replaced in his aesthetics by a sense of inner poetic intensity which some critics have described as a state of *intension*.

At this point we can conveniently refer back to the distinction which Montanari made between *tempus* and *aevum* (see p.29), since in his view the *aevum* represented an omnipresent memorial suspension of time deeply infused with human feeling, whereas *tempus* was merely the time-flow measured mechanically by the scientists. By reconstituting time as an 'aeval' form of lyrical intensity in *Sentimento del tempo* Ungaretti thus hoped to escape from, if not to resolve, the baroque obsession with the void and raise his lyricism to a more satisfying level of awareness. At the same time he may even have believed that he could restore the 'presence' of God.

Now the difficulties he encountered in carrying out this programme of rehabilitating the baroque manner as an inward spiritual reality lay less in his actual handling and representation of baroque modalities and techniques (since his established manner in *Allegria* was already tinged with a baroque colouring) than in the fact that the temporal condition of his earlier collection was not really a 'temps vécu'. It was instead a form of eternal present, a state of *epoché* conveyed through the timelessly suspended orphic and oriental perspectives of his early poetic vision of the bedouin-poet suddenly faced with the twin traumas of self-consciousness and war. So the artistic problem which at this point Ungaretti must have felt incapable of solving without breaking completely with his own 'dislocated' lyrical past was how to transform a suspended, dissociative sense of temporal relations into a multi-faceted, yet at least seemingly continuous, process of spiritual maturation.

Perhaps it would be as well to examine briefly at this juncture the nature of the image-flow in *Allegria*. Ungaretti's analogical bolts from the blue or poetic 'fulminations' can be regarded as atemporal, monadic forms of expression. They are juxtaposed rather than logically integrated; and, although their interrelationship later becomes apparent within the economy of each poem when taken as a whole, such images as are found, for instance, in the opening lines of lyrics like 'Lindoro di deserto' [Lindoro of the desert] seem at first sight not only atemporal but even centrifugal:

> Dondolo di ali in fumo
> mozza il silenzio degli occhi

> Col vento si spippola il corallo
> di una sete di baci. …

[A swaying of wings in smoke / slices the silence of the eyes / / With the wind one picks off the coral / of a thirst of kisses.] These flashes of sensory insight are the poet's rapturous 'gridi' [cries], but any sense of time, whether cosmic or aeval, is quite irrelevant to them: they subsist, as it were, in an eternal, suspended present.

In order to infuse into this manner a temporal or 'aeval' charge Ungaretti had to make the static and self-complete resonance-chamber of *Allegria* into one of continuous temporal flux. He does it, not by changing his modes of representation radically, but by producing a new form of *trompe-l'œil*: one applying to time itself and amounting to a kind of temporal illusionism that manages to conjure up a thread of seeming lyrical continuity out of an impressionistic prolonging of imagery which is every bit as monadic in quality as that found previously in *Allegria*. Ungaretti's true 'sentimento del tempo' [sense of time] is accordingly a harmonic lengthening of the totally separated and distinct instants of joy or elation evoked earlier; and in this sense, at least, it is never, despite all appearances, a radically new departure. In other words Ungaretti still continues to practise

his dislocated, impressionistic manner even now, but he concentrates
more on *prolonging* moments of intense feeling than on producing
self-contained lyrical essences. His sense of 'durata' is thus composed
of a series of discontinuous flashes of insight, and the lyrical pauses
which lie between these distinct moments of intense emotion and
represent for him examples of the 'void' surrounding experience all
have to be filled by the melodic and rhythmical effects he develops
in his art. In this sense, at least, all art is *trompe-l'œil*, but for Ungaretti the resuturing of the poet's 'intermittences du coeur' [pangs
of emotion] at the level of the conscience is not unauthentic, since
it tends to create his distinctive tone and timbre. After Petrarch, he
believed that Leopardi was the first poet to produce a truly syn-
thesized tone of this kind and it comes to fruition in 'A Silvia'. Of
this poem he notes significantly: 'Il Leopardi prosegue trovando nel
Canto *A Silvia* la coincidenza tra cadenza ritmica e cadenza tonale
dettata dalla sintassi' (*Saggi*, 810) [Leopardi proceeds by discovering
in the lyric *A Silvia* an exact fusion between rhythmic cadences
and tonal cadences determined by syntax]. He hoped that his own
poetry would also be of this type, and comments later that

> crisi di linguaggio ci sono sempre state, non forse mai sconcer-
> tanti come quella attuale, la crisi è continua, e continua, in
> poesia, può essere la liberazione. In poesia il linguaggio è in
> continua formazione, e di continuo fruttifica poesia. (*Saggi*,
> 833)
> [there have always been crises of language, perhaps never as
> disconcerting as the present one; the crisis is continuous, and
> continually, in poetry, it can mean liberation. In poetry lan-
> guage is in continuous formation, and continually produces
> poetry.]

This idea of the continuity and progressive deepening of the
poetic process with time permits Ungaretti to elaborate still further
his doctrine of the 'scavo della parola' [the excavation of the word].
Liberation in the sense he uses it here is a continuous release of the
harmonics of the past from the creative memory and their combination with the poet's immediate sense-impressions. In *Sentimento del
tempo*, however, Ungaretti tries to make his poetic word move
closer to the harmonics of the chord with its multiple overtones and
away from a series of notes unfolding in a simple melody, as previously practised in *Allegria*.

Even so, the problem remains of how actually to fill the 'voids'
between his lyrical insights and create what in Leopardi's case he

calls a 'margine d'illusione infinita' (*Saggi*, 809) [an area of infinite
illusion]. In *Sentimento del tempo* it is achieved by 'liberating' a continuous flow of resonances from the lyrical tradition whose continuity in time imparts an apparent continuity even to Ungaretti's
melodic line, despite its syntactic, imaginative, and rhythmic dislocation. A typical example of the illusion of temporal continuity
produced by literary resonances and a subtle return to the use of
traditional metres (especially the *endecasillabo* and the *settenario*) may
be found in the following lines from 'Di sera' [In the evening]:

> ... Sorridendo,

> Nulla, sospeso il respiro, piú dolce
> Che udirti consumarmi
> Nel sole moribondo
> L'ultimo fiammeggiare d'ombra, terra!

[Smiling, / / nothing is sweeter than with bated breath / to
hear you consuming / in the dying sunlight / my last flaming
of shadow, earth!]

Normally lines like these are carefully balanced between the dis-
continuity of the analogical imagery deployed to express the emotional charge and the continuous literary harmonics evoked. In this
passage the dominant tone is a mellifluous Petrarchism which, by
completely suffusing them, provides a continuous background music
in which to envelop the breath-taking – yet discrete – moments of
passion and insight flaring up from time to time in images like
'fiammeggiare d'ombra'. But even this refurbishing in a modern key
of the Petrarchan elegiac mode would not have been sufficient to
produce a feeling of temporal continuity if the prosody had not also
been remoulded in a traditional pattern so as to impart to the dislocated syntax of the passage a certain rhapsodic movement. Here,
in fact, the two *endecasillabi* in the first and last lines seem at first
sight to be normal or traditional ones with their main stresses falling
on the fourth, seventh and tenth, and the sixth and tenth, syllables
respectively; but what makes them differ from the normal
endecasillabo is the use of heavy caesuras, two in the first line and
one exceptionally heavy one in the last, before 'terra'. These
caesuras once again help to stress the discontinuities of feeling
lying beneath the apparent sinuous continuity of the poet's lyrical
cadences.

We are now in a position, therefore, to appreciate the real nature
of the temporal rhythm of *Sentimento del tempo*: it may be described

as the staccato throbbing of momentary passions seen against the continuous background of traditional harmonies and the growth, maturity and decline of the whole arc of the poet's lifetime. Within this sense of personal 'durata' the musico-imaginative pattern extends beyond Ungaretti's own immediate experiences and co-involves a wider mythological rhythm based on the orphic return of atavistic feelings as a form of literary anamnesis. As we have already stressed, the process is Petrarchan in origin and aims at restoring the past to its pristine immediacy within a modern context by making use of the poet's own sense-impressions as instruments of mediation. Yet during the process of mediation Ungaretti adds something of his own to the flavour of the traditional melodic line and this clearly represents his originality. In fact, his self-confessed goal in writing poetry was not only to reflect the authentic 'voice' of the lyric tradition and hand it down intact to posterity, it was also to reshape that tradition within his own sensibility, and he claims that such a relationship is one which the artist must always maintain between himself and the *Lebenswelt*. The poet in other words tends both to be its shaper and to be shaped by its multiple tensions, and this explains why Ungaretti's own verse amounts to the blending together of a dual theme, with personal elements in the foreground but with the mysterious resonances of the past murmuring a distinctive racial melody in the wings.

Authenticity for Ungaretti cannot consequently depend on the representation of personal experiences alone, they must also be given an aesthetic or orphic perspective. Perhaps one of the clearest illustrations of this point to be found in his work is in the opening of the second stanza of 'L'isola' [The island], where the poet's experience of an ever-deepening love of his native culture (symbolized by a nymph) is represented as an emergence of genuine feeling out of a previous deceptive form of *trompe-l'œil*. Yet this emergence cannot take place until the entire poem has suddenly become redimensioned by a dramatic saturation of its word-music with Petrarchan inflections, in the following line:

In sé da simulacro a fiamma vera
errando ...
[Within himself from feigned vision to true passion / erring.]

Such a form of Petrarchism ultimately gives rise to classical features in Ungaretti's lyrical texture, and this is not surprising when we bear in mind that he did not think the baroque mode was a definite break with the classical manner of the Renaissance but only a certain straining of its tensions in the direction of the grotesque or the disproportionate. His own classicism, however, like his baroque ethos, is a reconstituted one, probably an attempt to resynthesize and combine the salient elements of both manners. Its centre of gravity tends to lie halfway between Petrarch's own harmony of proportion and atmospheres of meditative self-absorption and the 'squilli di tromba' [trumpet-blasts] of a Góngora. This is because Ungaretti's manner seeks support as much from a sensory realism as it does from literary effects, and the result is that his lyrical procedures tend to move in the opposite direction from that of one of his literary masters, Baudelaire.

Nowadays it is generally acknowledged that the latter retained the classical forms of the French lyric while dissolving them from within and providing his poetic content with what he himself described as a baroque tension. Ungaretti, by contrast, begins with a baroque tension – no doubt the inheritance of Baudelaire – and endeavours to strengthen its crumbling imagery and tonal dissolution by re-creating in a modern key traditional classical structures. His classical tendencies are in this sense a call to order after the post-romantic excesses which culminated in Italy in the appearance of the highly baroque and disordered art-forms of the futurist movement. He seems to have regarded the process as essentially one of innocence to be regained, as the acquisition of a fresh, organic vision of life out of the culture-saturated ruins of the decadent ethos. Admittedly, he does not always achieve the necessary level of resynthesis and throughout the present volume some of his lyrics still tend to dissolve into a fragmentary impressionism. Nevertheless, this was the intention behind its inspiration and it explains why its lyrical texture is not decadent or effete in quality but a vigorous re-assertion of traditional human values.

Having as a preliminary sketched out the artistic intentions behind the composition of *Sentimento del tempo*, we can now pass on to an examination of its lyrical substance. Like *Allegria*, it is again divided up into sections, each of which, as the poet states in his preface, is to be regarded as an organic lyrical sequence in its own right. The first section *Prime* is transitional in quality, even though it inclines rather more than its namesake in *Allegria* towards a reconstituted classical prosody. It opens with an early poem dating from 1919 entitled 'O notte' [O night]. In it Ungaretti's future preoccupation with life's various climacterics is already hinted at, and the one he specifically deals with at this point is the passing of youth with its spontaneous enthusiasms. It will be replaced, he feels, by a vision prefiguring the barren plains of maturity:

O gioventú,
Passata è appena l'ora del distacco.

Cieli alti della gioventú,
Libero slancio.

E già sono deserto.

[O youth, / the moment of the break is only just past. / / Lofty skies of youth, / unimpeded ascent. / / And already I am a desert.]

From this initial experience of the traumatic passage of time, we move on in the sequence *Le stagioni* [The seasons] (1920) to the concept of nature's endless cycle or cosmic time. Ungaretti tells us that the whole of the section was composed in his early years in Rome and that of all the seasons depicted in it summer is the dominant one, because inwardly he always felt himself to be a man of summer and was constantly exploring its languor and fathomless mysteries:

È già oscura e fonda
L'ora d'estate che disanima.

[It is already dark and deep / summer's hour which dispirits one.] Later, as the gradual turning of the seasons carries him away from the plenitude of this sense of summer's nirvana, feelings of foreboding and death at once loom up, although death itself, we recall, is often a state of lucidity for him:

Già verso un'alta, lucida
Sepoltura, si salpa.

[Already towards a high, gleaming / sepulchre, we sail.] On the other hand, in step with his life's decline, we also sense a hardening here of the poet's resistance, and, in the coming winter of old-age, he hints that he will cling like the oak to its crag, even when all hope has faded:

Ora anche il sogno tace.

È nuda anche la quercia,
Ma abbarbicata sempre al suo macigno.

[Now even the dream is silent. / / Bare too is the oak, / but for ever rooted to its crag.]
In contrast with these sporadic intimations of mortality we find a

summery sultriness dominating the atmosphere of a poem like
Silenzio in Liguria [Silence in Liguria], in which the sharpness of the
poet's senses is soothed by a mellifluous return of the *endecasillabo*
set in a modern functional key. The poem consists of a description
at dawn of the calming effect of placated love, and its initially
tremulous harmonics are soon followed by a feeling of infinite
lyrical expansiveness, as the poet's wife awakens beside him to the
reality of the morning:

> Una carnagione lieve trascorre.
>
> Ed ella apre improvvisa ai seni
> La grande mitezza degli occhi.
>
> [A flesh-soft glow shimmers past. / / And suddenly she opens
> to her breasts / the great tenderness of her eyes.]

A contemporary remoulding of traditional metres is not only
evident in the oscillating ebb-and-flow rhythm of the first line of
this passage, but also in the fusion of image and melody in the opening line of the composition:

> Scade flessuosa la pianura d'acqua.
>
> [Sinuously the watery plain slopes down.]

Here functionality has perhaps reached its extreme limit. Not only is
the lyrical inflection remarkable for reattuning the classical line to
modern tastes, but the actual phonic combinations (the continuous
swish of 's' and 'f', for instance, offset by the pauses implicit in the
plosives 'd', 'p' and 'c' punctuating the line) also tend to intensify
the rocking of the water. This movement forms the basis of the
imagery and its very rhythm seems to imply a kind of continuity in
dissolution.

Finally the gentle impressionism of the poet's dawn-musing is set
in an orphic perspective as the light of a new state of serene understanding seems to overtake him with the coming of day:

> L'ombra sommersa delle rocce muore.
>
> Dolce sbocciata dalle anche ilari,
> Il vero amore è una quiete accesa,
>
> E la godo diffusa
> Dall'ala alabastrina
> D'una mattina immobile.
>
> [The submerged dark of the rocks dies. / / Sweetly budding
> from joyful hips, / true love is a burning calm, / / And I enjoy
> it diffused / by the alabaster wing / of a stagnant morning.]

In these images we find therefore a hint of the orphic pattern of love emerging from the very flux of life and the flaring of sexuality; yet this mythified condition of orphic wakefulness, although dilating the temporal continuum in which it is depicted, still remains, temporally speaking, nothing more durable than an essentialized and fleeting moment of insight, prolonged largely by the melodic continuity of the lyrical texture.

In another poem, 'Alla noia' [To ennui], a similar form of temporally prolonged impressionism produces a recessive effect, in which the lady continually withdraws her embrace as the poet pursues in vain her shadowy outline:

> La mano le luceva che mi porse,
> Che di quanto m'avanzo s'allontana.
>
> Eccomi perso in queste vane corse.

[The hand she offered me glowed, / which as I draw near her moves away. // Lo! I am lost in these vain pursuits.]

As she recedes from his grasp he is gradually overcome by a state of *ennui*, of existential listlessness and irritation. So, although the memory of her presence may relieve this mood of melancholy on occasion, his very faculty of recollection appears to work as a double-edged sword, and as his momentary recalls fade he finds that memory too becomes insubstantial and beguiling. The result here is that the vision of his lady's beauty is burned into his very flesh and rises memorially to dazzle him from time to time, but it leaves behind a renunciatory bitterness since the reality of enjoying it in the present will always be a vain hope:

> Memoria, fluido simulacro,
> Malinconico scherno,
> Buio del sangue ...
>
> Quale fonte timida a un'ombra
> Anziana di ulivi,
> Ritorni a assopirmi ...
>
> Di mattina ancora segreta,
> Ancora le tue labbra brami ...
>
> Non le conosca piú!

[Memory, fluid mirage, / melancholy sneer, / darkness of the blood ... // Like a timid fountain in the age-old / shadow of olive-trees, / you bring back drowsiness to me ... // In the still

secret morning / let me still desire your lips … / / Let me know
them no more!]

In these lines we see hints of Ungaretti's ambivalent attitude to
memory: it is at one and the same time a beguiling image of beauty
and a melancholy form of sneering, of *trompe-l'œil*. This is because
its perfection cannot be matched by reality and it remains for ever
delusively inaccessible. Normally it is to be associated with an atavistic cult of instinct and desire emerging from the very coursing of
his blood. At times, it is true, it also gives rise to the contingent ideal
of serenity adumbrated here by the fountain shaded by olive-trees.
Yet this is only a momentary elation deriving no doubt from the
'freschezza' [freshness] of the recollection. As it declines again it
simply brings back the poet's former exacerbated feelings of unrequited desire.

Just as memory evokes frustrated desire, so its gradual failing
causes the dreams of childhood to fade. Accordingly, in the distant
memories of the poem 'Ricordo d'Affrica' [Memory of Africa] we
find that the entire section ends on a dying fall, in which both recollection and participation prove impossible. Only the classical phrasing
of the poem still allows a residual state of serenity to linger on as an
undertone, although it is perhaps difficult to judge whether the last
line:

Ah! questa è l'ora che annuvola e smemora,

[Ah! this is the hour which clouds and brings forgetfulness]
implies a sinking into a state of contentment or senseless oblivion.
In all probability the main intention is that one world, that of the
poet's youth, is now fading away and another, a more mature one,
arising to replace it. Indeed, in this regard the next section 'Fine di
Crono' [The end of Chronos] heralds in a totally new era.

In this section the poet seems to be proposing an apocalyptic end
to our temporal condition as victims of cosmic time and, with the
death of the Titan-God Chronos, he introduces us to a new *cultural*
age, probably symbolized by Zeus and the highly civilized Gods of
Olympus. Such an age immediately brings about the internalizing
of time, now transformed into an Olympian type of *aevum*; and in
the eponymous lyric a description of the annihilation of external
reality appears in the echoing and recessive fall of the figure of
Chronos himself:

L'ora impaurita
In grembo al firmamento
Erra strana.

Una fuligine
Lilla corona i monti,

Fu l'ultimo grido a smarrirsi.

[The awe-stricken hour / in the bosom of the firmament / wanders strangely. / / A lilac soot / crowns the mountains, / / it was the last cry to fade.]

In place of the ancient God of the Earth, however, the figure which dominates the section is not so much Zeus as the bedouin-poet. He emerges and re-emerges almost as a god in his own right, while Ungaretti struggles to work out a fresh 'aeval' destiny for mankind in the aftermath of the supposed cataclysm:

Un uomo, solo, passa
Col suo sgomento muto ...

....

Torni ricolma di riflessi, anima,
E ritrovi ridente
L'oscuro ...

Tempo, fuggitivo tremito ... (*Lago luna alba notte*)

[A man, alone, passes by / silent in his awe ... / / You return full of reflections, soul, / and laughing find again / the dark / / Time, transient quiver. *Lake Moon Dawn Night*]

Here, one might reasonably claim, the recovery of time is a recovery in a different sense from the cosmic time earlier lost with the Titans: it now becomes, as previously indicated, a form of 'durata' and marks the unfolding of the inner momentum of the mind.

The hunger for experience and 'disponibilità' of the bedouin-poet are again mirrored in 'Con fuoco' [With fire] in the transient phenomena which emerge from the wasteland of life; but now it is not raw experience which is predominant but a sense of traditional insight. Thus, having at this stage accumulated enough of a memorial perspective to understand the inner meaning of the *aevum*, the erst-while 'agneauloup' is depicted as being saturated with cultural memories; so much so that he becomes a figure of nostalgia:

Con fuoco d'occhi un nostalgico lupo
Scorre la quiete nuda.

Non trova che ombre di cielo sul ghiaccio,

Fondono serpi fatue e brevi viole.

[With eyes afire a nostalgic wolf / scours the stark silence. / /

He finds only shadows of the sky on the ice, / / Melting ser-
pents and short-lived violets blend together.]

By what, we might ask, is this nostalgia prompted? Clearly, by
the poet's entry into his true cultural patrimony after he had worked
out the vital distinction between the cosmic and human time-scales.
As he once explained in a note to 'Ti svelerà', this is a time of eternal
'compresence', when memory and immediate sensation are finally
conflated in the sensibility. A similar idea is also evoked in highly
imaginative terms in the lyric 'L'isola', representing an isolated
region which in a further note he tells us is the place in which he can
momentarily suspend his conscience and analyse his own responses
as if detached from himself (*Poesie*, 537).

His initial entry into this new multilateral world of natural and
cultural reality reminds us of Baudelaire's evocation of his well-
known 'forêts de symboles' [forests of symbols] in the sonnet 'Cor-
respondances'; but with Ungaretti the symbolism is transposed into
a modern key and is no longer metaphysical, but ethical, or rather
ethico-aesthetic, in quality and intention:

A una proda ove sera era perenne
Di anziane selve assorte, scese,
E s'inoltrò
E lo richiamò rumore di penne
Ch'erasi sciolto dallo stridulo
Batticuore dell'acqua torrida,
E una larva (languiva
E rifioriva) vide;
Ritornato a salire vide
Ch'era una ninfa e dormiva
Ritta abbracciata a un olmo.

[Down towards a shore where evening was everlasting / with
ancient brooding woods he went, / and moved on / and a flutter
of wings liberated / from the throbbing heart-beat / of the torrid
waters attracted him, / and a phantom (it waxed / and waned)
he saw; / on climbing upwards again he saw / that it was a
nymph and she slept / upright with her arms around an
elm.]

The descent and subsequent climb depicted here again recall that
recessive process towards the void and the subsequent poetic return
which we have often seen before in Ungaretti; while the whole
drama takes place in the sultriness of the summery climate of Latium
where the poet is surrounded by the delicate – yet intensely sensual

and secretive – movements of natural life within the eerie stillness of the heat of day. The unexpected vision of the nymph at the end of the stanza is no doubt the vision of a classical form of beauty alternately emergent and receding from the poet's grasp during his metaphysical journey. In the second stanza we in fact discover that her secret grace is mirrored in the eyes of Italian maidens who are immersed in a form of atavistic mystery; so that we can conclude that the poem deals idyllically with Ungaretti's probing into his Italianate past, which he intends to revive and conflate with his own immediate 'durata'.

After the emergence of this type of nostalgia vibrant with its deep cultural resonances, there is a similar intensification of the more mature poet's forebodings on death. Even so, death for Ungaretti is itself a form of orphic consolation within the tradition: it is never completely negative as it is for many more secularly-orientated modern poets. In 'Inno alla morte', he believes that after death he will merge with the purified lyrical voice of his race and act as a guide and hidden mentor for future generations of poets. The final promise of the reconquest of time in this section seems then to be the eventual discovery of a 'paese innocente' of human dimensions, and the poet immediately sets about defining its elusive qualities in the remainder of the volume.

The next section *Sogni e accordi* [Dreams and harmonies] does not carry the aesthetic or metaphysical argument any further but confines itself to a series of lyrical experiments involving dreams and cultural harmonies. Its opening lyric is nevertheless remarkable both from a melodic and a rhythmic standpoint, because by the subtle use of hyperbaton it recaptures the articulation of classical metres within an impressionistic key. Likewise its spatial expansiveness and allusive perspectives clearly indicate that inner sphere of the mind which the poet has now opened up with the maturing of his concept of *aevum*. There even appears to emerge a series of delicate sensory echoes from the depths of the baroque void bridging that hollow ringing immensity which, as we have seen, Ungaretti claims automatically surrounds his moments of inspiration:

Scalza varcando da sabbie lunari,
Aurora, amore festoso, d'un'eco
Popoli l'esule universo e lasci
Nella carne dei giorni,
Perenne scia, una piaga velata. (*Eco*)
[Bare-foot, crossing from lunar sands, / Dawn, festive love,

with an echo / you repeople the exiled universe and leave / in
the flesh of days, / as a perennial trail, a veiled wound. *Echo*]

Here perhaps the predominant dactylic and anapaestic rhythms are
instrumental in bringing about the required effects, since they evoke
a recurrent movement of reverberating echoes in Ungaretti's
culturally saturated sensibility.

Neither are the modern orphic techniques, which the poet may
have acquired from Campana, wholly forgotten in this section. In
order to evoke the fossilization of his youth the poet uses a negative
form of Campanian symbol, evoking in 'Statua' [Statue] the ancient
orphic god dreaming an idle, detached dream of non-participation:

Gioventú impietrita,
O statua, o statua dell'abisso umano ...

Il gran tumulto dopo tanto viaggio
Corrode uno scoglio
A fiore di labbra.

[Petrified youth, / o statue, o statue of the human abyss ... //
The great tumult after such long journeying / corrodes a rock /
silently.]

In this lyric, it should also be noted, there is a subtle experimentation with analogy, especially in the last stanza. Analogy is, in fact,
significantly highlighted in *Sogni e accordi* which contains a series of
rapid changes in tone, ranging from an internalized Ungarettian, to
a more objective or traditional form of representation. Hence,
despite the glimmer of insight in the following comparison, we feel
that the description of the coming of a breeze in 'Aura' [Breeze] is
too immediate, too unsynthesized and contrived to make an impact
on our sensibilities:

Udendo il cielo
spada mattutina ...

[Hearing the sky / a morning sword.]

Yet by contrast other parallel analogies do sometimes make such an
impact since they evolve into satisfying visual conceits, as may be
seen in the following image:

Luna,
Piuma di cielo ... (*Ultimo quarto*)

[Moon, / feather of the heavens. *Last quarter*]

In point of fact, this kind of *visività* [visualizing] does on occasion
even acquire a new dimension as it moves towards a polychromatic
form of *veggenza* [insight]. In such cases only the second term of the

comparison is normally given in the multiple, yet dislocated, series of images evoked, and the reader is left to his own devices to reconstitute the original situation, as in the following example from 'Sogno':

> Con un volare argenteo
> Ad ogni fumo insinua guance in fiamma.
> [With a silvery flight / in every wisp of smoke she insinuates cheeks of flame.]

Here the poet is actually speaking about the effects of a personified dawn which tinges with red the stray morning mists. The transfiguration he achieves, however, transcends the mere visual image, because it also tells us something about the tremulous mood of suspension which he feels as he contemplates the scene. In other words, the better analogies in this section tend to become objective correlatives of the poet's states of mind as well as descriptive elements, while the more contrived ones limit themselves to a decorative function and are occasionally of excessive ingenuity. Not unexpectedly, self-surprise in such instances gives way to superficial exercises aiming at creating astonishment in the reader, and the result is a reversion to *Seicentismo* or traditional baroque artifices.

Perhaps the next section *Leggende* is the most significant one in the first part of the collection from the point of view of symbolic representation. The poet's aim seems to be the lyrical reanimation of a number of archetypal myths common to all periods of human existence in such a way that they acquire objective relevance in his own life:

> Si tratta di un contenuto piú oggettivo, che mettesse come una certa distanza fra il poeta e la propria ispirazione. (*Poesie*, 538–9)
> [One is dealing with a more objective content, which places, as it were, a certain distance between the poet and his own inspiration.]

In 'Memoria d'Ofelia d'Alba'[1] [In memory of Ophelia d'Alba] he tells us that these myths in every generation amount to

> Cose consumate:
> Emblemi eterni, nomi,
> Evocazioni pure …;
> [Worn-out things: / eternal emblems, names, / pure evocations]

yet it is the endless duty of the poet to lift them out of their state of suspended animation and re-endow them with the breath of actuality. This he does in a variety of ways, ranging along the whole

gamut of his representational techniques, starting with the statuesque
pose of orphic adoration, which he uses again in a poem addressed
to his mother, written in 1930 after her death:

> In ginocchio, decisa,
> Sarai una statua davanti all'Eterno,
> Come già ti vedeva
> Quando eri ancora in vita. (*La madre*)
>
> [Kneeling, decisive, / you will be a statue before the Eternal, /
> as already he saw you / when you were still alive. *Mother*]

From this hieratic stylization of the eternal pose we then gradually
ascend to a form of orphic 'invitation au voyage' beyond death,
until we finally reach a reconquered 'paese innocente' in 'Dove la
luce':

> Dove non muove foglia più la luce,
> Sogni e crucci passati ad altre rive,
> Dov'è posata sera,
> Vieni ti porterò
> Alle colline d'oro.
>
> [Where leaf is no longer moved by light, / our dreams and
> sorrows passed to other shores, / where eve reposes, / come I
> shall take you / to the hills of gold.]

On the other hand, although this atemporal condition of suspension appears to be the ultimate goal of the poet's resuscitation of
traditional symbols, the most important of the 'legends' he evokes
in this section is undoubtedly the highly complex one contained in
'Il capitano' [The captain]. Both because of its close adhesion to the
vicissitudes of his own life and because of its various cultural implications it deserves a fuller analysis than the other poems.

The details which Ungaretti gives us about the central figure are
meagre in the extreme, but he does explain that a real person was
involved, one Nazzareno Cremona, a captain in his own regiment,
who died 'schiantato sul Carso' [crushed on the Carso]. The poem
is, however, no mere recounting of a contingent event: the captain
is an eternal emblem of authority, and perhaps simultaneously an
emblem or prefiguration of death, if we are correct in assuming that
the source of the emblem is Baudelaire's 'vieux capitaine' in 'Le
voyage'. Wartime experiences in this instance, unlike in *Allegria*, are
kept strictly in the background, and the poet presents us with the
struggle between the captain's authority and his own growing-up.
The captain's initial assertiveness and subsequent death thus appear
to teach Ungaretti how to become self-reliant as a man and detached

as an artist, while at the same time respecting the tragic dignity of others within society.

The poem opens with two general statements which, curiously enough, tend once again to define the dominant attitudes of the bedouin-poet. The first, which stresses the receptivity or 'disponibilità' of his sensibility,

> Fui pronto a tutte le partenze,
>
> [I was ready for all departures]

is a continuation of the theme of the experience-hungry traveller we have already seen a number of times before. The second emphasizes the sense of mystery which acts as a shadowy hinterland behind human existence for the bedouin and provides a sheaf of cultural resonances and an orphic perspective for his immediate experiences:

> Quando hai segreti, notte hai pietà.
>
> [When you have secrets, night you have pity.]

We need hardly labour the point at this stage that the hint at 'segreti' again leads us back to Ungaretti's doctrine of creativity, to that 'nulla d'inesauribile segreto' [void of inexhaustible secrets] evoked in *Allegria*.

Likewise the word 'notte' is an orphic term employed to indicate pure unformed existence, probably a state to be assigned to the area of *tempus* before it has been imbued with 'pietà' [compassion] and acquired a deeper sense of *aevum*. But we also have to remember that the poet tends to employ an inversionary technique throughout *Sentimento del tempo*, upturning the respective values of life and death; and in this process night or at least the darkness of emotion often becomes the symbol of sensory, unself-conscious living, in contrast with light which is used to represent the blinding clarity and infinite perspectives one acquires after death. In regard to the newly appearing idea of 'pietà', to which we have referred earlier, (see p. 16) the poet now tells us that for him 'la pietà è un antico mito di Roma ... che converge nel cristiano sentimento' (*Poesie*, 540) [piety is an ancient Roman myth ... which converges with Christian feeling]. In his view it combines the atavistic sense of solidarity which the poet has with his fellow-men – especially, as we have seen, with his direct ancestors – and a Christian feeling of compassion for the suffering of all mankind. It is thus one of the principal formative elements in creating a sense of *aevum* out of *tempus* and, as such, is once more closely associated with the racial shibboleths of the bedouin. It also helps the poet in his attempts to externalize his emotions, and perhaps is even the force which consolidates the human tradition throughout time, depicting it as our immortal testimony before the gods.

Once the poet has laid down his basic attitudes to life through these generalized statements in the opening lines of the poem, he passes on to give the reader an archetypal autobiography of human development illustrated by his own childhood. At first he paints an emotionally concentrated picture of his infancy, in which a dawning consciousness of the continuity of the tradition, an eagerness to enjoy intense experiences, and the child's instinctive fears of the dark all play a symbolic role. So, as he unwinds this early temporal thread of his own life, he is clearly offering us an authentic prelude to the attitudes he will strike later on in his maturity:

> Se bimbo mi svegliavo
> Di soprassalto, mi calmavo udendo
> Urlanti nell'assente via,
> Cani randagi. Mi parevano
> Piú del lumino alla Madonna
> Che ardeva sempre in quella stanza,
> Mistica compagnia.
> [If as a child I woke / with a start, I grew calm on hearing / stray dogs howling / in the empty street. They seemed to me, / more than the light to the Madonna / which always glowed in that bedroom, / a mystic company.]

What is perhaps to be noted particularly here is the poet's sense of contingency, because the way in which the startled child awakes in the darkened room already prefigures the adult's future awareness of the terrifying starkness of the human condition. Similarly the howling of dogs foreshadows the bedouin's hunger for experience and echoes the howling already present in 'Godimento' [Enjoyment] in *Allegria* which is closely connected with the desert. Needless to say, the idea is also linked with his previous images of the wolf suggesting a certain waywardness or uncertainty in the poet's pattern of life. The point is imaginatively stressed in the image of the deserted street along which that hopeful bedouin Ungaretti will wend his way as he works out his destiny. Afterwards these humanist – virtually pagan – symbols are contrasted with the traditional Christian faith associated with the Madonna, and it is made clear that the emphasis lies not on any established, dogmatic religion at this stage but on an instinctive religion of self-development and self-expression.

Ungaretti's dawning sense of the perennial religion of humanism is, moreover, complemented in his early life by a longing for a kind of mystic communion with his fellow-men. The imagery depicting the concept here runs parallel with its archetype in 'I Fiumi' where, we recall (see p.81), the 'occulte mani' [the hidden hands] of the tradition kneaded him through and moulded his sensibility. Now its instinctive, pre-natal urges serve to stress the speed of his growing-up and his unpreparedness for the traumatic change in mental perspective which adulthood suddenly imposes on his carefree, un-thinking sensibility:

E non ad un rincorrere
Echi d'innanzi nascita,
Mi sorpresi con cuore, uomo?
[And was it not in chasing / pre-natal echoes, / that I surprised myself at heart, a man?]

At this point a crisis of self-awareness clearly looms on the horizon and, as the atavistic echoes of childhood die away, a soul-chilling despair fills his mind. The apparent pretext for it is the sight of the grisly slaughter of war, but at a deeper level it results from his grow-ing awareness of life's transiency and insignificance:

Ma quando, notte, il tuo viso fu nudo
E buttato sul sasso
Non fui che fibra d'elementi,
Pazza, palese in ogni oggetto,
Era schiacciante l'umiltà.
[But when, O night, your face was laid bare / and cast upon the rock / I was nothing less than a crazed bundle / of filaments manifest in every object, / the humility of it was crushing.]

The poet's traumatic awakening to the precariousness of his condi-tion is now in sharp contrast with the harmony he felt as a 'docile fibra / dell'universo' [as a gentle filament / of the universe] in 'I Fiumi', to which this passage no doubt acts as a contrast. But the remedy for his anguish is largely the same: it requires him to turn away from the brutal starkness of external life seen through the medium of *tempus* in the hope that he can reconstitute its essential features within the sphere of an internal or purely cultural tradi-tion.

At this point the poem unfortunately tends to trail away into a disjointed impressionism; but it is to be noted that the moonlit Leopardian landscape which frames the drama is now regarded as a less important accessory and is placed in parentheses, as if it were simply a distant metaphysical foil against which the respective destinies of the captain and the poet are worked out. The poet, in

fact, authenticates his destiny by overcoming the captain's unbend-
ing, almost statuesque, pose of authority, although he still shows his
piety towards him by compassionately closing his eyes after death.
From there on the fully matured poet sees the past tradition directly
through his own eyes, not vicariously through those of the captain;
and for this reason the essence of human drama is described here in
italicized verses while the less important situational references appear,
as already stated, parenthetically in ordinary type:

> *Il Capitano era sereno.*
>
> (Venne in cielo la luna)
>
> *Era alto e mai non si chinava.*
>
> (Andava su una nube)
>
> *Nessuno lo vide cadere,*
> *Nessuno l'udí rantolare,*
> *Riapparve adagiato in un solco,*
> *Teneva le mani sul petto.*
>
> *Gli chiusi gli occhi.*
>
> (La luna è un velo)
>
> *Parve di piume.*

> [*The Captain was serene.* / / (The moon came into the sky) / /
> *He was tall and unbending.* / / (He floated on a cloud) / / *No one*
> *saw him fall,* / *no one heard his death-rattle,* / *he reappeared carefully*
> *laid out in a furrow,* / *his hands were folded on his chest.* / / *I closed his*
> *eyes.* / / (The moon is a veil) / / *He seemed feather-like.*]

The moonlit landscape throughout the poem probably symbolizes
the 'dolci inganni' [sweet deceits] of poetic imagery in a Leopardian
sense; and so, as the captain floats away on a cloud into the past, the
moon's light acts as a veil preserving him from complete oblivion
and reviving his memory in the cultural tradition as an imposing
statuesque emblem of authority. In the last analysis the captain may
even be envisaged as a statuesque symbol of the tension which grows
up between the original poet and the cultural ethos within which he
operates. In order to resolve this tension every genuine poet has to
destroy its authority in his heart and reconstitute it, as it were, from
its ashes as the basic elements of his own sensibility. This is precisely
what seems to be the intention of the whole series of legends evoked
in the present section. Hence, at the end of it, in 'Epigrafe per un

caduto della rivoluzione' [Epigraph for a man fallen in the revolution], Ungaretti links his own poetry with the voice of the tradition itself and explains that through its haunting melodies

Il mio giovane cuore in sé immortala.

[My young heart is immortalized within itself.]

The central section of *Sentimento del tempo* is entitled *Inni* [Hymns] and marks the beginning of a religious crisis. As a result of it, another traumatic stage in the poet's spiritual development begins. The first poem, 'Danni con fantasia' [You damn with fantasy], reminds us of a similar one by Cardarelli and suggests that sin and the distortions of the imagination have hitherto been the poet's undoing. According to this lyric the poet's imagination has caused him to quest aimlessly after shadows, and his entire art, he feels, is now nothing more than an insubstantial pageant:

Se ti tocco, leggiadra, geli orrenda,
Nudi l'idea e, molto piú crudele,
Nello stesso momento
Mi leghi non deluso ad altra pena.

[If I touch you, o graceful one, you freeze horribly, / lay bare the idea and, much more cruelly, / at the same moment / you bind me undeceived to another anguish.]

Still, in the last resort even his sins have a contrastive value and without the variety they lend to life he could probably have no authentic sense of living:

La vostra, lo so, non è vera luce,
Ma avremmo vita senza il tuo variare,
Felice colpa?

[Yours, I know, is not true light, / / But would we have life without your diversity, / joyful sin?]

At bottom, therefore, this poem tends to highlight the despair of the hitherto atheist poet helplessly suspended in the sonorous void of his baroque aesthetics; and it stresses particularly his dawning realization as he matures that an ethico-aesthetic doctrine, however humanistic in orientation, is no adequate alternative for a traditional religious belief. On the other hand, he is still totally unwilling to revert to any dogmatized or fossilized form of worship, and so he struggles to combine a clearly transcendental view of Christianity with his former feeling of solidarity with his fellow-men. The tension this invokes is expressed in the all-important lyric 'La pietà' [Pity] in which the poet submits himself to an ordeal by self-questioning with his own conscience and meditates more deeply than ever before on the Michelangelesque problem (see p.47) of the absence of God in the modern world.

The whole atmosphere of the poem is similar to that experienced by Christ in the Garden of Gethsemane when he appeals to an unresponsive God to rescue him from his existential anguish as a man. But, if this is the case, Ungaretti's self-identification with Christ is clearly contaminated by a baroque sense of drama and the analogical, dislocated style typical of the hermetic manner. The lyric opens with a melodramatic – almost a romantic – statement, revealing that in spite of his thorough-going realist approach to life the poet is constantly assailed by metaphysical doubts and moral anxieties:

> Sono un uomo ferito.

> [I am a wounded man.]

He refers here above all to his maimed sensibility which is no longer able to maintain a satisfying ethico-aesthetic dialogue between himself and society, and the result is that he feels he has become alienated from human affairs:

> Non ho che superbia e bontà.

> E mi sento esiliato in mezzo agli uomini.

> Ma per essi sto in pena.

> [I have only pride and goodness. // And I feel myself exiled among men. // But for them I am stricken with anguish.]

The reason behind this sense of exile is the fact that a speculative demon has gradually been struggling to take over his mind ever since his acknowledgement of the absence of God in his early Roman period. The more the metaphysics of the baroque mode becomes consolidated in his sensibility, the more intense this speculative attitude tends to grow, because the baroque cult itself is, as we have seen, based on an abstract approach to life. Fortunately, Ungaretti continues to cling to the concrete elements inherent in his experiences despite his tortured self-questioning, and the fact that moral values rather than theological problems still remain uppermost in his thoughts is clearly indicated in the above-quoted lines.

Having reasserted the continuing validity of his ethical base, however, he then goes on to acknowledge that his ethical outlook has also been partially eroded. The first premonition he has of this is a dawning realization of the possibility that his poetic word may have nothing more than a hollow meaninglessness in a world deprived of God:

Ho popolato di nomi il silenzio.

Ho fatto a pezzi cuore e mente
Per cadere in servitú di parole?

[I have peopled the silence with names. // Have I shattered my
heart and mind / to fall into a slavery of words?]

But, once one admits that God and reality have been reduced to
mere words, to a simple *flatus vocis*, is this not tantamount to asserting
that the world itself is ruled by instinctive forces, or worse, by pure
chance? Such a view may legitimately be deduced from the following sequence of images:

O foglie secche,
Anima portata qua e là ...

No, odio il vento e la sua voce
Di bestia immemorabile.

Dio, coloro che t'implorano
Non ti conoscono piú che di nome?

[O dry leaves, / soul borne hither and thither // No, I hate the
wind and its voice / of an immemorial beast. // O God, those
who implore you / do they now know you merely by name?]

These withered leaves seem Dantesque in their resonances, and so
does the wind which reminds us of the wind of passion in the Paolo
and Francesca episode in the *Inferno*. Chance and instinct now clearly
govern his destiny in place of reason and the moral code, and the
poet feels that he might later be alienated even from death – in the
sense of the whispering of the tradition – as he is at present largely
debarred from life. In the predicament into which he has fallen he
tells us that not even sin retains its flavour, because it does not lead
back to feelings of remorse and therefore to the possibility of absolu-
tion. This means his very soul may have gone awry; and so, by a
not uncommon, psychological reversal of the true position, he ends
up by blaming God for his cruelty in alienating himself from mankind:

Dio, guarda la nostra debolezza.

Vorremmo una certezza.

Di noi nemmeno piú ridi?

E compiangici dunque, crudeltà.

[God, look on our frailty. // We desire some certainty. // Do
you not even laugh at us now? // Pity us then, o cruelty.]

Such weariness of flesh and spirit, such hopelessness in the wasteland of his modern baroque fever, leads him, if not to a death-wish,
at least to a desire for some traumatic change which will restore his
faith in his Maker:

> Fulmina le mie povere emozioni,
> Liberami dall'inquietudine.
>
> Sono stanco di urlare senza voce.

> [Blast my thread-bare emotions, / free me from anxiety. / / I
> am tired of shrieking voicelessly.]

What emerges from these lines is that his very sense of helplessness
is virtually a definition of the poet's rabid frustration as he realizes
the full implications of the closed and godless confines of his baroque
continuum. They also prove that his religious crisis arises authentically from his moral and aesthetic distress, it is not imposed by
external pressures in any way.

The second part of the poem is even more speculative in direction
than the first and deals with survival within the collective memory
after death, when the flesh has finally been turned to dust. At this
point a glimmer of hope emerges as Ungaretti again asserts his inversionary technique upturning the values of living and dying. For
him the living may even be redeemed by the hidden presence of the
dead, whose distant echoing voices represent the only true form of
insight:

> È nei vivi la strada dei defunti,
>
> Siamo noi la fiumana d'ombre,
>
> Sono esse il grano che ci scoppia in sogno,
>
> Loro è la lontananza che ci resta,
>
> E loro è l'ombra che dà peso ai nomi.

> [In the living runs the road of the dead, / / we are the torrent of
> shadows, / / they are the seed which bursts on us in dreams, / /
> theirs is the distant perspective remaining to us, / / and theirs the
> shadowiness that gives weight to our names.]

Once again the lyrical resonances of the passage seem to be Dantesque in origin, but by now some of the words have acquired a
deeper technical meaning for the poet. In a sense he is simply re-
stating his aesthetic doctrine here, because poetic inspiration is in his
view a dream which recaptures from the past the pure voice of the
dead and so dilates our immediate sense-impressions that it gives

weight and perspective to what would otherwise be empty words. In short, the poet's inversionary technique is no longer at this stage a show of technical virtuosity: it is an integral part of his hierarchy of spiritual values as he attempts to make the contingency of the present and the absoluteness of the past tradition fuse together. No form of rational abstraction or even baroque speculation seems to offer him at this point a convenient road to a state of serenity, and he significantly quotes L. Brunschvigg later who notes that 'l'Iddio del Cristiano è un essere morale, è *sensibile al cuore*' (*Saggi*, 796) [the God of the Christians is a moral being, is *sensitive to matters of the heart*]. It seems, therefore, that he now has almost a Petrarchan horror of metaphysics and puts the emphasis instead on a reconsolidation of moral and aesthetic values. As a result, after his formal conversion to Christianity in 1928, the year in which this poem was composed, he undoubtedly tends to blend a Christian ethic with his humanism.

The poet now realizes, in fact, that one major preliminary task needs to be accomplished before his art can ever again become authentic, the restoration of God. At this moment he feels as if the absence of God lingers in the collective sensibility of his time like a 'piaga misteriosa' [a mysterious wound]; and, just as the first part of the poem emphasizes his personal frustration as he shrieks voicelessly in his baroque wasteland, so here the whole of mankind in the modern world is dominated by an existential *Angst* resulting from the absence of God. God's light in the third section of the poem in fact becomes so slender and yet so powerful a beam that it can no longer dazzle without killing, or at least without inducing in the poet a death-wish:

> La luce che ci punge
> È un filo sempre piú sottile.
>
> Piú non abbagli tu, se non uccidi?
>
> Dammi questa gioia suprema.

> [The light which pierces us / is an ever more slender beam. / / Do you no longer dazzle unless you kill? / / Grant me this supreme joy.]

The fourth and final section of the poem deals with a resulting Baudelairian *ennui* as Ungaretti self-consciously contemplates the gratuitousness of his own perilous and godless contingency. The only hope of pious consolation which he believes man can permit himself in modern circumstances is the Foscolian one of tomb-building; but this activity does not amount to religious redemption:

it is simply another way of expressing that consolidation within the tradition and mankind's feeling of piety towards the dead which has been the poet's principal form of consolation all along. The section is important, however, for its representation of the hollowness of modern living without religious faith, since the spider's web of baroque reasoning we nowadays weave over the abyss of existence is in Ungaretti's view based solely on a narcissistic, intellectual self-deception:

> L'uomo, monotono universo,
> Crede allargarsi i beni
> E dalle sue mani febbrili
> Non escono senza fine che limiti.
>
> Attaccato sul vuoto
> Al suo filo di ragno,
> Non teme e non seduce
> Se non il proprio grido.

[Man, a monotonous universe, / believes he increases his blessings / and from his feverish hands / nothing but limits emerge, endlessly. / / Hanging over the void / on his spider's thread, / he neither fears nor beguiles / aught but his own cries.]

One of the limits mentioned in the first stanza of this quotation is the self-defeating cult of materialism which reduces homely 'laric' objects to dead obsolescent things, even to the very touch. The result is that the rhythm of the machine, as Ungaretti hints elsewhere, has long since taken over that of the human tradition and a mechanically-based form of mass-production has become part and parcel of the meaninglessness of everyday existence. So, as the lyric finishes, the wheel comes full circle and the poet presents us with the empty name of God, which now has lost all significance except in blasphemies, where alone it retains some residual emotive impact on our minds:

> Ripara il logorio alzando tombe,
> E per pensarti, Eterno,
> Non ha che le bestemmie.

[He makes good the wear-and-tear by building tombs, / and to think of you, God Eternal, / he has only blasphemies.]

Such an irredeemable sense of emptiness creates a fresh perspective of sin in human life, and the obsessive nature of the concept with Ungaretti at this stage is epitomized in *Inni* by the biblical figure of Cain, no doubt the latest avatar of the bedouin-poet. The poem

actually deals with the creation of the conscience after the Fall, and
Cambon (*La poesia di Ungaretti*, 130 et seq.) has offered us an illumi-
nating formula for the understanding both of this process and of the
appearance of death, as we shall see in a later section. His formula is:
innocence→sin→conscience, and in all essentials it parallels on an
ethical plane the metaphysical concept of creativity we discussed
earlier, which can similarly be covered by the formula, memory→
void→dream of becoming.

As we know, Cain's particular sin was the murder of his brother,
and this is perhaps the most heinous sin of all in Ungaretti's philosophy of human solidarity. Needless to say, Cain is haunted at all
times by the memory of his crime and depicted, through a subtle
transformation of an earlier symbol, as a 'pastore di lupi' [a shepherd
of wolves]. In his quest for redemption through the extinction of
conscience he scours a wasteland of incipient human dimensions, one
which already has a fabulous, mythological air about it. So even in
this early period the tradition has clearly begun to weave a confident
self-protecting mantle around humanity:

> Corre sopra le sabbie favolose
> E il suo piede è leggero;
> [He courses over fabulous sands / and he is fleet of foot]

and, towards the end of the lyric, the poet sees his own, and perhaps
even the fate of all mankind, as being similar to that of Cain, when
he asks himself anxiously:

> Anima, non saprò mai calmarti?
>
> Mai non vedrò nella notte del sangue?
>
> [Soul, will I never be able to calm you? // Will I never be able
> to see into the night of blood?]

Here he implies that, if his soul can never know serenity on earth, it
is because its memory of original sin is an irremovable metaphysical
source of despair. It is probably only after death that it will finally
assuage its existential anguish by a meditative recapturing of a state
of innocence through the very mediation of the trials and tribula-
tions of this world. In the meantime, it will continue to suffer from
the vicious circle of alternate recollection and *noia* which is a result
of our contingent condition after the Fall:

> Figlia indiscreta della noia,
> Memoria, memoria incessante,
> Le nuvole della tua polvere,
> Non c'è vento che se le porti via?

Gli occhi mi tornerebbero innocenti,
Vedrei la primavera eterna

E, finalmente nuova,
O memoria, saresti onesta.

[Indiscreet daughter of ennui, / memory, incessant memory, /
will no wind ever carry off / the clouds of your dust? / / My
eyes would become innocent again, / I would see the eternal
spring / / and, finally renewed, / O memory, you would be
honest.]

However, despite the logic of this position, it does not seem as if
Ungaretti is in the long run prepared to regard even original sin as
an ineluctable metaphysical flaw in the universe which human
emotion can never transcend. In 'La Preghiera' [Prayer] he unmistak-
ably envisages again a paradise to be regained, and this paradise
is by no means a theological abstraction: it is a renewed humanism, a
holding of hands by mankind unto Eternity, brought about by God's
purifying love from the very travail of the flesh:

Purificante amore,
Fa' ancora che sia scala di riscatto
La carne ingannatrice.

Vorrei di nuovo udirti dire
Che in te finalmente annullate
Le anime s'uniranno
E lassú formeranno,
Eterna umanità,
Il tuo sonno felice.

[Purifying love, / make once more a ladder of redemption / the
deceitful flesh. / / I wish to hear you say again / that finally
annulled in you / our souls will be united / and in heaven will
form, / an eternal humanity, / your joyous slumber.]

The humanizing of heaven is, however, again consonant with
Ungaretti's basic philosophical outlook, since it tends to change the
tempus of an inanimate and indifferent cosmos into a state of *aevum*,
giving it an infinitely human, historical perspective. The point is
re-emphasized in the last lyric of the section significantly entitled
Sentimento del tempo. Here the reduction of the external universe to a
human scale brings about a condition in which 'la lontananza (è)
aperta alla misura' [distant perspective (is) opened to a sense of
measure]. This is the secret aim of all of Ungaretti's 'hymns' and it

amounts to a modern form of humanism based on an ethico-aesthetic refurbishing of the past. In the process even God is humanized and thereby finally authenticated, and thereafter the external universe becomes an inner conquest of the mind.

Probably the road to salvation in this sense can only be traversed by a subtle repenetration of death's mysteries, since death as we have seen on many occasions, is to be identified in Ungaretti's view with the human tradition. So in the next section, *La morte meditata*, his inversion of human values is brought to its apotheosis and, while death gives the soul a sense of fulfilment, life offers only the meaningless oblivion of the senses.

Originally, this section was divided into two parts in the editions of 1933 and 1936 and bore the titles of *Sentimento della memoria* and *Sentimento del sogno*; and the lyric *Sentimento del tempo* was itself included in it in 1936. Eventually, however, Ungaretti found these titles unsatisfactory and changed them to the present one which covers both aspects of his dialectic of inspiration since it pivots around the central feature, that is, the void of death. Cambon (ibid. 130-1) implies that death for Ungaretti is a direct result of the biblical Fall and quotes appositely from 'Canto primo' [First song] to prove his point:

In un giardino puro
Alla luce ti diè l'ingenua brama
[In a pure garden / innocent lust gave birth to you.]

Here we no doubt have a figuration of the Garden of Eden and Eve's eating of the apple, after which Cambon sees Death as personifying the existentialist concept of the 'Other'. But it is doubtful whether this is really the case, because two other lines in the poem permit us to identify Death much more precisely. In the first she is described as

Madre velenosa degli evi ...;
[The poisonous mother of the ages]

in the second as

Bellezza punita e ridente.
[Beauty punished and smiling.]

Surely, such expressions can only apply to one figure, Eve herself? She is both punished for her crime, becoming a burden of guilt for her progeny, and a distant, inaccessible dream of innocence to be regained, which haunts mankind in its subsequent temporal existence. This explains other highly allusive lines in the second stanza, to the effect that peace was lost on her mouth. The image of the mouth of a modern Eve also appears in *Canto* in the next section, and if the

second part of the poem is taken as a pendant to the first, the name of
Eve is specifically mentioned in that lyric. There the separation of
the lover and his beloved becomes a single instance of mankind's
separation from the original Eve by the unfathomable spiritual
distances of suffering and death:

> E la crudele solitudine
> Che in sé ciascuno scopre, se ama,
> Ora tomba infinita,
> Da te mi divide per sempre.
>
> Cara, lontana come in uno specchio. ... (*Canto*)

[And the cruel solitude / which each person discovers in himself,
if he loves, / now an infinite tomb, / divides me from you for
ever. / / Beloved, as distant as if in a mirror. *Song*]

These inner distances are temporal rather than spatial for Ungaretti, and in fact he conflates time and space in *Sentimento del
tempo*. But the important psychological point he is making here is
that the emptiness of love is comparable with the metaphysical
desire left in mankind to fill the void created by the sin of Eve and to
re-establish that innocent, pre-sexual relationship between man and
woman which existed before the Fall. In this sense the biblical figure
of Eve is bivalent in *La morte meditata*: she is simultaneously death as a
punishment for sin and an obsessive mirage of innocence to be
regained, which is probably only attainable after death, given the
present nature of the human condition. In the meantime, mankind
dreams in its endless suffering of her peerless, atemporal beauty – a
dream of existential anguish and obsessive hope based on a belief in
the possibility of restoring (perhaps through art in our present life)
at least glimpses of her primeval innocence.

After this brief exegesis of the polyvalency of the symbol of Death
let us now return to the poem itself. At this point we can simply
enjoy the allusiveness of its artistry as it attempts to re-evoke a sense
of primeval innocence through the very meditation of death's
dream-kingdom. For Ungaretti the dream of death does not begin
simply after the poet's decease, intimations of Eve's paradise regained
are already present within this life's fabric. Indeed, in his view the
warp of our present existence is always interwoven with death's
beguiling resonances and the delicate tracery of her distant perspectives forms the background to its mysteries:

> In un giardino puro
> Alla luce ti diè l'ingenua brama

E la pace fu persa,
Pensosa morte,
Sulla tua bocca.

Da quel momento
Ti odo nel fluire della mente
Approfondire lontananze,
Emula sofferente dell'eterno.

[In a pure garden / innocent lust gave birth to you / and peace
was lost, / thoughtful death, / on your mouth. / / From that
instant / I hear you in the flowing of the mind / probing distances, / anguished emulator of the eternal.]

Even so, we should not imagine that the poet had acquired at this
stage a deep-rooted faith in a Christian type of spiritual eternity after
death. For him the afterlife is still a memorial process reawakening
the melodies of the past in the lyrical achievements of the present.
Since this is the case, he begins to wonder in 'Canto primo' how
long his own memory will endure in mankind's hall of fame after
his own death:

Quando m'avrai domato, dimmi:

Nella malinconia dei vivi
Volerà a lungo la mia ombra?

[When you have tamed me, tell me: // in the melancholy of the
living / will my shade linger long?]

'Canto secondo' again takes up the problem of memory and the
depositing of memory's trace over the ages. But now the tone is
harsher, more incisive and durable, and the song of death resembles
that of the cicada lost in a darkened universe of insubstantial reflections:

Morte, muta parola,
Sabbia deposta come un letto
Dal sangue,
Ti odo cantare come una cicala
Nella rosa abbrunata dei riflessi.

[Death, silent word, / sand deposited like a bed / by the blood, /
I hear you singing like a cicada / in the darkened rose of reflections.]

This tremendous resilience of memory emanates from what the poet
calls 'la buia veglia dei padri' [the dark vigil of the fathers]: that is,
the vigil of those poets of the past who control his own present

lyricism and, by extension, the tastes of his entire age, through the
insistent resonances they evoke within the lyric tradition. Yet in the
third song their guidance is not prompted by their humanity alone,
and not even by their desire to link hands over the aeons of time: it
is also proffered as a challenge to, while simultaneously being a
revelation of, the starkness of our contingency. Here memory again
becomes a double-edged sword and we encounter the ironic counterpart to our forefathers' vigilance in the phrase 'la beffa infinita dei
padri' [the infinite mockery of the fathers]. Their scorn is probably
an unintentional effect, however, and derives from the contrast
between the desperate contingency of the living poet and the non-
contingent, virtually eternal position in the racial memory of his
forebears. Their position has indeed become consolidated because
time has long since had the opportunity to ferment around their
words and lyrical inflections, and by comparison with them the
present-day poet can only feel that he is a prey to every type of
Mallarmean 'hasard'. Yet one possible way of escape from this
daunting condition is eventually indicated in the fourth song (the
beginning of the section *Sentimento del sogno* in the early editions).
In this poem Ungaretti himself claims to burn up time and space
through his art and participate directly during his own lifetime, or so
it seems, in the dream of death. His poetic dream to which he is no
doubt referring here is thus a 'liberation' from the weight of memory,
from the weight of history. Incidentally, the speculative nature of
this poem is emphasized in the change of the early 'monte' to 'colle'
in the landscaping of the final version. Such a change brings out the
relationship between the lyric and Leopardi's 'L'infinito' which
Ungaretti also read as a type of *ars poetica* (see *Saggi*, 472 et seq.)
based on a cult of self-conscious 'inganni' [deceits]:

> Mi presero per mano nuvole.
>
> Brucio sul colle spazio e tempo,
> Come un tuo messaggero,
> Come il sogno, divina morte.

> [Clouds seized me by the hand. // On the hill I burn both space
> and time, / like one of your messengers, / like the dream, O
> death divine.]

After the reduction of the universe to a spaceless, timeless dream in
this poem, we are presented in the fifth lyric with an allusive description of death's impalpable kingdom, evoked through a profusion
of intangible sensations. Once again the condition of death has all the

qualities associated with a baroque hollowness or void, in which the dramatic sensations of life are constantly heightened and intensified. So, after the customary initial statement indicating that the protagonist's eyes had been closed in sleep, the poem passes on to an analogical evocation of the condition of death as a submerged dream-universe of darkness, bobbing corks and nets:

Nasce una notte
Piena di finte buche,
Di suoni morti
Come di sugheri
Di reti calate nell'acqua.

[A night is born / full of sham holes, / of dead sounds, / like corks / of nets lowered into water.]

This description is followed by an equally intangible evocation of a Leopardian moonlight scene, and then – to round the poem off – the figure of death itself is evoked as a phantom-woman whose hidden charms touch the poet's soul. At the end of the poem her allusive presence leaves behind her a sense of indefinite exasperation and frustration, both lasting and transitory in their effects; and this once more is for Ungaretti the normal impact made by Eve's presence after the Fall. Moreover, just as we saw earlier in the 'albero mutilato' of 'I Fiumi', the tree-symbol is again evoked here as an image of human anguish:

Sei la donna che passa
Come una foglia
E lasci agli alberi un fuoco d'autunno.

[You are the woman who passes by / like a leaf / / and you leave on the trees a blaze of autumn.]

Such imagery reminds us, perhaps, of Baudelaire's poem 'À une passante' where a baroque feeling of sensuous exasperation is also conveyed by the momentary passing of an unknown woman. Finally, however, in the last lyric the poet awakens from his dream; but, because he now has the satisfaction of having familiarized himself with death's phantom figures, his own heart too becomes saturated with their inexplicable, secret remorse as day breaks. This remorse is probably a sense of disappointment at their inability to return to the contingency of this life so as to expiate their past sins, a feeling which the poet, as a modern humanist, shares:

Con voi, fantasmi, non ho mai ritegno,
E dei vostri rimorsi ho pieno il cuore

Quando fa giorno.

[With you, my phantoms, I never know restraint, / / and with
your remorse my heart is filled / when day breaks.]

What this journey into death's kingdom teaches Ungaretti is that
death is a sphere of human experience crystallized in the memory,
while creativity itself is liberation through the dream from the
gratuitous flux of everyday life during which the poet can commune
with the spirits of the past. By means of these excursions he hopes his
lyricism will pass out of the meaningless sphere of 'le hasard' to a
world of permanent moral and emotive values. The process amounts
essentially to the recapturing of the timeless through the transformation of time into perspective and 'durata'. Cavalli has explained its
paradoxical nature by pointing out that 'it is a search which brings
the poet back to a reality which is human and yet simultaneously
becomes a temporal abstraction, a sublime innocence'.[2]

The last section of *Sentimento del tempo* is called *L'Amore*, probably
because it is through the exploration of love in all its manifestations
that Ungaretti now hopes perfectly to attune his lyrical keyboard
and make it an instrument capable of detecting and reproducing
every one of the tradition's secret harmonics. The opening poem is
significantly entitled 'Canto beduino' [Bedouin song] and, like a
previous poem 'Primo amore' [First love], it evokes an early
Egyptian love-affair during which the poet tells us he was first
awakened to the ecstasies of the flesh (*Poesie*, 539). Here not only do
elemental or instinctive urges break through the lyrical tension, but
the poem acquires a universal significance in terms of Ungaretti's
symbolism, since the description involves the wasteland, the wind of
passion, the dream of truth, and also death's airy distances:

Una donna s'alza e canta
La segue il vento e l'incanta
E sulla terra la stende
E il sogno vero la prende.

Questa terra è nuda
Questa donna è druda
Questo vento è forte
Questo sogno è morte.

[A woman rises and sings / the wind pursues and bewitches her /
and it lays her on the ground / and the true dream seizes her. / /
This ground is bare / this woman is a paramour / this wind is
strong / this dream is death.]

Probably the woman in the poem is again Eve as she is seduced by Adam, for later in the 'Ultimi cori per la terra promessa' the poet returns to the theme of carnal knowledge and talks of Adam's curiosity in matters of the flesh and Eve's sense of perdition as they consumate their sexual relationship (*Lettere a un fenomenologo*, 60).

To a certain extent the same intense sensuality is continued in 'Canto' where it seems that the memory of physical contact opens up an abyss of solitude in the lover's mind. Yet in a postscript to the poem Ungaretti adumbrates a spiritual refinement to his hitherto high-pitched and taut sensuality, one which amounts almost to a modern, secularized form of *stilnovismo*:

Quando ogni luce è spenta
E non vedo che i miei pensieri,

Un'Eva mette sugli occhi
La tela dei paradisi perduti.

[When every light dies away / and I see only my own thoughts, / / an Eve lays on my eyes / the canvas of lost paradises.]

In this regard we note that the lady is openly called a modern Eve, not a more specific religious figure. This implies that the poet's new-found serenity is still saturated with a hunger for living. Later he pleads in 'Auguri per il proprio compleanno' [Greetings for my birthday] to be allowed in his declining years to continue his involvement in the delights of sensation, and it is on this note that the collection ends.

If therefore we look back over Ungaretti's achievements up to this point we shall see that the specific contribution of *Sentimento del tempo* is a peculiar reinsertion of the poet into the life of his times. In the early twenties he suddenly appears to have grasped the fact that *Allegria* already represented a baroque lyricism in embryo, and so he set about intensifying this facet of his inspiration in step with the maturing of his personality. The task was not as simple as it looked at first sight, because it not only required the creation of a coherent baroque doctrine but also the combining of that doctrine with the unfolding of his personal experiences. The secret of his eventual success in intermingling personal vicissitudes and a baroque outlook lies in his continual dilation of life's perspectives, culminating in his metaphysical understanding of love and death in the figure of Eve. But he does not allow his speculative attitudes to undermine his art at the imaginative level, he tends rather to transform his sense-impressions into ethico-aesthetic absolutes or emotive values. As a result, his experiences, instead of remaining sequentially patterned under the domination of external time, become inward and 'aeval' in quality.

Although Ungaretti cannot claim at this point to have solved the problem of his alienation from society and at the end of the collection is probably no less a social 'misfit' than he was before, as an artist he has certainly learned during its composition how to produce imagery of such intensity and coherence as to impose his art upon the life of his times. If not then to present society, he re-establishes in *Sentimento del tempo* an intimate sense of belonging to the Italian tradition, a feature which was not always present in *Allegria* where he normally seems to bestride two very different cultures. At the same time he now fully attunes his own tastes to those of the traditional Petrarchan lyric and his melodic line becomes a poetic dialogue in which what he considers precious and revitalizing in the past is used to dilate and interpret his own original feelings in the present. It is on this dual string that he hopes to build the new lyricism of the twentieth century; and, if he changes direction for a time in *Il dolore*, where he gives way momentarily to a more personal inspiration under the strain of living, he certainly keeps his promise to expand the deeper metaphysical implications of the present collection in *La terra promessa* (1950) where his vision of a land of regained innocence takes on an entirely new dimension.

5. *Il dolore*

Ungaretti's third collection, *Il dolore* [Grief], was published in 1947 and contains the poems written between 1937 and 1946. At first sight it seems to follow the mainstream of his earlier development, since its opening section deals with a theme already present in *Sentimento del tempo*, that ever-increasing anguish which the poet felt as a result of the loss of his youth and the approach of old age. However, this normal line of evolution is almost immediately brushed aside as he is shaken out of the normal tenor of his life by a series of tragedies, two personal and one social. The personal ones were the death in 1937 of his brother Costantino, to whom the first section of the collection *Tutto ho perduto* [I have lost everything] is dedicated, and the even more shattering death of his young son, Antonietto, in Brazil in 1939. These two family bereavements were then closely followed by the war and the invasion of Italy, and the latter event Ungaretti found particularly harrowing after his return in 1942. Together their impact distracted him almost completely from his principal line of poetic development which was not taken up again until very much later, with the publication of *La terra promessa* in 1950. In the interval the poet's immediate responses to the tragedies in which he was involved filled the entire canvas of his artistic life, so that *Il dolore* has to be considered in its general outline as a brief interlude of personal grief lying between two major moments of lyrical development.

The opening section of the volume dealing with the death of Costantino is not, thematically speaking, typical of the whole, since the first of the two poems it contains continues to examine that sense of anguish experienced by every human being as he approaches the various climacterics of his own existence. The lyric expresses the poet's despair at the loss of that particular acuity of the senses which he associates with youth, because he now claims that with his dying sensations his spontaneous 'gridi' have completely disappeared and his emotional life has been left that much the poorer. Such a loss does not simply amount to the diminution of sensual pleasures, moreover, but also marks the disappearance of his previous atavistic insights;

and the poet expresses his regret at their passing in language which has been sharpened by his technical development of certain archetypal concepts:

> Tutto ho perduto dell'infanzia
> E non potrò mai piú
> Smemorarmi in un grido.
>
> L'infanzia ho sotterrato
> Nel fondo delle notti
> E ora, spada invisibile,
> Mi separa da tutto.

[Everything I have lost of my childhood / and I can never again / unburden my memory in a cry. / / Childhood I have buried / in the depths of night / and now, an invisible sword, / it separates me from everything.]

Although the symbolism of this particular lyric is seemingly co-substantial with earlier forms, beneath the surface it undoubtedly undergoes considerable changes. Thus Ungaretti's hitherto metaphysical emblems (such as 'notte' [night] appearing in the above context) tend to lose their speculative charge and decline to the level of mere tonal pointers. The nocturnal atmosphere here does not in other words indicate an orphic area of pure, unformed existence but rather the darkness of a sense of oblivion. Likewise there is a tendency, as the volume progresses, to reorientate the symbolism completely towards a more discursive mode of transfiguration which might be described as baroque allegorizing. On certain occasions, on the other hand, the loss of metaphysicality of some former symbolic archetypes is partly compensated for by the raising of other, humbler ones to a virtual metaphysical status. An evident case of a new form of condensed emotivity which borders on the metaphysical limits of anguish is the image of the rock in the present poem, since it now becomes the symbol of the fossilization of the poet's sensibility with the passage of time and the waning of his youth:

> Disperazione che incessantemente aumenta
> La vita non mi è piú,
> Arrestata in fondo alla gola,
> Che una roccia di gridi.

[A despair which incessantly increases / life is no longer to me, / blocked in the depths of my throat, / anything more than a rock of cries.]

Needless to say, the original of this new type of symbol is to be found in Petrarch where Laura, whenever she represents the unrequitedness of the poet's love, appears to him as a 'petra viva' [a living stone]; yet, oddly, there is also a curious undercurrent of continuity in Ungaretti's imagery even at this juncture, because already in 'I Fiumi' the poet had written many years before:

L'Isonzo scorrendo
mi levigava
come un suo sasso.

[The Isonzo as it flowed / polished me / as one of its stones.] Whereas in the early poem the intractable hardness of the rock reveals the resistance of the poet to his fate, here it means the opposite: his succumbing to the ravages of time. The point is further emphasized in the other poem in the present section, the one addressed directly to his dead brother. In it he claims that not even memory can now overcome his sense of loss of the acute sensations of youth, and so he is inevitably proceeding towards a state in which the specifically poetic habit of spontaneous feeling finally becomes extinguished:

La memoria non svolge che le immagini
E a me stesso io stesso
Non sono già piú
Che l'annientante nulla del pensiero.

[Memory now only unfolds images / and to myself I myself / am no longer but / the annihilating nothingness of thought.] On the other hand, despite this metamorphosis of his symbolism, as far as his overall themes are concerned the poet is still running broadly true to form, because he is expressing those metaphysical ideas on human decline which had already emerged from time to time in a number of poems in *Sentimento del tempo*. Consequently it is only in the following section that the break with the past becomes unmistakable.

Written between 1940 and 1946 the next section, *Giorno per giorno* [Day by day], is a diaristic account of his son's illness and subsequent death, composed slightly after the event; and it expresses in a heightened baroque style the anguish and frustration which then wrung the poet's heart. This section and the next *Il tempo è muto* [Time is silent] should, incidentally, be read in conjunction with the poem 'Gridasti: soffoco' [You shouted: I am suffocating] which the poet felt was too personal a composition to be published at the time and which only appears in print much later, as a separate item in

1949. It was nevertheless completed as early as 1940 with a first draft probably in 1939 (see *Poesie*, 569); so, for the purposes of the present analysis, we shall restore it to its proper chronological order and consider it an integral part of *Giorno per giorno*.

The first poem in the section deals with the day-to-day development of Antonietto's illness, but even at the outset its various stages are dramatically presented as prefigurations of his inevitable death, by the continual emphasis placed on the pallor of his face and his father's desperate efforts to keep him amused. These distractions amount to pathetic actions like the feeding of sparrows in the sick-room, where the imagery highlights not only the fragility of all forms of life but also the desperate bonds of human solidarity at moments of drama and crisis:

> E il volto già scomparso
> Ma gli occhi ancora vivi
> Dal guanciale volgeva alla finestra,
> E riempivano passeri la stanza
> Verso le briciole dal babbo sparse
> Per distrarre il suo bimbo ...
> [And his face already wasted by death / but with eyes still alive / he turned from the pillow to the window, / and sparrows filled the room, / towards the crumbs scattered by his father / to amuse his child.]

From this initial domestic scene at Antonietto's death-bed we pass on to the period after his death when the poet can only imagine his son's presence in his dreams. Dreams here, however, have the normal connotation: they are no longer the technical and spiritual soarings which earlier in *Sentimento del tempo* we associated with inspirational processes. Even after the child's death everyday life for the poet had, of course, to go on; yet despite its apparent tranquillity he only finds real consolation when he continues to feel the haunting presence of his son at his side:

> Mai, non saprete mai come m'illumina
> L'ombra che mi si pone a lato, timida,
> Quando non spero piú ...
> [Never, you will never know how much the shade / inspires me which comes and sits beside me, timidly, / when I no longer hope.]

His whole comfort in other words lies in memorial recall, and the poet indulges in a form of Leopardian pathos set in a modern key by drawing a serene picture of his son's life to contrast with reality, a scene which is somewhat reminiscent of lines in Leopardi's poem 'A Silvia':

Ora dov'è, dov'è l'ingenua voce
Che in corsa risuonando per le stanze
Sollevava dai crucci un uomo stanco? ...
La terra l'ha disfatta, la protegge
Un passato di favola ...
[Now where, where is the innocent voice / which re-echoing as he sped from room to room / awakened from his sorrows a weary man? ... / The earth has undone it, a fabulous / past protects it.]

Thereafter Antonietto's voice becomes virtually obsessive and drowns out all others as he calls to his father from 'vette immortali' [immortal peaks]. In consequence, Ungaretti's anguish proves to be unbearable and breaks through all the restraints of art as he expresses himself in cries of raw emotion which attain their maximum tension in the one-lined lyric:

E t'amo, t'amo, ed è continuo schianto ...
[And I love you, I love you, and it is a continuous shattering ...]

Once his inspiration reaches this hysterical flash-point, the whole panoply of the poet's baroque artifices tends to be brought into play, especially after his return to Italy when he magnifies – almost bestial-izes – the vast stretches of sea and land which separate him from Antonietto's grave and fill him with a deep sense of horror:

Inferocita terra, immane mare
Mi separa dal luogo della tomba
Dove ora si disperde
Il martoriato corpo ...
[A ferocious land, an immense sea / separates me from the site of the grave / where wasting there now lies / his shattered frame.]

So, although the nature of his spiritual climate appears to have changed for the better with his return to the gentle Italian hills, the poet's despair at being unable to share his newly-found homeland with his son remains as poignant as ever:

Sono tornato ai colli, ai pini amati
E del ritmo dell'aria il patrio accento
Che non riudrò con te,
Mi spezza ad ogni soffio ...
[I have returned to the hills, to the beloved pines / and the homely accents of the rhythmic air / which I shall not hear again with you, / break my heart at every breath.]

At this point there follows a series of symbols of contingent grace

such as the swallow passing with summer; but the poet is conscious
of the fact that, although Antonietto is now dead, his love for his son
can never diminish. What has really happened as a result of the boy's
death is that his own summer has ended and autumn with its sense of
inexorable decline has begun to set in. This feeling also brings on a
fresh heightening of his baroque fury, represented by the tortured
presence of a fulminatory Pascalian abyss resounding with a secret
anguish as it haunts his mind at twilight:

> Già m'è nelle ossa scesa
> L'autunnale secchezza,
> Ma, protratto dalle ombre,
> Sopravviene infinito
> Un demente fulgore:
> La tortura segreta del crepuscolo
> Inabissato ...
> [Already there has descended in my bones / an autumnal dryness,
> / but by the shadows prolonged, / there suddenly arrives an
> endless / demented splendour: / the secret torture of twilight /
> sunk into an abyss.]

Probably the skeletal magnification of this anguished sense of
emptiness is best reflected in the sixteenth lyric where the description
of the young boy playing in the garden seems at first a continuation
of his earlier gambolling in the house. But now the whole scene is
dematerialized, made almost spectral, by a complex interplay of
reflections, even though its realist base – an evocation of the shimmering Brazilian summer's heat – in no way loses its potency:

> Agli abbagli che squillano dai vetri
> Squadra un riflesso alla tovaglia l'ombra,
> Tornano al lustro labile d'un orcio
> Gonfie ortensie dall'aiuola, un rondone ebbro,
> Il grattacielo in vampe delle nuvole,
> Sull'albero, saltelli d'un bimbetto ...
> [In the dazzle which screams from the window-panes / the shade
> frames a reflection on the tablecloth, / in the faint lustre of a pot
> return / swollen hydrangeas from the flower-bed, a drunken
> swift, / the sky-scraper in a blaze of clouds, / the capering of a
> child, on a tree.]

It is indeed within this apocalyptic scene of intense reflections and
dematerialized objects that Antonietto's voice again comes echoing
back to Ungaretti, accompanied by the soothing message that perhaps
his bereaved parent will now find repose in his continuing phanto-

matic presence and in the ending of his long exile from his native land:

Fa dolce e forse qui vicino passi
Dicendo: "Questo sole e tanto spazio
Ti calmino. Nel puro vento udire
Puoi il tempo camminare e la mia voce.
Ho in me raccolto a poco a poco e chiuso
Lo slancio muto della tua speranza.
Sono per te l'aurora e intatto giorno."

[The weather turns mild and perhaps you pass nearby / saying: 'May this sun and so much space / calm you. In the pure air you can / hear time's step and my voice. / I have gathered within me little by little and sealed / the silent impulse of your hope. / I am for you the dawn and wholesome day.']

Dramatic and intense as this sequence is, however, its emotionalism is by no means as great as 'Gridasti: soffoco …', which nevertheless thematically covers much the same ground. In this poem the further heightening of the tension is once more baroque in quality and Ungaretti's rhetorically-based distortion of the situation may be seen at the very outset, in his description of the child writhing in his death-throes:

Poi la bocca, la bocca
Che una volta pareva, lungo i giorni,
Lampo di grazia e gioia,
La bocca si contorse in lotta muta …
Un bimbo è morto …

[Then the mouth, the mouth / which once appeared, every day, / a flash of grace and joy, / the mouth twisted up in a silent struggle … / A child died.]

After his son's death the delirium which the poet experiences as a father is even more powerfully expressed, since in his subsequent demented state he believes that he continues to clasp Antonietto by the hand in fleshy form, although the boy's hand now withers even as he clutches it:

Io di continuo posso,
Distintamente posso
Sentirti le mani nelle mie mani:
Le mani tue di pargolo
Che afferrano le mie senza conoscerle;
Le tue mani che si fanno sensibili,
Sempre più consapevoli

Abbandonandosi nelle mie mani;
Le tue mani che diventano secche
E, sole – pallidissime –
Sole nell'ombra sostano ...
La settimana scorsa eri fiorente ...
[I can continually, / I can distinctly / feel your hands in my
hands: / your little childish hands / which clasp mine without
knowing them; / your hands which turn fleshly, / more and more
aware / entrusting themselves to my hands; / your hands which
become withered / and, alone – very pale – / alone in the shadows
linger ... / Last week you were flourishing.]

Then finally he expresses his remorse at having unwittingly
stolen hours and years from his son's life by going to live abroad and
blames the strangeness and unfeelingness of the Brazilian climate
for the tragedy, emphasizing his family's alienation from its unfamiliar skies:

È troppo azzurro questo cielo australe,
Troppi astri lo gremiscono,
Troppi e, per noi, non uno familiare ...
[This southern sky is too blue for us, / too many stars teem in it, /
too many and, for us, not one familiar.]

The last point, as we can see, once again refers back obliquely to that
sense of 'laric' familiarity which comforted the poet in *Allegria* and
which is now almost totally absent. His alienation, or so it seems, has
resulted in the reduction of the *aevum* to a new, but overwhelmingly
absurd, state of *tempus*, through spatial displacement.

The next section *Il tempo è muto* again looks back upon Antonietto's
death some time after the event, since the poet continues to feel
stranded in the shallows of life's absurdity. As Portinari has indicated
(op.cit., 146), life is suspended and almost stands still in this sequence,
so that in the eponymous lyric we are given a terrifying picture of a
baroque wasteland, one which reminds us in a realist key not only of
the kingdom of death but also of the death of memory, the ultimate
nullification of the personality for Ungaretti:

Il tempo è muto fra canneti immoti ...

Lungi d'approdi errava una canoa ...
Stremato, inerte il rematore ... I cieli
Già decaduti a baratri di fumi ...

Proteso invano all'orlo dei ricordi,
Cadere forse fu mercé ...

[Time stands still amid the motionless reed-beds ... / / Far from the shore a canoe was wandering .../Exhausted, inert the rower... The skies / already sunken into abysses of smoke ... / / Vainly extended over the brink of memory, / to fall was perhaps merciful.]

This kind of existential numbness, this Pascalian *mise en abyme* of the whole world, represents to a nicety the traumatic lifelessness of Ungaretti's spirit as soon as sufficient time has elapsed after the death of his son for him to realize the magnitude of his loss. Through the pathetic use of allegorical language – rather than through the harsh, yet precise, symbolism of *Sentimento del tempo* – we learn that he is now cast on a lifeless sea of dead emotion, and in his becalmed state of *ennui* he no longer considers any pursuit worthy of the effort. As a result, he sinks into an attitude of complete nihilism, of mental and physical exhaustion, deriving from his overwhelming emotional experience. But secretly even this is once again a state of 'naufragio' [shipwreck] of the kind previously found in *Allegria*, and, as such, promises yet another of the poet's avatars. The revitalization of his inner self, however, will only take place at a later period, and in the meantime he allows himself to linger in a timeless nirvana in which his nihilistic despair is reflected in a baroque violence cast in a curious Petrarchan mould of ascending or cumulative adjectival effects.

The poem which brings this nihilistic despair to its climax and, in spite of its gloominess, offers a distant prospect of hope is 'Tu ti spezzasti', which has extremely complicated cultural resonances, as Cambon and O'Neill have shown.[1] It again describes his son's death, but now opens up a virtually universal wasteland scenario as a foil to personal grief. Its subject-matter unfolds like a symphony of despair tempered by the more positive aspects of Christian 'dolore'. In his usual manner, as Marzot points out,[2] Ungaretti begins by presenting us with the stark physical spectacle of the Brazilian landscape, and we at once feel ourselves confronted by its brutally oppressive grandeur. It is a frightening landscape tending to crush all sense of human scale, in which a feeling of primitive destructiveness is endemic; and this primitiveness now differs widely from the more positive kind which we encountered earlier in Ungaretti's evocations of a 'paese inno-cente', because it is cosmic rather than anthropocentric in quality. Chance, in short, dominates the human tradition at this point, and its oppressive weight hangs over the entire stanza, as the poet filters his Brazilian perspectives through his memories of subsequent disaster:

I molti, immani, sparsi, grigi sassi

Frementi ancora alle segrete fionde
Di originarie fiamme soffocate
Od ai terrori di fiumane vergini
Ruinanti in implacabili carezze,
– Sopra l'abbaglio della sabbia rigidi
In un vuoto orizzonte, non rammenti?
[The myriad, immense, scattered, grey stones / quivering still
from out of secret slings / of primeval flames suppressed / or
from the terror of virgin torrents / rushing down in implacable
embraces, / – over the dazzle of the sand, rigidly upright / on an
empty horizon, do you not recall them?]

From the outset the scene clearly foreshadows the imminence of
the boy's death through a baroque internalizing of the forces of
chance, despite the superficial and intensely ironic sense of order
implicit in the effects of hyperbaton and classical prosody. This later
becomes even more evident in the violent inversions of the following
stanza, where a tree – the monkey-puzzle tree – becomes, even
syntactically, a solitary, almost inanimate, symbol of human anguish.
It is, as Ungaretti notes, the Brazilian pine and so holds for him distant
memories of the pine-trees of Italy. Yet, instead of waving serenely
under Italian skies, the monkey-puzzle here strains after life in a
parched, giganticized wilderness and finds its sustenance almost
magically, as it balances on a rock and ensures for itself a virtually
perfect equilibrium between its own sparse requirements and the
frighteningly limited resources of the arid landscape. Its condition
reminds us immediately of the oak-tree in 'Prime' in *Sentimento del
tempo* which also clung to life in a similar type of arid waste, although
in the meanwhile the earlier *tabula rasa* effect has been intensified
almost to apocalyptic proportions:

E la recline, che s'apriva all'unico
Raccogliersi dell'ombra nella valle,
Araucaria, anelando ingigantita,
Volta nell'ardua selce d'erme fibre
Piú delle altre dannate refrattaria,
Fresca la bocca di farfalle e d'erbe
Dove dalle radici si tagliava,
– Non la rammenti delirante muta
Sopra tre palmi d'un rotondo ciottolo
In un perfetto bilico
Magicamente apparsa?
[And the bent monkey-puzzle tree / which spreads itself in the

only / gathering of shade in the valley, / breathlessly gigantic, /
cast by its solitary fibres into the hard flintstone / more refractory
than its other damned companions, / its mouth cool with grass
and butterflies / at the point where it tore itself away from its
roots, / – Don't you remember it, delirious, mute, / on three
palms' breadth of rounded stone / in perfect equilibrium / a
magical apparition?]

Such a scene in other words is not even a struggle for continued
existence, it is, like the struggle waged by his own child, a representation of dying by inches – the sort of attrition which only the
strongest type of living thing can withstand. Indeed, all earthly life –
especially the fragile life of children – is inevitably condemned to
extinction in such harsh surroundings, and premonitions of Antonietto's death are already seen, without being recognized as such by
Ungaretti, as his son soars like a firecrest – the smallest of Italian birds –
into the tree and gazes down from its summit into the sluggish,
funereal life of some deep, oceanic abyss:

> Di ramo in ramo fiorrancino lieve,
> Ebbri di meraviglia gli avidi occhi
> Ne conquistavi la screziata cima,
> Temerario, musico bimbo,
> Solo per rivedere all'imo lucido
> D'un fondo e quieto baratro di mare
> Favolose testuggini
> Ridestarsi fra le alghe.
> [From branch to branch a lightsome firecrest / with eager eyes
> drunk with wonder / you conquered its dappled peak, / o rash
> and musical child, / simply to see once again in the shining depths
> / of a deep and still sea-chasm / fabulous turtles / stirring among
> the seaweed.]

Once again, be it noted in passing, a baroque frenzy is highlighted
here by the lust for life implicit in the adjectival charge (*lieve-ebbri-
avidi-screziata-temerario-lucido*), until the foreboding of an Ungarettian type of death appears towards the end of the stanza in a similarly
cumulative, adjectival effect (*fondo-quieto-favolose*).

Evidently, in this soul-chilling atmosphere the boy's struggle for
life was doomed to failure, and despite his lightness of foot and pleas-
ing gracefulness he is ultimately overwhelmed, a victim of his
Brazilian setting's inhuman and primeval power. This idea is again
intensified by means of a type of physical oppressiveness, by the
accumulation of adjectives around the symbol of the burning sun,

closely associated in his Arabo-Italian culture with death:

> Grazia, felice,
> Non avresti potuto non spezzarti
> In una cecità tanto indurita
> Tu semplice soffio e cristallo,
>
> Troppo umano lampo per l'empio,
> Selvoso, accanito, ronzante
> Ruggito d'un sole ignudo.

[Graceful, joyous child, / you could not but destroy yourself / in such pitiless blindness / you a simple breath and crystalline form, / / an all too human flash for the impious / savage, frenzied, throbbing / roar of a naked sun.]

The present poem is consequently the most intense baroque composition that Ungaretti ever wrote, and its rhetorical pomp is carefully offset by its intimations of inescapable tragedy.

In the second part of *Il dolore* the poet's sense of personal loss is compounded by his wider anguish as he returns to an already virtually defeated Italy in 1942. The suffering of his native land now seems to transcend and at the same time to complement his personal despair, and he chooses as its immediate setting (though his memory is actually at fault) the region of the Maremma which in the past had strongly reminded him of his solitude and of the atmosphere of war:

> Che nel *Dolore* la Maremma mi richiami la guerra per l'idea di desolazione, è naturale. La Maremma, almeno come era ancora a quel tempo, si associava all'idea di solitudine e di desolazione, come il deserto, sebbene non fosse affatto il deserto. Il deserto e la Maremma sono immagini di zone geografiche di desolazione, e possono l'uno e l'altra compenetrarsi dell'immagine di strazio morale suggerita dalla guerra. Sulle prime la Maremma mi richiamava allora piú la sua propria desolazione che quella disummana della guerra, e d'improvviso, in quell'ultimo momento del secondo conflitto mondiale, la mia passione e il mio lutto s'immedesimavano nella pietà delle cose diffusa davanti ai miei occhi dalla Maremma presente. (*Saggi*, 835–6)

[That the Maremma should remind me in *Il dolore* of war, through the idea of its desolation, is natural. The Maremma, at least as it was at that time, was associated with the idea of solitude and desolation, like the desert, although it was not, of course, the desert at all. The desert and the Maremma are visions of geographical zones of desolation, and they can both be steeped in images of moral anguish suggested by the war. At first, the Maremma recalled to me at that juncture more its own desolation than the inhuman desolation of war, yet suddenly, in the last moment of the second world conflict, my passions and mourning closely merged with my pity for the things cast before my eyes in the presence of the Maremma.]

The solitude so described is again symbolized by a tree, this time an Italian pine, in the section *Incontro a un pino* [Against a pine] (1943). Surrounded by a host of memory-laden stones, it welcomes the poet back to his native land:

In Patria mi rinvenni
Dalla foce del fiume mossi i passi ...
....
Verso un pino aereo attorto per i fuochi
D'ultimi raggi supplici
Che, ospite ambito di pietrami memori,
Invitto macerandosi protrasse.
[I found myself once more in my Native Land / from the river's mouth I retraced my steps / ... / towards an airy pine twisted by the fires / of final suppliant rays / which, as a desired guest of memory-laden stones, / it projected, unconquered and agonizing.]

However, the most important section of this latter part of the collection is undoubtedly *Roma occupata* [Occupied Rome] (1943–4). The occupation described does not refer to that of the allies but to the Nazi occupation, since the Anglo-American armies did not arrive in Rome till 4 June 1944.

What is perhaps remarkable about the present sequence of poems is the way in which Ungaretti weaves the events of everyday life into an elegiac symphony echoing his country's sufferings. Portinari tells us (op. cit., 153) that one image refers to the strange drum of Radio London which tapped out the V-sign during the war; if so, it is also combined in a baroque manner with another 'strange drum' represented by the oval of the Colosseum with its eyeless sockets set in the walls, since it too figures in the same poem, 'Defunti su montagne' [Dead on mountains]. The one vision lost in the mists of time no doubt echoes the glories of the past, the other with its hollow booming offers a promise for the future:

Pallore, al Colosseo

Su estremi fumi emerso,
Col precipizio alle orbite
D'un azzurro che sorte piú non eccita
Né turba.

....

Agli echi fondi attento
Dello strano tamburo
A quale ansia suprema rispondevo
Di volontà, bruciante
Quanto appariva esausta?

[A pallor, on the Colosseum / sunk in thick fumes, / with the
tumbling of a blueness / from its sockets which fate no longer
excites / nor disturbs ... Alert to the deep echoes / of that strange
drum / to what supreme tension did I answer / with a will, as
burning / as it appeared exhausted?]

Indeed, anyone who heard and recalls the ghostly echoing of the drum
on the radio will remember how accurately the poet represents the
tremulous feeling of hope it evoked at the time. But far surpassing in
importance this allusive blending together of 'petits faits divers' was
the poet's deeper fear that the immortal heritage of Michelangelo –
the city of Rome itself – might be destroyed in the holocaust then
engulfing the whole of Italy:

Patria stanca delle anime,
Succederà, universale fonte,
Che tu non piú rifulga?

Sogno, grido, miracolo spezzante,
Seme d'amore nell'umana notte,
Speranza, fiore, canto,
Ora accadrà che cenere prevalga? (*Accadrà?*)

[Weary fatherland of souls, / could it happen, o universal fount, /
that you will shine no more? // Dream, shout, shattering miracle,
/ seed of love in humanity's night, / hope, flower, song, / can it
now be that ashes will prevail? *Will it happen?*]

That Michelangelo was not far from his thoughts at the time may
also be seen in lines from 'Folli i miei passi' [Wild my steps] when,
immediately after his return, he tended to wander aimlessly through
the streets of Rome as if it were already a ghost town. And yet
eventually he was filled with the same type of suppressed hope as the
great artist must have experienced himself as he planned to restructure
its architectural features:

Appresero cosí le braccia offerte
....
Quell'umile speranza
Che travolgeva il teso Michelangelo
A murare ogni spazio in un baleno
Non concedendo all'anima
Nemmeno la risorsa di spezzarsi.
[Thus my suppliant arms learned / ... / of that humble hope /
which drove the tense Michelangelo / to wall up all space in a
flash / not conceding to the soul / even the room to shatter itself.]

Perhaps the most important lyric in this whole sequence is 'Mio
fiume anche tu' [My river you too], which rings the changes on one
of Ungaretti's principal symbols from the past, his rivers. To the Nile,
Serchio, Isonzo and Seine he now adds the Tiber which he calls
significantly the 'Tevere fatale' [fateful Tiber] since it not only foreshadows his return to an Italianate culture for a second time after his
exile in Brazil but, because of the dual role of the Eternal City, also
indicates his return to Catholicism. The poem, in fact, has a new
textual quality about it, marking a happy combination of his neo-
narrative, baroque rhetoric and his previous allusive style. Although,
as we have seen, the harsh metaphysical archetypes of his hermetic
symbolism in *Sentimento del tempo* have long since been reduced in
this collection to the status of tonal pointers, we now begin to detect a
revival of analogical techniques. Even so, overtopping this device in
the first part of the poem is a sumptuous, baroque rhetorical note,
especially visible in the frequent repetition of 'ora che' [now that] and
certain parallelisms in Ungaretti's use of his tonal indicators such as
'notte', intended to heighten his despair and increase the apocalyptic
atmosphere of the composition:

Ora che notte già turbata scorre ...
[Now that night already flows perturbed.]
Ora che scorre notte già straziata ...
[Now that night flows already anguish-stricken.]
Ora che già sconvolta scorre notte ...
[Now that night flows already shattered.]

Oddly enough, these lines tend to remind us of the typical forms of
variant we find in his previous verse; but, whereas Ungaretti's earlier
variants are mutually exclusive to each other, here they are juxtaposed
and mutually supporting in a rhetorical sense, and they show us once
again how in the language of *Il dolore* the poet has changed from a
symbolic hermeticism to a cumulative baroque style.

Another important element in the textual richness of 'Mio fiume anche tu' is its allegorical realism. For instance, the image of the lambs which it contains reminds us in the first place of the 'agnus Dei' [lamb of God]; then later the utter timidity of these creatures (symbolically here the Roman people) is reinforced in the brooding atmosphere of terror by the imaginative transformation of the houses of the city into insecure dens, the abodes of a bestialized populace:

Ora che persistente
E come a stento erotto dalla pietra
Un gemito d'agnelli si propaga
Smarrito per le strade esterrefatte;
Che di male l'attesa senza requie,
Il peggiore dei mali,
Che l'attesa di male imprevedibile
Intralcia animo e passi;
Che singhiozzi infiniti, a lungo rantoli
Agghiacciano le case tane incerte ...

[Now that persistent / and as if grudgingly erupting from the stone / a bleating of lambs pours forth / lost along the terror-stricken streets; / now that the expectancy of unceasing evil, / the worst of all ills, / now that the expectancy of unforeseeable evil / ensnares both mind and footstep; / now that infinite sighs, at length death-rattles, / freeze the houses, insecure dens.]

Later still, in the second stanza, the lambs of God are even more closely associated with the lost sheep of the masses, after which a sense of despair and desolation becomes absolute, as women and children wander bemusedly in the streets:

Ora che pecorelle cogli agnelli
Si sbandano stupite e, per le strade
Che già furono urbane, si desolano ...

[Now that the sheep with the lambs / stray in stupefaction and, along the streets / which were once urban, sink in desolation.]

There inevitably follows, as a means of illustrating this almost universal despair, a memorial perspective of the suffering and indignity of the Italian people, one which now ranges all along the scale of wartime neuroses and acts of bestiality, though beginning with that even more deepseated, historical curse of Italian life, emigration:

Ora che prova un popolo
Dopo gli strappi dell'emigrazione,
La stolta iniquità

Delle deportazioni;
Ora che nelle fosse
Con fantasia ritorta
E mani spudorate
Dalle fattezze umane l'uomo lacera
L'immagine divina
E pietà in grido si contrae di pietra;
Ora che l'innocenza
Reclama almeno un'eco,
E geme anche nel cuore piú indurito;
Ora che sono vani gli altri gridi;
Vedo ora chiaro nella notte triste.
[Now that a people experiences / after the wrench of emigration
/ the stupid iniquity / of deportations; / now that in graves/ with
fantasy twisted / and shameless hands / man tears away from
human features / the divine image / and pity contracts to a cry of
stone; / now that innocence / demands at least an echo, / and
laments even in the most hardened heart; / now that all other
cries are vain; / I now see clearly in the wicked night.]

Finally, in contrast with this further series of 'petits faits divers'
raised to a symphonic level, the all too human figure of Christ
emerges from the apocalyptic setting to redeem man's bestiality
towards man. But it is not as if Ungaretti's mind has even now been
won over intellectually to the call of an orthodox Catholicism, it is
simply that at an emotional level his profound sense of humanity has
been crowned by a dawning sense of Christ's divine mission. His
appeal to Him in the last stanza is consequently a curious adaptation of
the medieval 'lauda' [hymn of praise] to his gradually reawakening
analogical style of writing, and this strangely composite poetic imagery
rises to a crescendo at the end of the poem, reminiscent of a Iacoponian
type of emotional frenzy. The result is paradoxically a strange, pagan
redimensioning of Christian mythology, which aims at absorbing
within the Christian ethos the continuing atavistic humanism implicit
in Ungaretti's aesthetic beliefs:

Cristo, pensoso palpito,
Astro incarnato nell'umane tenebre,
Fratello che t'immoli
Perennemente per riedificare
Umanamente l'uomo,
Santo, Santo che soffri,
Maestro e fratello e Dio che ci sai deboli,

Santo, Santo che soffri
Per liberare dalla morte i morti
E sorreggere noi infelici vivi,
D'un pianto solo mio non piango piú,
Ecco, Ti chiamo, Santo,
Santo, Santo che soffri.
[Christ, thoughtful heart-beat, / star incarnate in human dark-
ness, / brother who sacrifice yourself / perennially to rebuild
/ mankind humanely, / Saint, Saint who suffers, / master and
brother and God who knows we are weak, / Saint, Saint who
suffers, / to free the dead from death / and sustain us the joyless
living, / with my own tears I no longer weep, / lo! I call to you,
Saint, / Saint, Saint who suffers.]

Naturally the peculiar tonal colouring of poems of this type immediately raises the problem of Ungaretti's possible religious conversion, if indeed so strong a word as conversion can be used at all
about him. At most, as we have already pointed out, his new religious
fervour can only amount to a combining of his Christian emotivity
with his previous humanistic insights, although where exactly the
weight of emphasis falls has continually been a matter of dispute.
Ungaretti himself lends support to the view that his is a generic kind
of religiosity, though he adds:

Anche in un'opera di carattere prevalentemente profano, la
fonte della poesia si appalesa nei momenti di maggiore sofferenza
che sono insieme i momenti di maggiore dedizione, di maggiore
bontà: momenti cristiani.
[Even in a work of predominantly profane character, the
spring of poetry broadens out in moments of greater suffering,
which are at the same time moments of greater dedication,
greater goodness: Christian moments.][3]

Among the critics the position is perhaps even more controversial.
On one side we have the views of Mario Luzi and on the other of
Piemontese. Even Luzi, however, is somewhat hesitant in his attribu-
tion of religious sentiments to the poet, though at one stage he does
mention his Catholicism while by no means equating his views with
those of the dogmatists and theologians. So, after the publication of
Il dolore, he observes in a Testimonianza: 'In the latest volume, which
is addressed particularly to a sense of anguish, a religious emphasis is
stronger ... God is no longer a pure and abstract fact situated beyond
the limits of experience, an element in the extreme inevitable dialectic
of human experience; instead he has come down to the level of the

emotive and spiritual life of the poet, he has taken on a more precise
and familiar appearance; and, if one recalls what of late a feeling for
the tradition has meant for Ungaretti, one could without too much
circumspection translate the two adjectives into a single one and say
Catholic ... But rather than a distinct orientation of the spirit,
Ungaretti's religiosity is an innate attitude and we can see it in his
dramatic sense of sin and damnation, in the horror and magic of the
senses, in his assertive type of fetishism.'[4] Supporting a similar standpoint in a review of *Il dolore*, Marvardi – perhaps somewhat dog-
matically – notes: 'Christ is now for Ungaretti the reason for life and
death; from here on the poet can explain everything through Christ.'[5]
Yet what this critic does not seem to have emphasized fully is that
Ungaretti's Christ, even in this collection, has undergone the humanizing process of an association with the bedouin-poet, and so he is
Christ the man in the first place and only afterwards Christ the God.
This is no doubt why, with Luzi, the word 'Catholic' evokes a certain
amount of embarassment, and why for Piemontese the very idea of a
Catholic Ungaretti is rejected outright. So, after conceding that in *Il
dolore* there is a 'presenza consolatrice' [a consolatory presence] of the
Divinity, the latter asks himself the following questions: 'Catholic
poet? Christian poet? Certainly, if any definition of this kind were to be
adopted in his regard, one would have to be content with the second.
And even that would seem, frankly, still a little too committed.'[6] In
fact, a subsequent reversion to a thorough-going humanist stance in
the next collection appears to favour this type of judgement, although
the position is still complicated by the poet's own hints in his prose
writings at a gradual return to orthodoxy.

   The secular reversion to which we have referred is already apparent
in the last section of *Il dolore* entitled *I ricordi* (1942–6). Here Ungaretti meditates more deeply over the nature of memory again and
seems to regard the continuum of memory as that of man's spiri-
tuality. So much so that his lyrics once more appear as the poet's
immortal testimony to a life well-spent before the Gods and his so-
called religious crisis as a mere episode in his career:

   I ricordi, un inutile infinito,
   Ma soli e uniti contro il mare, intatto
   In mezzo a rantoli infiniti ...
   [Memories, a useless infinity, / but alone and united against the
   sea, intact / amid infinite death-rattles.]
Here the sea clearly symbolizes the passage of time; but, although
time offers us all constant scope for liberation from our immediate

bondage and the power to seek out fresh experiences, it simultaneously tends to cancel out 'le orme dolci / d'un pensiero fedele'
[the sweet traces / of a faithful thought], and within the very recesses
of the spirit it opens up an abyss of oblivion. The process of the layer-
ing of memories in the mind and their constant recall, by contrast,
works in the opposite direction; and, in the universal setting which
Ungaretti adopts in this lyric, recollection is seen as the means whereby
so many divine moments of insight are sifted out of the hour-glass of
cosmic time:

I ricordi,
Il riversarsi vano
Di sabbia che si muove
Senza pesare sulla sabbia,
Echi brevi protratti,
Senza voce echi degli addii
A minuti che parvero felici ...
[Memories, the vain upturning / of sand which moves / weight-
lessly on the sand, / brief, prolonged echoes, / voiceless echoes of
farewells / to moments which seemed joyous.]

It is also significant that other joys reappear at this stage together
with further meditations on memorial processes, since their presence
again tends to clash with any too dogmatic interpretation of the role
of religion in the collection. Indeed, the halfway mark between the
two extremes of Christian and pagan ethics may well be detected in
the lyric 'L'angelo del povero' [Angel of the poor], where the
Christian symbol of the angel itself seems to herald in a reawakened
humanism.

The most significant poem of the section is on the other hand 'Non
gridate piú' [Shout no more], which at once emphasizes that the poet
has now left behind him his ultra-subjective period and has returned
to that hermetically-derived auscultation of the past previously
associated in the cultural field with the dark vigil of his forefathers.
The first version of the lyric is considerably more diffuse than the
final one,[7] and in it the poet pleads with modern American writers
not to offend the dead by countenancing the bombing of Rome:

O compagni, cari una volta,
Cessate l'offesa alle tombe.
[O companions, once dear, / cease the desecration of tombs.]

The second version, by contrast, reduces the dispersive effects of the
twenty-seven lines of the first to eight lines of supreme lyrical con-
centration; and in the process the once particularized American audi-

ence becomes a universal one, as the poet addresses an exhortation to
the whole of mankind in the post-war era:

Cessate d'uccidere i morti,
Non gridate piú, non gridate
Se li volete ancora udire,
Se sperate di non perire.

Hanno l'impercettibile sussurro,
Non fanno piú rumore
Del crescere dell'erba,
Lieta dove non passa l'uomo.

[Stop killing the dead, / shout no more, do not shout / if you
still want to hear them, / if you hope not to perish. // They have
the imperceptible whisper, / they make no more noise / than the
growing of the grass, / happy where man does not pass.]

Perhaps the gravest charge which has been made against the manner
of *Il dolore* and indeed against the whole of Ungaretti's post-war
manner is that levelled against him by Bàrberi Squarotti, to the
effect that 'the restoration to which Ungaretti tends is not that of a
historico-moral universe, of a social ideal, of an ideal of man, of
feeling (as happens with Eliot and equally with Pound), but an exclusively rhetorical construction, a faith in a system of literature, not
in a system of society, in a structure of man'.[8] Now certainly Ungaretti, earlier on in 'La pietà', did acknowledge the danger of falling
into a 'servitú di parole' [a slavery of words], but surely he meant by
it a complete failure to participate in human activities of any kind?
And yet his sense of participation, his commitment to family and
society, seems even more dramatically evident in this and subsequent
volumes than it was before. Again, if he is being accused of excessive
emotionalism, could not a similar charge on occasion be levelled
against Leopardi or even Petrarch himself? The plain truth is that,
instead of running to the spurious protection of a rhetorical manner
as a form of escapism from his personal tragedy, the poet now appears
determined to integrate his baroque modalities into the very substance
of his lyrical inspiration. Admittedly, he often seems to be walking a
tight-rope between literary mannerism and a form of exasperated
expressionism, yet his sense of equilibrium is such that we certainly
do not feel that we are being treated to a shell without substance, but
rather to a substance which only finds its release in an adherent,
baroque literalness of expression – one almost completely freed from

earlier hermetic or infolded symbolic pre-conceptions of any kind,
though still containing a touch of broad allegory here and there.

Still, once Ungaretti's immediate feelings of visceral grief have
worked themselves out, the poet turns away from this personal
interlude despite its novelty and richness of texture, and his tone can
then be seen to be slowly reverting to a more objective, neo-hermetic
style. What is more, at the time when he published *Il dolore* in 1947
he stressed once again the uselessness of poetic experimentation into
linguistic forms alone, while simultaneously suggesting that he had
never fallen into the trap:

> Ma c'e il pericolo, certo, di prendere le ricerche di linguaggio
> come fine a se stesse, e non come dettate dall'ispirazione e dal
> contenuto per esigenze di forma e di stile. Il pericolo e l'assurdo
> è che si facciano delle ricerche di linguaggio non avendo nulla da
> dire. (*Saggi*, 737)
> [But there is a danger, certainly, of taking research into language
> as an end in itself, and not as dictated by inspiration and by
> content through the exigencies of form and style. The danger
> and the absurdity are that one might carry out research into
> language without having anything to say.]

Indeed, the fact that this does not happen in his case is vouched for
by his later integration of the many stylistic lessons learned during
the neo-narrative manner of the present collection into his major
impressionistic style which once more predominates in subsequent
collections. The voices of the past, a touch of essentialized baroque
realism, and a fresh infolding of the image will consequently be the
distinctive features of the next volume, *La terra promessa*, in which
the process of involution will be more imaginative than metaphysical,
in subtle contrast with *Sentimento del tempo*. Moreover, the paradise
regained to which the title alludes will also acquire the additional
tonality of the elegiac classicism of antiquity, especially that of Virgil.
By such means the 'anguished serenity' of Ungaretti's old age will
tend to be refracted through the Debussy-like impressionism of his
melodic line, now endued with a refurbished sensitivity towards
human time and its perennial promise; and, in particular, his reconstituted *endecasillabo* will acquire from this new amalgam an ever-
deepening range of lyrical impact.

6. *La terra promessa*

Although *Canzone*, one of the main thematic lyrics of *La terra promessa*, was drafted in 1935 and the collection itself was announced by Mondadori in its publicity material in 1942 (See *Poesie*, 545–6), by the time it was eventually published as a complete volume in 1950 it had undergone a radical change in tone and atmosphere. So instead of participating in the summery climate of *Sentimento del tempo*, its dominant atmosphere is autumnal, and this progression was already foreseen by the announcement of 1942, since the work then bore the title of *Penultima stagione* [Penultimate season].

As Ungaretti tells us himself, the idea for the new collection came to him soon after he had composed the poem 'Auguri per il mio compleanno', in which the fading of his youth was perhaps felt more poignantly than elsewhere:

> Veloce gioventú dei sensi
> Che nell'oscuro mi tieni di me stesso
> E consenti le immagini all'eterno,
>
> Non mi lasciare, resta, sofferenza!

> [Nimble youthfulness of the senses / which holds me in the dark about myself / and informs eternity with images, / / do not abandon me, remain, o suffering!]

But by the late forties this sense of loss had progressed much further, as we have seen in *Il dolore*, and long before *La terra promessa* was completed he already felt that his old age had arrived. Indeed, in the preface to the work, we learn that the poet now considered himself to be moving into the final season of human life in which feelings of autumnal ripeness were far advanced:

> Era l'autunno che intendevo cantare nel mio poema, un autunno inoltrato, dal quale si distacchi per sempre l'ultimo segno di giovinezza, di giovinezza terrena, l'ultimo appetito carnale ... Poi è il rinascere ad altro grado della realtà: è per reminiscenza il nascere della realtà di secondo grado, è, esaurita l'esperienza sensuale, il varcare la soglia d'un'altra esperienza, è l'inoltrarsi nella nuova esperienza, illusoriamente

e non illusoriamente originaria – è il conoscersi essere dal non
essere, essere dal nulla, è il conoscersi pascalianamente essere dal
nulla. Orrida conoscenza. La sua odissea sempre ha per punto
di partenza il passato, sempre torna a conchiudersi nel passato,
sempre riparte dalla medesima aurora mentale, sempre nella
medesima aurora della mente si conchiude. (*Terra promessa*,
11–12)

[It was autumn I intended to celebrate in my poem, a well-
advanced autumn, from which the last remnant of youth had
been detached for ever, of earthy youth, its last carnal appetite …
Then came rebirth into another level of reality: it was through
memorial reminiscences a rebirth into a second grade of reality,
it amounted, once sensual experience had waned, to the crossing
of the threshold of another experience, it was the exploration of
that new experience, deceptively and yet non-deceptively
primal – it was knowing oneself to have sprung from non-
being, to have sprung from nothingness, it was knowing oneself
in a Pascalian sense to be emergent out of nothingness. A horrible knowledge. Its Odyssey always has the past as its point of
departure, and it always ends up by consuming itself in the
past; it always begins again with the same mental dawn, and
with the same mental dawn it always concludes.]

Now this is, once again, a typical Petrarchan form of experience. It
involves the previously discussed technique of abolishing the future,
or at least of identifying it with a 'passato rovesciato' [an upturned
past], and then of relegating all hope to the memory of a lost innocence, which effectively brings about the self-closure of the hermetic
image upon itself. Often the imagery is presented in a Leopardian
form and places special emphasis on the suffering and clearsighted-
ness of age. Detached as the aging mind becomes from the flesh, it
begins to see the world as a sensationless Pascalian abyss, or rather as
a pure metaphysical chasm, which neither the fancy nor the imagination can any longer bridge over. As a result, 'Canzone' was originally intended to express the transfer of Ungaretti's inspiration from
the *committed* sphere of the senses to the *detached* sphere of pure
intellectual insight (*Terra promessa*, 12).

In referring to Pascal's experience, the poet is probably not only
alluding to his definition of man as a void[1] but also to his belief that
sensory objects, especially in the form of imaginative transfigurations
of reality, are so many barriers or illusions erected by men as a form
of self-protection between themselves and the horrors of living.

Hence, as the French writer observes, 'we rush nonchalantly towards the precipice, after having placed something before us to prevent ourselves from seeing it'.[2] On the other hand, despite this apparent connection, Ungaretti's views on life are the opposite of Pascal's, since he does not believe that the impoverishment of the senses and the dominance of the intellect in old age is a gain but rather a loss: a loss of poetic power. Oddly enough, in both cases the emotional outcome is the same: a sense of irredeemable anguish resulting from the application of an inflexible type of intellectual analysis to the human condition, an intellectualism not normally interspersed with any touch of sensory consolation. Although Pascal may have considered this type of anguish as a positive element in his Christianity, Ungaretti equates it, as we know, with Michelangelo's sense of emptiness, which he once defined as deriving from the latter's deprivation of God. So it is not through an acknowledgement of the Pascalian 'néant' [void] that he eventually hoped to reach the promised land, but rather through its continued concealment – by way of a sporadic reawakening of his previous experiential imagery in a mediate, recollective form.

Nevertheless, he does cautiously admit that the new grade of self-consciousness into which he has moved could well contribute something precious to his inspiration. In particular, it adds a sharper tang to his poetic recollections, with the result that his insights take on the appearance of flashes of youthful perceptiveness set against the icy corrosion of his dying sensibility. The attitude which the poet is seeking to outline in 'Canzone' is accordingly a truly novel form of psycho-sensuous fulfilment, in which the passions and keen appetites of his youth are now dying or dead and are being replaced by a golden treasury of past experiences. These are memories he intends to reminisce over and restructure, so that they can be persuaded to release their deeper secrets, their mature understanding of the human predicament.

Again, in his introductory note the poet emphasizes that there is nevertheless no sharp cleavage even at this stage between his sensations and ideas, at least not in an absolute sense:

> Non che fra l'una e l'altra sfera, a dire il vero, ci sia una parete che non sia fluida, e non che l'una e l'altra sfera non si compenetrino. Ad una certa epoca dell'esistere, uno può avere avuto la sensazione che la mentale in lui escludesse ogni altra attività: il limite dell'età è limite. Non sia limite poiché poesia non si fa mai senza opera anche dei sensi, specie una poesia di stretta e infinita

qualità musicale come pretende di essere quella che ora vi
piacerà di leggere. (*Terra promessa*, 12)
[Not that there is between the one sphere and the other, to tell
the truth, an impermeable partition, not that both spheres do
not interpenetrate. At a certain period in existence one can have
had the sensation that the mental side of oneself excludes all
other activity: the limit of age is indeed a limit. Let it not be a
limit, since poetry is never made without the participation of the
senses too, especially a poetry of restricted yet infinite musicality
such as the poetry claims to be which you will now be pleased
to read.]

Whether an incipient waning of inspiration with appetite can be
detected or not, the fact remains that *La terra promessa* undoubtedly
strikes a fresh balance within the mainstream of Ungaretti's hermetic
development. Its allusive complexity can, admittedly, be bewildering, but in the specific case of 'Canzone' our bewilderment when
confronted with its highly condensed structures is partly dispelled
by Ungaretti's own commentary published as an appendix to one of
his later volumes of verse, *Morte delle stagioni*, in 1967.

Although we shall have to rely principally on the poet's own interpretation of his more recondite symbols, we can from the outset
analyse one important element in the poem's make-up: its variants.
These are again extremely important in *La terra promessa* since they
mark the various stages of Ungaretti's struggle to produce the exact
lyrical inflections correlative with his moods. In particular, his un-
flagging efforts to exploit the whole range of resonances implicit in
his own Debussy-like style may be gauged from the variants of the
first line of the poem.[3]

Among the early versions are the following alternatives:
   La care braccia di segreti sazie ...
   [The dear arms with secrets sated.]
   Le care braccia esauste di segreti ...
   [The dear arms exhausted by secrets.]
   Le nude braccia di segreti sazie ...
   [The naked arms with secrets sated.]

If we examine these three variants closely, all of them might at first
sight seem to be satisfactory renderings of the image of arms laden
with the secret experiences of a lifetime, although none strikes a deep
lyrical chord in our sensibilities. This only occurs in the definitive
version, where a form of classical rephrasing causes the whole line to
vibrate magically in unison with the lyricism of the past tradition.

The introduction of a subtle hyperbaton is the device which recaptures the appropriate harmonic required, and the change of resonance
which it succeeds in effecting is truly remarkable:

Nude, le braccia di segreti sazie ...

[Naked, the arms with secrets sated.]

Needless to say, this delicate interplay of variants which gradually
builds up to a superb final version shows that Ungaretti's experimentation with form was no mere literary exercise, but rather a
rugged lyrical commitment springing from his desire to clear a way
through all fashionable poetic obscurities so as to attain to the higher
reaches of his own particular brand of musicality. The process not
only continues to develop in this lyric but also – sometimes in intensified form – in all the major compositions of the collection.

The structural pattern to be found in 'Canzone' is basically a circular
one, so that the final stanza reflects with only one significant modification the archetypal winter landscape evoked in an earlier one. This
modification results from a change of attitude on the poet's part, who
gradually passes from a reluctant acceptance of the aridity of old age
to a joyful reception of this ultimate stage of existence as something
positive and even potentially fruitful. A similar structural circularity
is typical of hermetic poetry as a whole, since the process of refocussing previous experiences at the end of a poem often offers a means of
interpretation of the arcane elements involved in its recondite symbolism. In this lyric the harsh discontinuities of Ungaretti's earlier
hermetic alchemy are replaced by less effect-seeking, more intimate
and mature forms of involution. As a result, there emerges a greater
sense of unity in the poem's lyrical articulation, since the smoother,
more fluid style which he now produces successfully integrates
symbol with tone and tone with musicality.

The main figure appearing in the lyric is the poet as he approaches
the end of his career and has reached a stage in which he is beginning
to draw a vicarious pleasure from the recall of the consolidated secrets
lodged in his poetic memory. Their inner ferment is the stuff and
substance of his personality and it acts as a substitute for his loss of
the immediate sensations of youth. As fully matured consolations,
his memories even counter at times the fading of his carnal appetites
symbolized here, or so he tells us in the commentary, by 'bellissime
fanciulle' [beautiful maidens]. As we might expect, these are not
explicitly referred to in the text but are left indeterminate in typical
hermetic manner. Instead, their disembodied arms are described as
swimming deep underwater in the spectral tides of Lethe, and their

naked limbs are content to garner from its flowing current the rich
harvest of the poet's recollections:

> Nude, le braccia di segreti sazie,
> A nuoto hanno del Lete svolto il fondo,
> Adagio sciolto le veementi grazie
> E le stanchezze onde luce fu il mondo.
>
> [Naked, their arms with secrets sated, / they have, swimming,
> the depths of Lethe's bed explored, / softly liberated the vehem-
> ent graces / and the weary labours whence the world was light.]

The light mentioned in these lines must be interpreted as the light
of experience newly illuminated by the sharper insights of age. Its goal
is self-fulfilment or self-consolation (which are perhaps now equiva-
lents for Ungaretti) and it reveals a new type of psycho-sensuous
equilibrium which the poet hopes to attain towards the end of his life.
In the imagery of the poem, therefore, the previously mentioned loss
of sensuous commitment is counterbalanced by the carnal undertone
of the nudity of the maidens' arms; yet, although such a symbol
infuses a lingering sensuality into what would otherwise be a dis-
passionate vision of extreme maturity, we sense that the evocation of
nakedness is now wholly aesthetic, not sexual, in its intended impact.
No doubt the climax of the new light's detached and almost superhuman clarity will only be reached at the point of the poet's extinction, when time will have at last begun to ferment around his
completed human 'durata', fixing for ever his literary *persona*,
Petrarchan-like, in the firmament of the cultural memory. But, in
the meantime, until death finally completes him and sets him for the
purposes of comparison and contrast among the immortals, he feels
he has entered upon a halfway stage in that process: a stage which he
evokes in a correlative landscape or wasteland resonant with the
emptiness of spent passion:

> Nulla è muto piú della strana strada
> Dove foglia non nasce o cade o sverna,
> Dove nessuna cosa pena o aggrada,
> Dove la veglia mai, mai il sonno alterna.
>
> [Nothing is more silent than the strange road / where no leaf
> burgeons, falls or winters o'er, / where nothing ever pains
> or pleases, / where waking never, never with slumber is
> changed.]

This kind of suspended animation in the limbo of old age will be
transcended at length by a wholly new and positive perspective. In
the meantime, the poet feels that he is peering into an unfathomable

Pascalian abyss, though with the aim of glimpsing in its depths some
still flickering ray of hope. What this hope will consist of is described
in the remainder of the poem.

The next stanza marks a point of partial redemption as the poet
awakens to 'un momento dell'esperienza quasi interamente mentale'
(*Poesie*, 555) [a moment of almost completely mental experience].
This awakening is presented in truly Ungarettian style as a series of
delicate reflections, in which the rebirth of love – in the form of
human warmth and affection – fills the poet with surprise and delight
as soon as he realizes that after his already long journey through life
yet another stage of authentic lyrical experience is being offered to
him:

> Tutto si sporse poi, entro trasparenze,
> Nell'ora credula, quando, la quiete
> Stanca, da dissepolte arborescenze
> Riestesasi misura delle mete,
> Estenduandosi in iridi echi, amore
> Dall'aereo greto trasalí sorpreso
> Roseo facendo il buio e, in quel colore,
> Piú d'ogni vita un arco, il sonno, teso.
> [Everything then emerged, within reflections, / in the credulous
> hour, when, a weary / tranquillity, having from disinterred
> arborescences / re-extended itself as a measure of goals, / with
> echoes evanescing in rainbows, love / quivered with surprise
> from the airy gravel / reddening the darkness and, in that
> colour, / making sleep a tauter bow than any life.]

We learn that this is a description of dawn and it appears to be a
periodic orphic return of the 'dawn original' associated with primeval purity. As such, it is a fresh representation of the poet's secret
experiences upon a higher intellectual plane. But the images are so
elusive, so personal and inward-looking, that only Ungaretti himself
can offer a satisfactory set of clues as to their interpretation. He tells us
that the overall situation denotes rebirth and that it evokes a new
sphere of feeling; that the tree-like emanations are gradually dis-
interred because they are on the point of reflowering, emerging from
an underground state between 'grave and resurrection'; that the
'mete' [goals] are receding imaginative perspectives wholly renewed
at this point by the intellect; that the echoes are 'voices' probably
deriving, rainbow-like, from the past; that the gravel is the gravel
lying at the bottom of Lethe; and that love is now emergent from the
stony river-bed where earlier we saw the young girls swimming.

Thus from this point on the darkness of a wholly intellectualized 'nulla' takes on a reborn, imaginative hue and is transformed into a rosy promise, in which love, no doubt in the convergent senses of pity and piety (see p. 16), quivers in slumber yet is as taut as a bowstring.

Beyond the literal meaning a deeper artistic significance is also to be found. It is connected with the implications of poetic images and their status vis-à-vis natural objects. On this subject Ungaretti explains his point of view elsewhere, coincidentally once more in reference to the tree-symbol which is half-emergent here as a figure of reborn humanity. In his 'Secondo discorso su Leopardi' [Second discourse on Leopardi] he notes that

> L'arte della parola esige una metamorfosi radicale. Se dico: albero – tutti hanno nella mente un albero; ma nulla è meno albero di quelle tre sillabe da me pronunciate. È possibile che fosse da principio la parola, voce onomatopeica; ma subito la metafora intervenne a liberarla d'ogni imitazione della natura, a renderla espressione della natura umana, a ridurla a esprimere stupori, terrori, ebbrezze, necessità, affetti, il sacro, i rapporti prossimi e anche quelli remoti tra oggetti, e la partecipazione animatrice del soggetto in tali rapporti – un soggetto nel quale doveva operare incessante l'ansia di conoscenza affinché incessantemente potesse convertire la realtà in proprio simbolo.

> [the art of words demands a radical metamorphosis. If I say: tree, – everybody has in mind a tree; but nothing is less tree than those three syllables (albero) pronounced by me. It is possible that at first the word was an onomatopoeic form; but suddenly the metaphor arrived to free it from all imitation of nature, to make it an expression of human nature, to reduce it to express surprise, terror, shuddering, necessity, affection, the sacred, the immediate and also the distant relations between objects, and the revivifying participation of the subject within these relationships – a subject in whom a thirst for knowledge should continually operate so that incessantly he can convert reality into a symbol of his own.][4]

Now these remarks further elucidate the basic dialectic of dreams and reality stressed earlier; for, in his regression to 'il nulla', the poet is clearly not talking about annihilation in any physical or metaphysical sense: he is describing a process of converting the real into a series of metaphors. This is precisely what is happening in the present poem. Metaphors of the poet's old age are raising images of objective reality (a scene at dawn) up to the level of a clearsighted, emblematic discourse. His new form of writing is thereby largely detached from the natural objects on which it is based, yet through that very detachment it manages to recapture the resonances of the symbols embedded in the lyric tradition and to mingle its archetypal forms and overtones with his own contingent and immediate sense-impressions.

The same thread of arcane allusiveness is maintained in the next stanza which deals with the effects of the time-flow on the sensibility. For Ungaretti the youthful sensibility is highly receptive to impressions of all kinds, but as time passes walls or crustacean-like deposits grow around one's centres of feeling and stifle the sharpness of one's responses. Only a few distant glimmerings remain in old age, but occasionally these sudden unaccountable reflarings of passion break through all the barriers of sensory sclerosis and create a new area of lyrical intensity:

> Preda dell'impalpabile propagine
> Di muri, eterni dei minuti eredi,
> Sempre ci esclude piú, la prima immagine,
> Ma, a lampi, rompe il gelo e riconquide.
> [A prey to the tangled skein, / of barriers, eternal inheritors of
> time, / the primal image excludes us ever more, / but, in flashes,
> it cracks the ice and reconquers.]

Once again the poet's goal is not so much a teleological one, an entelechy, as a regression to a primal image, to a pre-childhood state of pure vision, in a womb-like 'paese innocente'; yet the vision which bursts upon his mind at such moments is not crudely primeval but a purity *regained* in the orphic sense. This purity does not remain platonic and disembodied, it is made corporeal (like Campana's images) and is fused into a 'breve salma' [brief spoil of flesh]. Later the corporeal image also decays, but it leaves behind it a perspective which recedes into the distance until it 'tocca a nudo calma' [touches nakedly the stillness]. Once again, then, the lyrical process amounts here to the emotional hypostasizing of the orphic pattern behind the flux of life. This is perhaps a difficult concept to explain, but it is not wholly unfamiliar to us since it is also evoked poetically in English in Eliot's description of the eternal rhythm of the Chinese jar in 'Burnt Norton':

> Only by the form, the pattern,
> Can words or music reach
> the stillness, as a Chinese jar still
> Moves perpetually in its stillness.

Without the eternal stillness of the dynamic orphic pattern a sense of *epoché* or meditative image-suspension could not meaningfully exist, and for Ungaretti this would mark the end of our human sense of continuity. There would, as Eliot further explains, not even be the dance, and yet 'there is always the dance': a timeless rhythm of aesthetic proportions behind the constantly shifting shadows of humanity. This makes the Anglo-American and the Italian writers both contingentist poets, although at the same time poets with certain platonic leanings who long for a sublime state of motion-in-repose.

At this point it might seem contradictory to assert that Ungaretti believed that the Pascalian void over which he felt himself suspended did not really exist; but in his view the void itself is the creation of man, an optical illusion of the spirit. What is important is not the void itself but the image or pure form which bridges it over and acts as a foil to its unremitting climate of existential despair. In this sense we can see how his contingentist philosophy is closely linked with the baroque void which was simply, in his view, a figment of Michelangelo's fevered imagination. Indeed, for an artist like Michelangelo, however dramatic and however giganticized the imagination became, the void could never be filled, because it stood for a form of immutable, yet unattainable, spiritual perfection. Ungaretti, by contrast, really did have hopes of bridging it over, because he no longer aimed at a static or platonic ideal of perfection, but instead at the modern orphic ideal of human fulfilment through the memory. He did not have, that is, the will-o'-the-wisp of eternal perfection before his eyes, only the mirage of endless memorial regression back towards Eve's primeval innocence. So although he tells us that Plato and Bergson were his two philosophical masters (*Poesie*, 561), he is not a platonist in the usual sense of the word. He does not propose his world-picture as an image of the Truth, only as a way of feeling. This is an absolute of emotional rather than metaphysical dimensions which impinges not so much on his rational soul as on his sensibility. He puts the point as follows:

> Come intendo io, infatti, il mondo, quale è il mio modo particolare d'intendere l'universo? C'era un universo puro, umanamente una – diciamolo – cosa assurda: una materia immateriale. Questa purezza diventa una materia materiale in seguito a un'offesa fatta al Creatore, non so per quale avvenimento. Ma insomma, per un avvenimento straordinario, di ordine cosmico, questa materia è corrotta – e ha principio il tempo, e principia la storia. Questo è il mio modo di sentire le cose, non è una verità,

ma è un modo di sentire le cose: io le sento, le cose, in tale
modo. (*Poesie*, 560)
[How, in fact, do I understand the world, what is my particular
way of understanding the universe? Once upon a time there was
a pure universe, humanly speaking – let's admit it – an absurdity:
an immaterial materiality. This purity became a material
materiality as the result of some offence perpetrated against the
Creator by who knows what event. But, anyway, through some
extraordinary happening of a cosmic order, this material became
corrupt – and thereby time originated, and history originated.
This is my manner of feeling things, it is not the truth, but it is a
way of feeling: I feel things in this way.]
Since then the image of regenerated primeval truth is always a
recessive one, his type of platonic or consolatory remembrance can
be likened to the flight of reality down the tunnel of time, with only
the poet's obsessive illusion of innocence and his hunger for fulfilment as his teleological goals. This is expressed in the following
quatrain:
    Piú sfugga vera, l'ossessiva mira,
    E sia bella, piú tocca a nudo calma
    E germe, appena schietta idea, d'ira,
    Rifreme, avversa al nulla, in breve salma.
    [The more true, the more the obsessive aim may flee / and the
    more beautiful it is, the more it touches nakedly the stillness /
    And as a seed of anguish, scarcely changed to pure idea, / it
    quivers, opposed to the void, as a brief spoil of flesh.]
The next lines form a brief link-stanza which reads somewhat
cryptically, even if still suggestively:
    Rivi indovina, suscita la palma:
    Dita dedale svela, se sospira.
    [Streams it divines, uplifts the palm: / if it sighs, it reveals daedal
    fingers.]
Within the process of the purification of his memories, these images
appear to amount to a magical repenetration of Ungaretti's childhood
dreams. Since, as he tells us himself, the effects described are of a new
dawn – probably the dawn of creation as well as the dawning of the
poet's new sphere of life – the palm-tree adumbrates an oasis in the
desert, a recurrent obsession, as we know, ever since *Allegria*; while
the distantly perceived streams – almost like the mythical Italian ones
imagined in his childhood dreams in Alexandria – extend an orphic
promise of the eventual slaking of his spiritual thirst. In other words,

the revitalization of the poet's sensibility and its elevation to a higher
state of consciousness is now imminent. Eventually it becomes re-
vitalized through 'la sua profondità umana' (*Poesie*, 562) [its human
profundity] which suggests a renewed form of commitment, probably in an empathic sense. As a result, the complexity of this newly
foreshadowed life is so great that the goddess Iris, who previously
'legava l'eterno all'effimero' (*Poesie*, 562) [bound the eternal to the
ephemeral] for the poet by means of her rainbows and other auroral
effects, now seems incapable of extending her powers to complete the
process in its entirety. So she is replaced by Daedalus whose fingers
are alone 'capaci di aprire i labirinti, di entrare nei segreti dell'essere'
(*Poesie*, 563) [capable of opening up mazes, of entering into the
secrets of being]. Why should this be? Probably because Daedalus is
a *homo faber* while Iris is a more abstract messenger of the gods.

As Ungaretti fixes his eyes on his new – yet again almost hopelessly
receding – task, he suffers the anguish of each mortal soul as it tries to
cross the threshold of Becoming and reach the inaccessible gateway of
Being, of absolute Truth. Whatever his consolations may be, he
continues to recognize that he is cradled over a naked abyss, and as a
poet he knows that the forms with which he bridges it over will only
be satisfying artistically, never existentially. Since an early title of
'Canzone' was 'Trionfo della fama' [Triumph of fame], it may well
be that Ungaretti is claiming that these forms will satisfy the poet to a
degree commensurate with the lyrical fame he himself acquires within
the tradition: to the degree, that is, that he learns to reflect and
essentialize its latent resonances. At least, a Petrarchan-like value-
judgement in this sense seems to be implied in the following lines:

Non distrarrò da lei mai l'occhio fisso
Sebbene, orribile da spoglio abisso,
Non si conosca forma che da fama.

[I shall never turn from it my fixed eye / although, horrible from
the naked abyss, / one may not know form except from fame.]

However, since the subject is the 'ossessiva mira' [obsessive aim] in
life, a more plausible and intellectually satisfying explanation of these
lines – despite the earlier title – would be to take 'forma' as representing the Platonic Idea and to translate 'da fama' as meaning 'by report'.
Then we would have a picture of the poet peering over the naked
abyss and seeing in it a mirage of the Absolute; it would also explain
his horror, since he would be appalled by the infinite distance which
separates Being from his own contingency. But perhaps the two ideas
can be combined, because the fame of the established poet in the

fabric of the past tradition is very similar to a platonic Essence, and the contingent poet seems as far from attaining this level of emotive intensity as he does from merging with the absolute Idea.

Fame and hypostasized Form are consequently the twin goals which elude us in this life; they seem like unreachable dreams, absolutes which torment and yet never sate us. Not even Dante, despite his remarkable achievement in writing the *Divine Comedy* fully enjoyed them, according to Ungaretti; and all we have to console us are echoes of the divine, very much like the shadows thrown on the wall of Plato's cave. Life is fundamentally a hopeless struggle against the limitations of our condition, yet inwardly – from all but the objective or cosmic standpoints – the very accumulation of our shadowy experiences enriches our souls and gradually fulfils us as men. This type of fulfilment is the most that any human being can expect from his mortal existence.

In the final stanza of the poem Ungaretti further underlines the point by likening himself to some agèd but modern Ulysses who crosses and recrosses the receding walls of Ithaca, and yet who knows that this will be his last home-coming, his last adventure, since the thread of his existence must soon be finally broken. Hence the ultimate hues of recurrent dawns are naturally portrayed here through a state of pure *epoché* or image-suspension, offering, it seems, a last chance of expressing desire, of contingent meditation, before final transcendence to an everlasting state of Being. The description of this ultimate wasteland brings the wheel full circle; but, even though the scene is a variation on the arid and despairing one evoked earlier, the desolate landscape is essentially a description of serene acceptance, of the infinite dilation of human insight, through close communion with death. Moreover, death itself has now become an 'immortale ricordo' [immortal memory] which acts for Ungaretti as a sounding-board of man's perennial adventures:

> Nulla piú nuovo parve della strada
> Dove lo spazio mai non si degrada
> Per la luce o per tenebra, o altro tempo.
> [Nothing fresher there seemed than the road / where space is never degraded / through light or shadow, or through other time.]

Here, therefore, individual 'durata' acquires an overwhelming maturity by association with traditional values, and through a foretaste of his own emotive absoluteness the poet already looks directly into the face of death. This implies that Ungaretti regards communion with death within the human tradition as the attainment of the highest state of purity of which the artist is capable; and, since in his view we internalize or hallow the material world which gradually becomes spirit within us, the final message of 'Canzone' is visionary in a special sense of the word: it bases the activities of the sensibility on orphico-aesthetic foundations rather than on purely intellectual or speculative ones, and its object is to redeem time and space emotionally by suffusing them with the evaluative qualities of the human soul, emblematically displayed in concrete form and lyrically eternalized by communion with the 'voices' of the dead.

Having once defined in 'Canzone' the nature of the promised land as a deathless and enlightened state of the human tradition, a state which is paradoxically a state of life-and-death combined because it is a human yet metaphysically purified state of image-suspension, Ungaretti turns his attention to depicting those individuals who may or may not inhabit his new-found Eden or Hall of Fame. In the two other major poems of the collection he, in fact, deals with the characters of two types of human being for whom this orphically transformed reality is in no way accessible, since they do not possess the bedouin-poet's receptivity in this life and consequently tend to fossilize instead of transfiguring their emotions. The first of these is Dido, queen of Carthage, the second Palinurus, Aeneas's trusty helmsman during his wanderings after the fall of Troy. Dido represents the trauma of aging without the possession of a spiritual inwardness, while Palinurus symbolizes the aridity of a blind, yet dogged, fidelity which is used as a substitute for the bedouin's more positive virtues of self-reliance and 'disponibilità' [receptivity].

Ungaretti tells us that the *Aeneid* is never very far away in the poetry of *La terra promessa*, though the original text is perhaps combined at times with one or two echoes from Caro's classic translation. Moreover, as Hanne has implied,[5] the poet tends to use Virgil's work more as a sounding-board for symbols than as a source of lyrical patterns. The result is that the *Aeneid* serves mainly as a referential or mnemonic commentary on Ungaretti's allusive texture, especially in so far as it helps to bring out symbolic meaning where his highly allusive language would otherwise obscure it. Yet at the same time, it is almost as if the modern poet has introduced a baroque, Michelangelesque moment into the heart of Virgil's manner, and this element clearly enhances the haunting feeling of shadowy insubstantiality deriving here from the sixth book. This is the book, we recall, in which Aeneas visits the underworld and it is on its dominant

imagery and mythology that the modern poet's lyrical patterns are
now partly based.

The first of the poems dealing with Dido is the 'Cori descrittivi di
stati d'animo di Didone' [Choruses descriptive of Dido's state of
mind] which contains in all nineteen fragments. It takes the form of
a muted symphony in an elegiac key mourning the passing of the
Carthaginian queen's beauty; and it is presented to us as an anguished
monologue spoken just before she commits suicide. The lyrical thread
is not exactly narrative (which Ungaretti considered a primitive
poetic form) nor is it entirely dislocated or analogical in its unfolding.
It consists instead of a schematic and emotionally-punctuated outline
of the story of Dido's abandonment by Aeneas in the fourth book of
the *Aeneid*, together with flashbacks to her childhood joys and
pleasures. These are superimposed upon certain gloomy forebodings
of her impending doom, interspersed with sudden bursts of self-
conscious insight into the real nature of her predicament. Again, in a
virtually Leopardian manner, the loss of youthful pleasures and sensations with the decline of age is minutely, if somewhat allusively,
recounted; yet the process is not compensated for, as it usually is with
Ungaretti, by the accumulation of the richly-textured memories of
a fulfilled personality, but only by the aridity of a lack of inwardness,
by a kind of soul-death. As a degenerate Eve, Dido has not transmuted the world into spiritual substance with the passing of time;
she has caused it instead to revert, as a result of her disenchantment
and lack of authenticity, to its former material opaqueness. Her
decline engenders a feeling of despair, since her life seems to her to
have been entirely gratuitous and passion-ridden in its unfolding;
and yet this is probably what Virgil intended to emphasize in using
her story. In fact, as Poschl points out,[6] she is one of those characters
entirely ruled by passion who tend to act as foils to Aeneas, while he
himself is solely guided by his duty to open up for his people the
promised land of Italy. His 'piety' is consequently the same as
Ungaretti's own atavistic self-consciousness and is directed towards
the fostering of a perennial humanism, not a facile form of self-
gratification.

The tone of the sequence is based on a chiaroscuro technique intermingling protracted periods of sorrow with brief moments of joyful
reminiscence. A similar lyrical process occurred earlier, we recall, in
Il dolore; but now these moments of joy are wholly based on recalls
of Dido's youthful feelings or physical beauty and are not surrounded
by the halo of consolation which an inner spiritual sense of fulfilment

would evoke. Even her reminiscences, therefore, are pervaded by an incipient touch of anguish.

At the outset she does not perhaps realize the poignant feelings her memories will stir up and attempts to bring about an emotional re-evocation of her youth through a momentary escape down memory's tunnel. The three opening lines (all presented in typical Ungarettian style as general statements of intent) describe the journey back to the carefree sensations of her early life:

> Dileguandosi l'ombra,
>
> In lontananza d'anni,
>
> Quando non laceravano gli affanni ...

[The shadows melting away, / / in the remoteness of the years, / / when anguish did not sting.]

At the end of this recessive journey we are then confronted with a delicate description of Dido's swift rise to puberty and the early flush of youth, both processes evoked in a hauntingly impressionistic style whose phrasing acquires greater incisiveness through a careful, classical fingering of the syllables:

> L'allora, odi, puerile
> Petto ergersi bramato
> E l'occhio tuo allarmato
> Fuoco incauto svelare dell'Aprile
> Da un'odorosa gota.

[The then child-like breast you hear / growing desirously erect / and your eye full of alarm / reveals an unwary April fire / upon a perfumed cheek.]

Inevitably, however, this type of blushful responsiveness is at once crushed by a reversion without transition to her gloomy present. At the same time the 'sneer' of memory is consciously interposed between past and present to fossilize even remembrance, although Dido does perhaps still cling questioningly to a forlorn hope of escape from her destiny by appealing to what seems to be an enigmatic ritual of memorial exorcism:

> Scherno, spettro solerte
> Che rendi il tempo inerte
> E lungamente la sua furia nota:
>
> Il cuore roso, sgombra!
>
> Ma potrà, mute lotte
> sopite, dileguarsi da età, notte?

[Derision, zealous spectre / which makes time inert / and long its
fury marks: / / My corroded heart, release! / / / But can night,
with dying strife / assuaged, melt away from age?]

In the second lyric this tremulous mood of anguish mingled with
residual hope stirred by the protagonist's reminiscences (the kind of
deceitful hope which she herself offers her sister, Anna, in the
Aeneid just before she kills herself) finds its correlative in nature. At
this point another example of Ungaretti's delicate form of impressionistic image-patterning may be seen, when the quivering expectancy of Dido's love-lorn musing is conveyed by recourse to the
myth of Echo:

La sera si prolunga
Per un sospeso fuoco
E un fremito nell'erbe a poco a poco
Pare infinito a sorte ricongiunga.

Lunare allora inavvertita nacque
Eco, e si fuse al brivido dell'acque.

[The evening is drawn out / through a hanging fire / and a quiver
in the grass little by little / seems to link the infinite to fate. / /
Lunar then and unperceived Echo / was born, and merged with
the shimmering of the waters.]

On the other hand, in the third lyric we reach a first stage of frenzy
and despair immediately after the prolongation of the preceding
deceptive moment of restless calm. Then, in a series of 'gridi' [cries]
which are not joyful as in *Allegria* but deeply sorrowful, Dido expresses the inner torment brought on by unrequited love and her
complete abandonment to her passion:

Ora il vento s'è fatto silenzioso
E silenzioso il mare;
Tutto tace; ma grido
Il grido, sola, del mio cuore,
Grido d'amore, grido di vergogna
Del mio cuore che brucia
Da quando ti mirai e m'hai guardata
E piú non sono che un oggetto debole.

[Now the wind is hushed / and hushed the sea; / all is silent; but
I alone / shriek the cries of my heart, / a cry of love, a cry of shame
/ from my heart which burns / since first I saw you and you gazed
on me / and now I am nothing more than an object of weakness.]

We cannot help noticing once again the Virgilian reminiscences in

these lines; one of these is ironically the atmosphere of stillness and
rapt attention evoked at the beginning of Book II of the *Aeneid* when,
with the words 'conticuere omnes' [all were silent], Aeneas begins to
recount his wanderings to the already partially enamoured queen.
Now, however, the silence is not one of serenity but of hysteria,
when Dido finally realizes the full implications of her abandonment.
In a sense this silence again serves to heighten the first of a number of
crisis-points in the lyrical sequence, in which emotion rises and falls
rhythmically like the sea that is eventually destined to carry Aeneas
away. Hence we do not experience a narrative progression of the
facts when reading the choruses, only a progression of the critical
moments in the protagonist's half-hearted psychological struggle
against self-annihilation.

Oddly enough, the fifth, eighth and ninth lyrics appear to be a
negative counterpart to certain lines drawn from Donne's love-lyric,
the 'Good-morrow', and surprisingly the English metaphysical poet
has a continuous – though perhaps unconscious – attraction for
Ungaretti towards the end of his life. At the end of the ninth lyric,
we again note a second climax in Dido's despair, one arising when
she suddenly realizes the gratuitousness and irrelevance of the sensory
world after her lover has spurned her:

Le immagini a che prò
Per me dimenticata?
[Of what value images / to me who am forgotten?]

Following each climax of this type there is a tendency to revert to a
landscape which will directly reflect the potentialities of the next
stage of the queen's anguish, and so once again in the tenth lyric we
find solace and anguish closely intermingled, with the characteristic
Ungarettian chiaroscuro device intervening to permit a moment of
despair to be gilded by a transient glow of hope. But the shimmering
light now evoked is ambivalent in its significance; for, as Hanne
points out (op. cit., 6–7), it may well be the very opposite of hope
and represent a prefiguration of the glow of Dido's funeral pyre
which Aeneas and his men observe from the harbour as they sail
away from Carthage:

Il mio declino abbellirò, stasera;
A foglie secche si vedrà congiunto
Un bagliore roseo.
[My decline I shall beautify, tonight; / to dry leaves one will see
conjoined / a rosy glow.]

From here on a sense of anguish becomes progressively deeper, and

finally the transient nature of Dido's love-affair with Aeneas is
referred to openly in the fourteenth lyric, when she describes his
eyes, once full of love, as 'gli occhi tuoi opachi, secchi' [your dry and
opaque eyes]. In the eighteenth she then appears to accuse him of yet
another cruelty, of departing without leaving her even a child to
console her. This is a theme which also appears in Virgil (Book IV
lines 326–30), and the whole idea is conveyed to us through the
analogy of the hysterical activity of herons guarding their young, in
which the voracious fledglings themselves seem to represent the
earthy voraciousness of the queen's passion. Indeed, it is with the
stench of procreation in her nostrils that she claims Aeneas is abandon-
ing her, and this dishonourable conduct will be the lasting notoriety
he will acquire from his cowardly flight:

> Àrdee errare cineree solo vedo
> Tra paludi e cespugli,
> Terrorizzate urlanti presso i nidi
> E gli escrementi dei voraci figli
> Anche se appaia solo una cornacchia.
>
> Per fetori s'estende
> La fama che ti resta,
> Ed altro segno piú di te non mostri
> Se non le paralitiche
> Forme della viltà
> Se ai tuoi sgradevoli gridi ti guardo.

[I only see the ashen herons wheeling / amid swamps and
thickets, / crying terrorized near their nests / and the excrement
of their voracious fledglings / even if only a crow appears. // In
a stench is spread / the fame which remains to you, / and now
no other sign of yourself do you show / except the paralysing /
marks of cowardice / if at your unlovely cries I look on you.]

In these lines passion and scorn have become elemental in their
expression and Dido has reduced their love to an excremental level.
Afterwards, the sequence ends on a laconic, bitingly ironic note,
when by a play on words Ungaretti changes Dido's errors into
horrors, and her wayward passion into an arid desolation:

> Deposto hai la superbia negli orrori,
> Nei desolati errori.

[You have laid pride down amid horrors, / amid desolating
errors.]

What then can we conclude from our analysis of this highly

allusive sequence? First, that like the *Aeneid* the choruses are couched in a language of symbolic gesture (Poschl, 48); and, second, that they represent a modern reinterpretation of the episode of Dido's death as related in the Virgilian epic. But even more than this the choruses renew one of the deeper underlying symbolic patterns of the *Aeneid*: its quest for the promised land and its lesson that a state of serenity is only to be gained through the dictates of 'pietas' and 'disponibilità', both of which are also, we remember, the principal elements in the bedouin-poet's make-up. Virgil's Aeneas and Ungaretti's 'uomo di pena' [man of grief] are accordingly to be equated at this point, and the latter, like the ancient Trojan hero, now possesses an inner *fatum* which distinguishes him from the disintegrating characters of Dido and Palinurus. Indeed, whenever we examine the character of Ungaretti's Dido we cannot help thinking simultaneously of Racine's Phèdre who was also destroyed by the overwhelming nature of her passion; and it is perhaps not wholly fortuitous that the poet published a translation of Racine's play in 1950 just about the time when he finally completed *La terra promessa*. Even so, despite the multiple echoes from Virgil, Racine and others, what emerges clearly from the poem is the poet's continuing personal belief that a sense of human solidarity and a form of lyrical ancestor-worship, a feeling for duty rather than a blind yielding to passion, will offer the only valid path to self-fulfilment.

The lyric entitled 'Recitativo di Palinuro' [Palinurus' Recitative] aims at representing another aspect of unauthentic living, the fossilization resulting from the adoption of a type of dog-like fidelity as an obsessive ideal to the detriment of one's inner becoming. The poem is written in the unusual form of a *sestina*, first introduced into Italian literature by Dante and borrowed by him from its probable inventor, the Provençal poet Arnaut Daniel. The poem is not without technical echoes from one of Dante's own 'rime petrose' [stony rhymes], itself a *sestina*, and it consists of six stanzas of six hendecasyllabic lines with six rhymes only, which are repeated in a different order in each of the stanzas. Like the medieval *sestina*, Ungaretti's poem has a 'congedo' [envoi] made up of three hendecasyllabic lines using three of the rhymes appearing in the other parts of the composition. Needless to say, the repetition of same rhymes throughout the entire lyric can rapidly lead to tedium unless the poet is skilful at ringing the changes on the meanings of the rhyme-words he uses; and, like his predecessors, Ungaretti soon found he had to deploy a great deal of semantic ingenuity to maintain the lyrical tension.

In a note to the poem he gives us some inkling of its meaning, and suggests that its main theme is one which deals allusively with the fate of Aeneas's faithful helmsman who fell off his boat as they approached Italy and was either drowned or murdered by savages before the Trojans finally disembarked. Ungaretti had, in fact, visited Cape Palinurus south of Naples as early as May 1932 and even then had marvelled at the great rock into which, as legend has it, Palinurus was transformed after his fatal misadventure. In the prose article *La pesca miracolosa* [Wondrous fishing] which he wrote about his visit he refers to the scene as follows:

> Dall'altura di Velia avevo guardato a sinistra Palinuro colla meraviglia che fa sempre una pietra enorme resa aerea dalla distanza. (*Il deserto*, 159)
> [From the heights of Velia I looked on Palinurus to the left with the amazement with which a mighty rock, made airborne by the distance, always fills one.]

Similarly the character of Palinurus is progressively giganticized in the poem and made rock-like or statuesque in attitude, while at the same time the story takes on the quality of a modern – even an eternal – myth, itself completely airborne or suspended in the ethos of the Italian tradition.

The story is naturally recounted once more in Ungaretti's impressionistic manner and he makes use of certain minor inconsistencies in Virgil's narration of the same event in two different places in the *Aeneid* (Book V 827–71 and Book VI 340–71) to suit his own symbolic purposes. He first accepts the idea put forward by Palinurus himself in Book VI that a rapidly brewing storm and the chance breaking of the rudder had caused his downfall; but in fact it is not the external circumstance which primarily interests the modern poet: he is far more attracted by the psychological one of a lack of vigilance on Palinurus's part which led him unwittingly to reject the idea of a real, inwardly-conceived, promised land in favour of an unauthentic, external one. He failed to acquire the spiritual resilience, in short, to succeed in the way that Aeneas was to succeed at the end of the journey through a show of 'pietas' and 'dovere'; and so he succumbs to a false spiritual slumber, just as Dido had been attracted before him to the false peace of suicide as an escape from her passions. This false sense of serenity is symbolized in the *Aeneid* Book V (lines 835–61) by the God of Sleep who slowly overcomes the protagonist's will; but the further point, that Palinurus's actual yielding to sleep amounts to a desire for an absurd, rock-like immortality, is added by Ungaretti who tells us that the storm he evokes in his lyric is really the storm of the passions (*Terra promessa*, 13). The poem is consequently a second example of a desperate form of escapism from a personal state of inner fragmentation, with the foil of Aeneas's own integrated personality once again hovering in the background to indicate the true nature of the authentic 'uomo di pena'. One should stress at this point, however, that in adopting this interpretation of the Palinurus episode Ungaretti is considerably changing the psychological and symbolic meaning of the original story by Virgil; for in the *Aeneid* there is no overt suggestion that Palinurus is an unauthentic character, even though his absolute fidelity to Aeneas is repeatedly affirmed.

The poem opens, as we have stated, at the height of the storm of human passion, and no doubt Palinurus in his unswerving fidelity to his leader is unable to bear the thought of the new fidelities which his arrival in the promised land will hold in prospect for him. He thus loses control of his inner *fatum* as Dido did before him, and the danger of his lack of vigilance – the most unforgiveable sin in a ship's helmsman – is highlighted in the opening lines:

> Per l'uragano all'apice di furia
> Vicino non intesi farsi il sonno ...
> [Because of the hurricane at the peak of its fury / I did not perceive sleep approaching close by.]

As a result, sleep pours its insidious oil over the waves and the outer peril of the storm is concealed behind an ever-growing sense of spiritual inertia:

> Olio fu dilagante a smanie d'onde,
> Aperto campo a libertà di pace,
> Di effusione infinita il finto emblema
> Dalla nuca prostrandomi mortale ...
> [Oil was spread over the raging of the waves, / a field opened up to the liberty of peace, / the feigned emblem of an infinite flood / as a mortal man prostrating me from the nape.]

Hence, plunged into an unreal dream by this process, whose blandness Ungaretti himself stresses by quoting in his brief commentary to the poem the last line of the second stanza,

> Solo accordando a sfinitezze onde,
> [Harmonizing only the waves to weariness]

Palinurus no longer has any thought for his mortal body, while the deadly dangers lurking in the ocean's depths are momentarily hidden from him by a feigned emblem of sleep-bearing tranquillity.

Unfortunately, external nature fails to respond to these internal blandishments of calm and becomes even fiercer in its mortal contest with the ship; so that in the end the protagonist does not know where the greater peril lies, in the inward beckoning of sleep or the outer battering of the waves. As we shall see, it was eventually the siren-song of sleep which posed the greater danger, because in the fourth stanza it causes his spirit to escape from its human bonds, from the security of the Trojan tradition of vigilance, into a kind of sidereal or cosmic dream where *tempus*, not *aevum*, holds sway:

D'àugure sciolse l'occhio allora emblema

Dando fuoco di me a sideree onde ...

[The augur's eye then liberated an emblem / conceding my flame to sidereal waves.]

By accepting this state of non-participation in immediate human affairs Palinurus at once forfeited his right to a future in the promised land, and so degenerated from the status of the receptive man to that of an inanimate object, a rock. But even when his decline had been completed and he had become wholly fossilized in his despair as an absurd emblem of unyielding fidelity, an irony still persists in the verse. It appears as a type of Petrarchan oxymoron within its very fabric, because the statuesque figure into which Palinurus is transformed then takes on an unexpectedly dynamic, Promethean-like stance and challenges through unceasing rebellion the static eternity of the gods, especially the previously mentioned realm of the god of sleep, here representative no doubt of the whole pantheon:

Tale per sempre mi fuggí la pace;

Per strenua fedeltà decaddi a emblema

Di disperanza e, preda d'ogni furia,

Riscosso via via a insulti freddi d'onde,

Ingigantivo d'impeto mortale,

Piú folle d'esse, folle sfida al sonno.

[Thus for ever peace escaped me; / through strenuous fidelity I declined to an emblem / of despair and, prey to every fury, / struck continuously by the cold offence of waves, / I grew gigantic with mortal vehemence, / wilder than the waves, a wild challenge to sleep.]

Having abandoned the sphere of human tradition for the immobility of the realm of the gods, we therefore find Palinurus in the sixth stanza vainly seeking to reboard his ship by swimming in its wake. But at this point death – a more arcane type of sleep – overwhelms him, and he is fossilized – petrified the poet says – as an

eternal emblem of non-fulfilment. Existence then is little more than
vanity for Ungaretti outside the magic circle of the traditional
'chorus', and we can sense in the desperate plight of Palinurus the
plight of all the poet's unauthentic characters from Moammed
Sceab onwards, each of whom commits the unforgiveable sin of
negating his inner destiny by yielding to external circumstances:

> Piloto vinto d'un disperso emblema,
> Vanità per riaverlo emulai d'onde;
> Ma nelle vene già impietriva furia
>
> Crescente d'ultimo e piú arcano sonno,
> E piú su d'onde e emblema della pace
> Cosí divenni furia non mortale.

> [A conquered pilot of a scattered emblem, / to recombine it I
> vied with the aimlessness of breakers; / but in my veins a fury
> was petrifying // growing with a last more secret slumber, / and
> higher than the waves and an emblem of peace / I thus became
> an immortal fury.]

At the end of the poem Palinurus has consequently become what
the poet calls 'l'immortalità ironica d'un sasso' [the ironic immortality
of a rock]; and, as death finally overtakes him, he is reduced to a state
of mineral insentiency, just as Dante claimed to have been reduced
to a similar rock-like state by the unfeelingness of the lady in the
'rime petrose'. In the same way as Dido's more instinctive revolt, his
largely ethical one inevitably provokes a similar process of disintegration, and all he leaves behind him is a massive but distant metaphysical
presence, a mineralized emblem floating in a dream-like state above
the sea, very much like Ungaretti's previously-quoted vision of the
rock of Palinurus near Velia. Hence, whereas Dido's excesses of
passion lead to horror and disgust through the unruliness of her
senses, an excessive sense of fidelity in Palinurus leads to an equivalent
form of horror, – to his reduction to an arid intellectual cipher, lost
in a restless dream of meaningless inhumanity. Indeed, this poem
reminds us not only of Dante but also of Shelley's 'Ozymandias',
where a boundless but gratuitous vista of the desert and its desolation
appears around the king's shattered statue:

> 'My name is Ozymandias, king of kings:
> Look on my works, ye Mighty, and despair!'
> Nothing beside remains. Round the decay
> Of that colossal wreck, boundless and bare
> The lone and level sands stretch far away.

As we have suggested earlier, in contrast with these two figures of disintegration the economy of the collection requires – if only to act as a foil – the presence of the positive image of Aeneas himself, whether he becomes metamorphosed or not into the figure of the bedouin-poet. Ungaretti at once apologizes for his absence in the introduction, telling us that at the time of publication the 'Cori d'Enea' were still 'allo stato d'abbozzo' [in draft form]. They do actually appear later under the modified title of the 'Ultimi cori per la terra promessa' in *Il taccuino del vecchio*; but their original conception as the choruses of Aeneas is nevertheless vouched for by a photostat of poems-in-progress appearing in front of Allen Mandelbaum's English translations of Ungaretti's verse published in 1958.[7] What these lyrics indicate above all is the poet's realization that life is a continuous process, not a sequence of immutable states, because they underline Aeneas's – or rather Ungaretti's – unquestioning acceptance of his contingent condition and of life's constant anxieties, as a basis for his quest for an ever-deepening form of self-fulfilment. However, an analysis of this sequence can be left to a later stage, so let us now turn our immediate attention to a number of important, if less ambitious, lyrics which round off the present volume.

The first of these is 'Variazioni su nulla' [Variations on nothing] which again deals with the distinction implicit in Ungaretti's entire work between *aevum* and *tempus*. The main symbol in the poem is the hour-glass or clepshydra with its continuous flow of sand representing time. At first, the kind of time it is intended to symbolize is uncertain, but it is probably *tempus*. Even so, the emotive process of the *aevum* has apparently already been at work upon it from time immemorial, and its activity is represented by the continually fading, flesh-textured qualities of a cloud, presumably perceived as it glimmers in the mists of the ultimate dawn and symbolizes humanity's dying embers:

> Quel nonnulla di sabbia che trascorre
> Dalla clessidra muto e va posandosi,
> E, fugaci, le impronte sul carnato,
> Sul carnato che muore, d'una nube ...

[That trifling flow of sand which silently slips away / from the hour-glass and then rests in a heap, / and, fleeting, the imprints on the flesh, / on the dying flesh, of a cloud.]

In the second stanza this human-informing or 'aeval' process, so far only implicit, is made explicit by a hand which turns the hour-glass, although even here the real object of the poem is perhaps still not yet attained. In a note Ungaretti comments upon its meaning by saying:

Il tema è la durata terrena oltre la singolarità delle persone. Null'altro se non un disincarnato orologio che, solo, nel vuoto, prosegua a sgocciolare i minuti. (*Poesie*, 567)

[The theme is a terrestrial 'durata' beyond the singularity of individuals. Nothing else but a disincarnate clock which, alone, in the void, continues to drip the minutes].

Nevertheless, even in this unfolding of an inhuman post-temporal existence we continue to sense the residual influence of man, since his spiritual presence is still there, still alert to hear and note the steady dripping of time. So it seems as if the poem deals ultimately with the internalization of time, with the humanization of the material universe. Probably the result of the process will be a speculative interpenetration of *tempus* and *aevum*, which will yield an entirely new type of time-flow bearing witness to the products of both natural and human activity:

La mano in ombra la clessidra volse,
E, di sabbia, il nonnulla che trascorre
Silente, è unica cosa che ormai s'oda   .
E, essendo udita, in buio non scompaia.

[The hour-glass turned the hand to shadow, / and the trifling flow of sand that slips away / silently, is the only thing which can now be heard / and, being heard, does not vanish in the gloom.]

The second poem of the group is 'Segreto del poeta'. It is a reaffirmation of the same process of spiritualization as we have seen elsewhere, but in a different key. It does not deal so much with time as with its concomitant ephemeral forms. Similarly, the symbol of night is once more subtly transformed here, so that it becomes the emotive emblem of a period of recollective meditation rather than a metaphysical image of pure existence. Nevertheless, since Ungaretti's symbolic effects are intended to be cumulative, it also seems to retain some metaphysical undertones in its sub-symbol of memorial shadows appearing in the second stanza. What the poet is mostly concerned with is undoubtedly the lyrical transmission of his emotivity, and this is best achieved, he says, at night when his lady's transient earthly gestures are re-illumined by being suffused with the inner light of memory. The memory of her light then seems even more important than her real fleshly radiance, because she acquires a wholly recollective and evaluative grace. Even so, the meditative light she radiates can only be transmitted when inspiration touches an emotive absolute, through the smouldering of hope:

Avviene quando sento,

Mentre riprende a distaccarsi da ombre,
La speranza immutabile
In me che fuoco nuovamente scova
E nel silenzio restituendo va,
A gesti tuoi terreni
Talmente amati che immortali parvero,
Luce.
[It happens when I feel, / as hope begins to disengage itself / immutably from shadows / within me, which a fire newly uncovers / and in the silence restores / to your earthly gestures, / loved so much that they seemed immortal, / light.]

Since in his old age the poet now feels he must live almost entirely on his memories for want of any other intensely new experiences, it can easily be explained why in a note to this poem he tells us that it contains 'l'intima sua speranza' (*Poesie*, 567) [his inner hope].

The last poem seems by contrast to mark a moment of personal despair, and its atmosphere of inertia reminds us of the earlier lyric addressed to Palinurus. The sea is the main background symbol to the composition and it never was a happy symbol for Ungaretti. In *Il dolore*, we recall, it represented a trackless waste separating him from his son's grave, while even earlier in 'Agonia' in *Allegria* it was already something to be conquered, as the dying quail conquered it before expiring in the first bushes when it had finally reached land. Here it seems to have been changed into a universal symbol of the failure of the life-force, of the corrosion of the poet's 'disponibilità'. It also represents a cosmic wasteland of meaningless Being towards which unauthentic characters like Dido and Palinurus inevitably gravitate. In contrast with Montale's view it is thus a condition in which the material returns inertly to the material instead of being transfigured into spirit. Probably in his present mood Ungaretti felt that he had himself reached this lowest common denominator of spiritual inertia, and so he makes the sea the image of the *nec plus ultra* of existential despair:

Più non muggisce, non sussurra il mare,
Il mare.

Senza i sogni, incolore campo è il mare,
Il mare.

....

Morto è anche lui, vedi, il mare,
il mare. (*Finale*)

[The sea no longer howls, it no longer whispers, the sea / the sea. / / Without dreams, a colourless track is the sea, / the sea. / / ... / / Dead too, you see, is the sea, / the sea.]

It is indeed on this dirge-like note that the collection ends; but the mood contained in the last poem is fortunately just a momentary one and in his next collection we find that the poet's hopes gradually revive, despite his continuing disillusionment.

If then we are led to inquire why *La terra promessa* should end on such a pessimistic note, the answer probably lies in the metaphysics of the human condition itself as Ungaretti envisaged it. Since life's arrow represented for him, as it did for Bergson, a process of indeterminate change which denies any definite teleological goal, the promised land, though distantly perceived, could never actually be attained. It is simply a perennial figment of the human imagination and, precisely because he considered mankind to be condemned to wander for ever in a desert of kaleidoscopic mirages, it seems to him that even the most tenacious individual tends periodically to weary of his search for ultimate truth, for that revivifying 'prima immagine', evoked in 'Canzone'.

At such moments there is perhaps some confusion in Ungaretti's mind between his yearning for an all-embracing finality which he knows it is impossible to attain and his sense of existential intentionality: his awareness of his ability to make projects and pursue them endlessly, either to the point of fulfilment or till they melt away in his hands and are replaced by other, more satisfying ones. At such periods of disturbed insight his only refuge is in a kind of passivity or soul-death which has been growing throughout this volume and is ultimately symbolized, as we have seen, in its last poem 'Finale' by a dead tract of ocean. But whenever the confusion is resolved, the poet's declining spirit is revived by the shining emblem of Aeneas's heroism, and he too adopts in his remaining collections the quasi-heroic stance of a modern existential Aeneas. In this sense the way has at last been cleared in *La terra promessa* for a fully self-conscious focussing of the poet's attention on the promised land, even though his new area of humanistic serenity only remains accessible in intentionality, it is not a fixed ideal resulting from a recrudescence of platonic absolutes. This no doubt explains the continuing anguish of the bedouin-poet in later poems; for, although he can transform reality and effect a continual 'dépassement de soi' [self-surpassing] in the human sense, he can never wholly arrest life's flux and so change process into Being.

The promised land of this collection is consequently a symbol of man's perpetual struggle for fulfilment. It is neither wholly ontological and concerned with the 'prima immagine' nor is it wholly teleological and concerned with abstract or distant goals, but is an amalgam of both.

Moreover, since on Ungaretti's own admission the collection is incomplete, even fragmentary, we can only guess at its intended, overall design. Throughout, he constantly seems to be aiming at presenting the wider contours of existence in an allusive, metaphysical light. In this respect 'Canzone' deals with our common human experience, with the kind of being who lives most of his life in thrall to his senses but who, towards the end of it, escapes to a higher contemplative sphere. Then, later, in the other major poems, Ungaretti seems, like Montale, to divide mankind into two broad categories, the fits and misfits. This permits him to depict Dido and Palinurus as partial characters who have been unable to fulfil themselves, while Aeneas contrasts with them both in the role of the authentic personality. Since the choruses to Aeneas are missing, it could be argued that Ungaretti found it no less difficult than Montale to describe the integrated human being; but in stark opposition to the latter who always considers himself one of the 'damned', Ungaretti – as the incarnation of the bedouin-poet – constantly appears as one of the potentially fulfilled. And, in fact, this contrast between his own continuous integration into life and the dramatic failure of alienated characters to do the same takes us right back to the pathetic figure of Moammed Sceab at the beginning of *Allegria*.

Nevertheless a curious new gloss seems to have been put on Ungaretti's dialectic of creativity in the *Terra promessa*, since the poet has now come to recognize the true nature of his human limits: an inability to grasp absolutes and provide for himself a stable ontology. So, as he regresses from reality towards his dream of an Eve-like, reborn innocence and eventually comes up against 'il nulla', he shies away from its promise of absolute insights and puts greater emphasis on the subsequent return to reality. In this way the obsessive metaphysical cult of the 'prima immagine' becomes transformed into something which is 'avversa al nulla' [opposed to nothingness], a cult of the poet's own experiential 'segreti' [secrets] as they accumulate over time. These act as a balm and consolation after he acknowledges his inability to grasp anything but 'echoes' of the Eternal. Consequently, as a self-confessed phenomenologist, he now considers fulfilment to depend upon the consolidation of memories in old age, and this cult becomes a substitute for absolute platonic yearnings. Since

memories are contingent elements, they too can admittedly be somewhat deceptive; but they offer the only hope of entering a consolatory
terrestrial paradise of the kind that Ungaretti envisages. Eventually
this paradise proves to be an extension of his atavistic perspectives as
well as of his personal experiences, since in his later collections literary
reminiscences and instinctive racial recalls form an integral part of its
very fabric.

7. The Final Collections

The final volumes of verse published by Ungaretti are not only far less ambitious but they can hardly be said to possess the same internal coherence as their predecessors. At first sight they appear to be composed of a series of *vers de circonstance* or else of additions and after-thoughts to his other collections. This is the case with 'Gridasti soffoco ...' which was first published separately in 1949, and re-appeared later as part of *Un grido e paesaggi* in 1952; yet, since the poem deals with the death of Ungaretti's son, it should logically have featured in *Il dolore*. The reader will recall that we did actually examine this particular poem in its proper sequence, although we have, by contrast, preferred to reserve until the present chapter other displaced compositions like the 'Ultimi cori' (formerly the 'Cori d'Enea'), because their texture reveals innovations which more properly fit into a later stage of the poet's lyrical development. Such an approach now offers us a useful opportunity to highlight these innovations by comparing them with already consolidated procedures, and thereby to redimension our earlier perspective of Ungaretti's overall poetic achievement.

The most extensive innovatory text in *Un grido e paesaggi*, and possibly the most wide-ranging in all the later collections, is 'Monologhetto' [Short monologue], written according to Bigongiari under the aegis of Leopardi and Rimbaud.[1] The poem was first composed in prose in the last weeks of 1951 and broadcast over Italian radio on New Year's Day 1952. Afterwards it was turned into verse and, following the appearance of several versions in periodicals, it finally obtained its definitive form in the present collection. It is written as a symbolic monologue in which Ungaretti meditates upon his own life and on the range and limits of the human condition which his personal experiences tend to exemplify. In consequence, we can consider its articulation to consist of a kind of dialectic between memory and appearance as the poet tries first to recapture and then to consolidate in a generalized lyrical discourse the principal stages of his career. The purpose behind this dialectic according to Spagnoletti is that of creating 'un tempo dell'anima' [a time of the spirit].[2] Its inner temporality is clearly intended to act as a foil to the outer time-flow of the poet's external or 'social' commitment, and these two strands are delicately intertwined to give the impression of a universal orphic pattern observable behind the contingency of the particular vicissitudes experienced by the individual during his lifespan. The poet takes the month of February as his central inscape for the recall and reconstitution of his memories, partly because it was the month of his own birth and partly because it allows him to introduce yet another example of his inversionary technique in the false – because summery – Februaries of the southern hemisphere, which he experienced during his stay in Brazil. A third reason is adduced by Bigongiari who tells us that the root of February in Italian is identical with 'febbre' [fever] and no doubt it refers in the context to life's fever. Another possibility, which links up with our overall orphic interpretation of Ungaretti's poetry, is that the poet is thinking of the Latin 'Februa' meaning 'the solemnities of purification' marking the end of the year.

From the beginning the poet in his usual manner takes a sweepingly generalized view of his subject, which is his own life's journey. But the kaleidoscopic scenes he evokes are either withdrawn almost immediately after their initial appearance or else are transmuted into others offering very different perspectives. The result is that he gradually evolves a fluctuating space-time continuum in keeping with his own particular sense of memorial involution and 'simultaneità' [simultaneity]. The initial landscape is, naturally enough, a brief evocation of spring. Not only is it a season symbolic of his youth but, inasmuch as it begins earlier in Italy than in England, it is somewhat more advanced in February. He parallels this event with a mystical rebirth drawn from biblical sources – actually from the story of the flood – and the myth that emerges is integrated symbolically into the spring-like lyrical texture of the scene as the land is repeopled after the waters have subsided. Rebirth, as we know, signifies re-creation for Ungaretti, and perhaps the re-emergence of the human tradition is intended to be inferred symbolically from the reappearance of the land after the flood. There is, moreover, a delicate interplay of literal and symbolic senses throughout, so that even the Italian habit of white-washing dove-cotes in springtime becomes a practical mnemonic of a revived biblical sense of peacefulness and fertile promise:

> Come di sopra a un biblico disastro,
> Nelle apparenze, il velario si leva
> Lungo un lido, che da quell'attimo
> Si scruta per ripopolarsi:

Di tanto in tanto riemergenti brusche
Si susseguono torri;
Erra, di nuovo in cerca d'Ararat,
Con solitudini salpata l'arca;
Ai colombai risale l'imbianchino.
[As when after a biblical disaster, / in the mirages, a sail rises / along a strand, which from that moment / is scrutinized for repopulating: / suddenly re-emerging from time to time / towers run in a row; / the ark, again in search of Ararat, / wanders, sailing through wildernesses; / to the dove-cotes the white-washer climbs again.]

What we also notice in this description is the skeletal yet incisive, contours of the landscape evoked in a Leopardian fashion, and the way in which the symbol of the dove-cotes transferred from the story of the ark to a local everyday scene transforms a fabulous biblical atmosphere into an evocation of central and southern Italian settings. This leads the poet to a description of spring in the Maremma during which that immensely flat wasteland is transformed into a secret regenerative force full of sprouting briar and birds building nests. From here he passes – again without apparent transition – to Foggia and Lucera in the deep south, where an unaccustomed flash of a car's headlights disturbs an age-old mode of life, symbolized by frightened ponies champing in the stables. Everything is now hushed, innocent, and atavistic in its life-style; it is almost as if the external world has been replaced by a rapid succession of inner landscapes caught in the maelstrom of a cyclical temporality whose fulcrum is firmly based on the constant reappearance of an obsessive February. Later the poet suddenly seems to become airborne and moves over to the mountains of Corsica where yet another biblical scene – this time taken from modern reality rather than ancient myth – is evoked, at Vivario.

The festivity is a vigil and a singing competition combined, and as the drama unfolds the Corsican shepherds display all the primitiveness of their biblical counterparts. They are, in short, men of another, more pastoral age and their statuesque poses and sense of certainty seem far removed from the tumult of industrial life, as they listen to a timeless lovesong:

Dentro i monti còrsi, a Vivario,
Uomini intorno al caldo a veglia
Chiusi sotto il lume a petrolio nella stanza,
Con i bianchi barboni sparsi
Sulle mani poggiate sui bastoni,

Morsicando lenti la pipa
Ors'Antone che canta ascoltano,
Accompagnato dal sussurro della rivergola
Vibrante di tra i denti
Del ragazzo Ghiuvanni:

Tantu lieta è la sua sorte
Quantu torbida è la mia.

[Among the Corsican mountains, at Vivario, / men keeping
vigil in the warmth / huddled beneath the oil-lamp in the room, /
with their long white beards spread / over their hands resting on
their crooks, / slowly nibbling their pipes / listen to uncle Antone
singing, / accompanied by the whisper of the Jew's-harp /
vibrating between the teeth / of the boy Ghiuvanni: / / *Her fate
is as joyful / as mine is troubled.*]

The period of the year in which this breath-taking mythological
tableau takes place is Carnival time (again in February); yet juxtaposed
with its primitive, old-world calm is the other side of the coin, the
barbarous one of the slaughtering of pigs in the streets for the next
day's feasting. Later, the poet's eye wanders even further afield, from
the new houses in the village up to the old houses ranged along the
hillside, and far beyond them to the perfumed woods of Vizzavona.
Then, eventually, he takes up his journey once again, this time by car,
and after negotiating some hair-raising bends, he arrives in Ajaccio,
where a mythical atmosphere is re-evoked by reference to a sybilline
February sky. Sybilline moods and soothsaying indeed play a significant role in the poem later on and here they offer the poet a moment of
hope:

Il cielo è un cielo di zaffiro
E ha quel colore lucido
Che di questo mese gli spetta,
Colore di Febbraio,
Colore di speranza.
Giú, giú, arriva fino
A Ajaccio, un tale cielo,
Che intirizzisce, ma non perché freddo,
Perché è sibillino …

[The sky is sapphire-like / and has that shining colour / suited to
it in this month, / a colour of February, / a colour of hope. /
Down, down, as far as / Ajaccio such a sky reaches, / and it
numbs, but not because it is cold, / but because it is sybilline.]

However, although this is in fact Carnival-time, the carnival which is so vividly described is not that of the Corsican peasants. Instead we are invited to take another gigantic geographical leap and find ourselves immersed in the frantic, hallucinatory carnival of Brazil, as the ship which took the poet to that country in 1936, the *Neptunia*, docks in the harbour at Pernambuco. There, in a series of kinaesthetic images, the whole world is depicted as swaying to the strains of the music, especially after dark when a play of light and shadow intensifies the carnival's baroque effects. So, after its long journey, the ship

A Pernambuco attracca
E,
Tra le barchette in dondolo,
E titubanti chiattole
Sul lustro elastico dell'acqua,
Nel breve porto impone, nero,
L'ingombro svelto del suo netto taglio.
Ovunque, per la scala della nave,
Per le strade gremite,
Sui predellini del tramvai,
Non c'è più nulla che non balli,
Sia cosa, sia bestia, sia gente,
Giorno e notte, e notte
E giorno, essendo Carnevale.
Ma meglio di notte si balla,
Quando, uggiosi alle tenebre,
Dalla girandola dei fuochi, fiori,
Complici della notte,
moltiplicandone gli equivoci,
Tra cielo e terra grandinano
Screziando la marina livida.
[moors at Pernambuco / and, / among the tossing skiffs / and swaying barges / on the elastic glitter of the water, / in the narrow port it darkly imposes / the slender burden of its sharp outline. / Everywhere, on the gangway of the ship, / along the seething streets, / on the footboards of the trams, / there is nothing that does not dance, / be it thing, beast, or people, / day and night, and night / and day, it being Carnival-time. / But one dances better at night, / when, gloomily in the darkness, / from the Catherine-wheel of fires, flowers, / accomplices of night, / intensifying the make-believe, / hail down between heaven and earth / variegating the livid sea-shore.]

At once the imagery seems to symbolize the 'élan vital' itself, but the ceaseless dynamism of the tropical scene does even more than this: it catches up the whole of the poet's spiritual geography in a whorl of sharp outlines and haunting shadows, depicting his entire existence as a vortex of simultaneous temporal perspectives seen through the foreshortened, baroque lens of an upturned telescope.

Needless to say, the month is still February; but, as a European, Ungaretti feels alienated in this new, inverted world of hot winter months and finds it difficult, even though necessary, to go native and mingle his blood with that of his hosts:

L'equatore è a due passi.
Non penò poco l'Europeo a assuefarsi
Alle stagioni alla rovescia,
E, piú che mai, facendosi
Il suo sangue meticcio:
Non è Febbraio il mese degli innesti?
[The equator is a few steps away. / The European suffered not a little in accustoming himself / to the upturning of the seasons, / and, even more, in making / his blood half-caste: / Is not February the month for grafts?]

As a result, he eventually discovers the seductions of these false Februaries and joins in the obsessive dancing which governs the life-style of the Brazilian people.

At this point the memorial and discontinuous flash-back technique so far employed is halted for a moment, so that the poet can draw breath and meditate on the somewhat disturbing fact that conjuring up his past in this way is a sign of old age. But after a short pause the reawakening of memories continues as gaily as before, and now it moves right back to his Egyptian childhood. Here the sense of mystery deepens as the time-hallowed myths of the East and the magic of the soothsayers penetrate and bewitch the mind of the astonished European child. Likewise the re-born innocence of the scene is emphasized by the insinuation of a further biblical reference to Adam and Eve; while the apparently necromantic casting of the shadow of a mahdi on the rock appears to be a magical inversion of the stark face of reality cast on a similar rock in 'Il capitano', where, we recall, it awakened the poet's faculty of self-consciousness. Here instead an attempt is made to lapse back into childhood superstition and primitive magic during the Shiitian celebration of the moon of the amulets. The madhi (meaning he who is divinely inspired) is presumably the Mohammedan Messiah who, it is claimed, will bring back justice to the world.

Yet the Shiites are themselves Mohammedan heretics who apparently try on occasion to bring about magical epiphanies of the Madhi, their last prophet, and who, as tradition has it, did not actually die but simply went into hiding from mankind. However, the haunting vision of this mass-hypnotic ceremony of necromancy is shattered for the poet by the derisive laughter of his own mother. In a sense she is perhaps no less superstitious than they are, but being a down-to-earth peasant woman she utters another prophecy based not on magic but on certain pragmatic observations about the weather and its influence on the harvest. Her peasant-like Italian scepticism is thus a counterblast to the attractions of eastern magic; although it is once again to be noted that the scene is depicted in a hallucinatory manner by the evoking of mere skeletal or spectral contours, as is the case with all the other significant scenes in the poem. In consequence, some of the mystery of the Shiitian rites rubs off on the poet, and this is even detectable in his surrealistic, almost apocalyptic, description of his own birth:

> E anch'io di questo mese nacqui.
> Era burrasca, pioveva a dirotto
> A Alessandria d'Egitto in quella notte,
> E festa gli Sciiti
> Facevano laggiú
> Alla luna detta degli amuleti:
> Galoppa un bimbo sul cavallo bianco
> E a lui dintorno in ressa il popolo
> S'avvince al cerchio dei presagi.
> Adamo ed Eva rammemorano
> Nella terrena sorte istupiditi:
> È tempo che s'aguzzi
> L'orecchio a indovinare,
> E una delle Arabe accalcate, scatta,
> Fulmine che una roccia graffia
> Indica e, con schiumante bocca, attesta:

> *Un mahdi, ancora informe nel granito,*
> *Delinea le sue braccia spaventose;*

> Ma mia madre, Lucchese,
> A quella uscita ride
> Ed un proverbio cita:

> *Se di Febbraio corrono i viottoli,*
> *Empie di vino e olio tutti i ciottoli.*

[And I too was born in this month. / There was a squall, it rained heavily / at Alexandria in Egypt on that night, / and the Shiitians were / feasting down there / during the moon called moon of the lucky charms: / a child galloped on a white horse / and around him in a throng the people / clung together in the circle of the soothsayers. / Adam and Eve they commemorated / astounded before their earthly destiny: / it was time for the ear / to be sharpened for divining, / and one of the Arab women crowding round cried out, / pointed to lightning which scarred / a rock, and, with foaming mouth, gave testimony: / / *a mahdi, still half-shaped in the granite,* / *reveals his frightening arms;* / / my mother, a Lucchese, / at that outburst laughed and quoted a proverb: / / *If the lanes run in February,* / *it fills all one's crocks with oil and wine.*]

This drama marks the end of the second stage in the hallucinatory flow of the narrative, during which we see first a return to the mature manhood of the poet and then, unexpectedly, a regression to much deeper memories, to the ineffable mysteries of the East which surrounded him in his childhood. Inevitably at this juncture he speaks of a new – no less decisive – form of experience which falls due every February as he celebrates his birthday: his sense of growing emptiness as the month marks another step in his temporal decline. Such intimations indicate a foreknowledge of his own impending death, and this thought of final extinction, like the obsessive idea of the month itself, is associated with other religious festivities or ceremonies taking place in February, such as Candlemas and Ash-Wednesday, especially the latter since in Catholic countries this is celebrated by scattering ashes over the heads of penitents and uttering the phrase: 'Sei polvere e ritornerai in polvere' [Dust thou art and to dust shall thou return]. When the true meaning of these words finally penetrates our understanding in old age, we all become tense and delirious, according to Ungaretti, and try to substantialize, to reincarnate ourselves, imaginatively and memorially, within the dusty void which their constant threat evokes in our minds:

Impaziente, nel vuoto, ognuno smania,
S'affanna, futile,
A reincarnarsi in qualche fantasia
Che anch'essa sarà vana …
[Impatient, in the void, each one of us becomes crazed, / uselessly struggles / to rise reincarnate within some fantasy / which will also be vain.]

This then is the nature of the poet's true existential anguish, and it

gives point to the Pirandellian flavour he finally attributes to the words
he utters about the wider, masked carnival of life, which the narrative
thread of the poem has now become:

> Poeti, poeti, ci siamo messi
> Tutte le maschere;
> Ma uno non è che la propria persona.
> [Poets, poets we have put on / every kind of mask, / but one is
> nothing but our own person.]

At this juncture, it seems, even the consolidation of memory has
failed, because between the memory and the reality, as Eliot would put
it, there always falls the shadow: a realization that our memories are
wholly insubstantial things and that, whereas they can certainly
dredge up vicarious consolations from the past, they cannot offer any
direct comfort to soothe one against the manifest disintegration and
degradation of the present. So, in Ungaretti's view, it is only the un-
memoried spirit of the child which does not act as a misfit in life's
flux, because he alone enjoys the necessary innocence, the direct commitment, and lack of a prolonged temporal perspective not to be
haunted by the consolatory illusions and countervailing existential
Angst springing from the recollection of things past. Yet this very
state of childhood is all too brief a spell, and almost resembles an
instantaneous dream dissolving into the insatiable hunger and dis-
satisfaction of adult remembrance:

> Ma perché fanciullezza
> È subito ricordo?
> [But why is childhood / suddenly memory?]

We deduce from this form of symbolism that our communion
with truth, with the root of our being, is nothing more than an occasional flash of insight; and at the end of the poem Ungaretti again
equates life with a Bergsonian 'vivo tendersi' or 'élan vital', even
though it is now stunted by time's insubstantial mirages and the ash of
decay. Nevertheless our momentary, if continually decaying, gestures
in life, in so far as they indicate the uniqueness of our personalities and
characters, prove to be our immortal testimony before the gods of
chance, and they underline man's Promethean-like urge to overcome
through his will the limits of his existential condition on earth:

> Non c'è, altro non c'è su questa terra
> Che un barlume di vero
> E il nulla della polvere,
> Anche se, matto, incorreggibile,
> Incontro al lampo dei miraggi

Nell'intimo e nei gesti, il vivo
Tendersi sembra sempre.
[There is only, there is only on this earth / but a glimmer of truth /
and the nothingness of dust, / even if, an incorrigible madman, /
against the flash of mirages / in gestures and intimate self, the
living man / always seems to strain.]

The desolation of this message – in spite of its heroism and residual
spark of Bergsonian hopefulness – is self-evident, and it is brought
home to us all the more starkly because Ungaretti has now realized
that his previously cherished consolations from the tradition can no
longer offer him complete protection against the inner ravages of his
sense of contingency and decline.

What then can we conclude when faced with the problems associated with this apparently narrative, yet still highly impressionistic,
poem? It seems that by evoking a compact whorl of memories with
their lack of transitions and obsessive sense of rhythm Ungaretti is
trying to bring about a 'simultaneità dei ricordi' [a simultaneity of
memories] in the same way as he formerly brought about a 'simultaneità delle sensazioni' [a simultaneity of sensations] in his earlier
poetry. The point has been illustrated by Ossola[3] on the technical
level, since he sees certain baroque devices developed in *Il dolore* and
elsewhere reappearing within its lyrical texture. One of the most
important of these is a kind of tautology in which sense does not
noticeably progress with the repetition of words:

Il cielo è un cielo di zaffiro
E ha quel colore lucido
Che di questo mese gli spetta,
Colore di Febbraio,
Colore di speranza.
[The sky is sapphire-like / and has that shining colour / suited to
it in this month, / a colour of February, / a colour of hope.]

Another is the circular use of words themselves, as in

Giorno e notte, e notte
E giorno, essendo Carnevale.
[Day and night, and night / and day, it being Carnival-time.]

While a third is the use of a kind of anagrammatic technique which
seems to be a favoured device with Ungaretti in all his later collections:

... il vivo
Tendersi SEMbRa SEMpRe.
[... the living man / always seems to strain.]

Where Ossola's analysis is more questionable, however, is in the conclusions he draws from these repetitive devices, since he falls in with Bàrberi Squarotti's views that the poet has now taken refuge in an effete nominalism in which a baroque rhetoric leads to a vicious circle of nihilistic spiritual effects. What is more, he considers that Ungaretti learned this mode of perceiving things from the Shakespeare of the sonnets and he quotes one (Sonnet 100) in Ungaretti's own translation to prove his point. The original in English reads as follows:

> If there be nothing new, but that which is
> Hath been before, how are our brains beguil'd,
> Which, labouring for invention, bear amiss
> The second burden of a former child!
> O, that record could with a backward look,
> Even of five hundred courses of the sun,
> Show me your image in some antique book,
> Since mind at first in character was done!
> That I might see what the old world could say
> To this composed wonder of your frame;
> Whether we are mended, or whe'er better they,
> Or whether revolution be the same.
> O, sure I am, the wits of former days
> To subjects worse have given admiring praise.

Now in this sonnet the critic takes the translation 'una stessa rivoluzione' [the same revolution] to be a negative obsession with Ungaretti in his old age and mentions that it recurs at the beginning of the 'Ultimi cori'; but in point of fact the sonnet itself finally teaches the opposite lesson, the possibility of continuous improvement. We could indeed call the vicious circle implied by Ossola's type of meaningless 'eternal returns' a form of 'bas orphisme', of a kind which is also apparent in Campana's work at times, whenever his lyrical spiralling towards fulfilment is momentarily broken and replaced by a gratuitous churning of dissociative sense-impressions. But is Ungaretti's present verse actually a poetry of this type? It seems not. What both Ossola and Bàrberi Squarotti appear to have missed is the fact that the poet, as a reincarnation of the spirit of Aeneas, is trying to build a new empire for himself: an empire of consolidated memories. The 'prima immagine' and this contingent orphic ideal now tend to coincide and offer a new form of consolation – a new type of illusionism or *trompe-l'œil*, if you like – which will dominate his later volumes. These consolidated memories, moreover, are not the product of literary isolation, of mere rhetorical and literary reminiscences artfully

combined to delude the reader: they consist of a final desperate offering of the authentic bedouin-poet whose tortured existential mis-
givings have cast him back into his inner world of 'segreti' for
spiritual comfort, since the external world now bears all the signs of
inevitable decay. Perhaps then it is a lack of performance rather than
of authentic spiritual method which at bottom disquiets these critics?
But whether one believes that Ungaretti fully succeeded or not in
consolidating his memories in his last collections is really beside the
point in this particular argument, because what we are at present
discussing is the poet's inner intentions, not specifically his lyrical
achievement. In 'Monologhetto', therefore, the Bergsonian reminiscence at the end seems to us to be conclusive proof that the poem is not
wholly renunciatory in intention, but that its lyricism is now heightened by Ungaretti's cumulative baroque effects. His former elemental 'gridi' have consequently changed to cries of anguish mingled
with momentary feelings of joy as he re-contemplates the pent-up
memories of a lifetime and draws a momentary consolation from
them, even though he senses that he is on the very brink of the abyss.

On the other hand, as a form of spiritual counterpoint to the
desperate pleasures and sense of existentiality brooding over 'Monologhetto', Ungaretti appears to revert elsewhere in the collection to a
neo-platonic attitude, prompted perhaps by his still somewhat ambivalent Christian sentiments. So, in the section entitled *Svaghi*, the
poem 'Esercizio di metrica' [Metrical exercise] tends to outline a form
of neo-platonic transcendence to an absolute state of purity after
death. Whether this state of purity is to be equated with the clear-
sightedness of the poet safely ensconced within the lyric tradition or
whether it alludes instead to some more substantial after-life is a
matter for dispute; but the poem still shows a continuing faith in the
process of 'illimpidimento' or clarification of experience. This faith
no longer applies, moreover, simply to lyrical textures but also to the
human soul itself:

> L'urto patito che scinde,
> Sorte ripresati Eterno, se, già
> Fetida, l'alvo reclami che
> È orrido a ingenui, la spoglia tua,
> Giú essa sarà, dal suo mistero esule,
> Sparsa nel sonno, non sozza, vera.
> [Having suffered the cleaving blow, / fate having re-seized you
> Eternal, if, already / mouldering you reclaim the womb which /
> is horrible to the ingenuous, your mortal spoil, / from its mystery

exiled, down there / will be scattered in sleep, not foul but true.]

Clearly, what is important here is the meaning that Ungaretti attaches to the word 'vera', which significantly qualifies 'spoglia' [mortal spoil] and not 'sonno' [sleep]. Fortunately he gives us an explanation himself in his introductory remarks to the poem, where he emphasizes:

> Esercizio metrico nel senso tecnico esso è, e non solo. Mi vuole di più rammentare la misura che all'uomo è il suo corpo provvisorio. Indispensabile misura essendo il corpo lo strumento con il quale l'uomo si foggia la sua realtà immortale. (*Poesie*, 268)
>
> [It is not merely a metrical exercise in the technical sense. It also aims to remind me of the measure that his ephemeral body is to man. An indispensable measure since the body is the instrument with which man fashions his immortal reality.]

So although, as he goes on to add, the soul after death acquires an 'infinite lightness', it owes its spiritual validity to the experiences of the body, and indeed it is in this sense, as an authentically shaped existential essence, that we must take the meaning of 'true' in the present context. If we do so, it seems that there is no real contradiction between Ungaretti's present platonism and his earlier phenomenologist approach, since in philosophical terms he would argue that 'Being' is always shaped by 'Becoming' and that the immortality he envisages would be fundamentally of a human order perpetuated memorially through time, probably again in the Petrarchan sense of fame.

We return more or less to the same theme in the next collection *Il taccuino del vecchio* (1960). The main poem contained in this volume is the 'Ultimi cori per la terra promessa' which originally bore the title of 'Cori d'Enea'. This fact may be discovered from the autograph of poems-in-progress from *La terra promessa* reproduced by Mandelbaum, to which we have already referred. The lyrics appearing in the autograph are numbers four, five, six, seven and eight, and their rather limited range seems to reinforce the impression given by the title that they were once closely linked with the character of Aeneas. Later, however, their overall perspective was enlarged, especially after the poet had made a further visit to Egypt with Sinisgalli and travelled by air from Hong Kong to Beirut on his return from Japan with Fautrier and Paulhan, These journeys, he tells us, were responsible for the first three and the twenty-fourth, and the twenty-third chorus, respectively; while choruses sixteen and seventeen resulted from the launching of artificial satellites (*Poesie*, 573). In this period there was accordingly a tendency on Ungaretti's part to broaden the subject-matter of the choruses dedicated to Aeneas with the object of making them wider-ranging and more symphonic in quality than he had originally intended.

Aeneas, we recall, was already a thorough-going existential figure in *La terra promessa*, even though he normally acted as a distant foil and was never actually present in any of its poems. Yet, unlike Dido and Palinurus, his very 'absence' was always assertive of the validity of creative action arising out of duty and piety, a belief he nurtured in spite of the constant sense of disillusionment emanating from the world of appearances. His justification for this belief was centred on the validity of the human tradition and on his own racial destiny, and together he regarded them as establishing a more permanent standard of values than any mere hypostasis of cosmic phenomena. So, whereas cosmic standards represent 'dismisura' [disproportion] for him, human ones offer 'misura' or a sense of scale. Later, this dialectic deriving from the fathering of Ungaretti's philosophy of life on to the classical symbol of Aeneas is one which the poet assures us himself has its polarities in Parmenidean Being on the one hand and in a sense of Heraclitean flux on the other. Though confined by these two limits, the empire-builder of all ages always struggles to modify the phenomenological *Lebenswelt*, that prerational and suspended condition of the spirit implicit in the mass-psychology of a given society at any given historical moment. The concept was intended by Ungaretti to embody both the aesthetic standards and the *mores* of society in a state of dynamic equilibrium, and the poet confesses to Paci at this stage in his career that the latter's critique of certain of his poems from precisely a phenomenologist standpoint had proved to be a revelation to him (*Lettere a un fenomenologo*, 63). A little later, in the summer of 1959, he again wrote to Paci and quoted Mario Diacono, who had in the meantime observed that the phenomenologist philosopher had discovered 'una corrispondenza sostanziale tra la poetica della memoria e i temi fondamentali della fenomenologia di Husserl' (ibid., 66) [a substantial correspondence between the poetics of memory and the fundamental themes of Husserl's phenomenology]. This is a view with which the poet completely concurred and believed he had discovered for himself.

The fundamental redimensioning of the 'Ultimi cori' seems to have begun with the addition of the first three lyrics which together emphasize the poet's metaphysical belief in the contingency of life.

Their opening statements are indeed as arresting as the two which previously prefaced 'Il capitano' in *Sentimento del tempo*. Here, for instance, is the opening of the first chorus:

Agglutinati all'oggi
I giorni del passato
E gli altri che verranno.

[Glued to today / the days of the past / and the others to come.]
The growing tension of this existential perspective, moreover, gradually builds up to a climax, so that in the third lyric Aeneas's attitude to life is to be identified with a final assertion of the bedouin-poet's 'disponibilità':

Quando un giorno ti lascia,
Pensi all'altro che spunta.

È sempre pieno di promesse il nascere
Sebbene sia straziante
E l'esperienza d'ogni giorno insegni
Che nel legarsi, sciogliersi o durare
Non sono i giorni se non vago fumo.

[When one day leaves you, / think of the next which is rising. //
Birth is always full of promise / although it is agonizing / and the experience of every day teaches / that in fusing together, melting or lasting / one's days are nothing more than wayward smoke.]
But, although these three initial lyrics emphasize the ephemerality of life, the second also reintroduces the same quality of spiritual inwardness, the same process of absorption of the external world, that had previously been Ungaretti's established means of transmuting familiar objects into essential parts of himself. The process is fundamentally evaluative in its effects, since the recurrent symbolic suspension of certain 'laric' objects in the poet's imagery opens up the multiple facets of his temporally-acquired perspective on life. Hence, especially in old age, he consolidates in his mind a kind of obsessive mental picture, which again substitutes the objects of a memorial inner space, weight for weight and extension for extension, as it were, for the infinite void of physical reality outside himself:

La persona, l'oggetto o la vicenda
O gl'inconsueti luoghi o i non insoliti
Che mossero il delirio, o quell'angoscia,
O il fatuo rapimento
Od un affetto saldo,
sono, immutabili, me divenuti.

[The person, object or event / or unaccustomed or accustomed haunts / which spurred delight, or that anguish, / or the fleeting rapture / or a steadfast affection / have become myself, unchangeable.]

After this consolidation of his inner substance out of the very elements of Heraclitean flux, the poet eventually reverts to a meditative mood and asks himself what is his ultimate goal. He suggests that existence is not teleological in any way, or if it is then our goal is not ahead but behind us, in that primal image of which he has already spoken. Life, once it starts, is by its very nature open-ended, though perhaps it is governed and modified by the intentionality of the individual as he transforms his projects throughout his entire existence. So in the fifth lyric he reverts once more to the idea of the wasteland and the experience-hungry 'agneauloup' of his youth. This early figure now feeds on a desperate hope in his maturity and scours the desert with nothing left but the scattered fragments of primeval truth as a guide:

Si percorre il deserto con residui
Di qualche immagine di prima in mente,

Della Terra Promessa
Nient'altro un vivo sa.

[One scours the desert with the residue / of some primal image in mind, / / of the Promised Land / nothing else do the living know.]

Perhaps, the poet asserts, new laws will be discovered on Sinai, like those formerly brought down by Moses; but the only real law is the temporal one which cruelly undermines our illusions and offers us nothing more than a void as our goal.

From this we can deduce that the poem is attempting to build up to a kind of ultimate symphony in which Ungaretti's archetypal images are once more subtly recombined to evoke the essential harmonics of a complete, if disillusioned, existence. The poet is still in questioning mood, anxiously exploring and exploiting his disillusionment to its uttermost limits. So much so that he even begins to doubt the validity of memorial survival after death, and with it the very foundation of that cumulative human tradition which up till that point he had himself used as a foil against the unfeeling enormity of the cosmos:

È sopravvivere alla morte, vivere?

Si oppone alla tua sorte una tua mano,

Ma l'altra, vedi, subito t'accerta
Che solo puoi afferrare
Bricioli di ricordi.

[Is surviving death, living? / One of your hands resists your fate, / but the other, you see, at once assures you / that you can only grasp / tatters of memory.]

So far the questioning has been wholly concerned with the life of the poet who has conducted a self-exploration into the meaning of existence; but in the eighth lyric a second protagonist appears on the scene. This second person is probably Ungaretti's wife who was at that time in poor health and indeed died soon after, towards the end of 1958. Yet her revived presence is not the major enigma associated with the present lyric, since the English reader will immediately recognize its opening lines as being virtually a literal translation of John Donne's 'The Good-morrow', in which an eternal love triumphs over disillusionment and death. Let us first of all compare the relevant texts. Part of Donne's opening stanza reads as follows:

I wonder by my troth, what you, and I,
Did till we lov'd? were we but wean'd till then?
But suck'd our countrey pleasures, childishly?
Or snorted in the seaven sleepers den?

These lines are paralleled, even though in a slightly modified form, by Ungaretti's:

Sovente mi domando
Come eri ed ero prima.

Vagammo forse vittime del sonno?

Gli atti nostri eseguiti
Furono da sonnambuli, in quei tempi?

[Often I wonder / what you and I were before. // Did we perhaps wander, victims of sleep? // Our acts, were they carried out / as if by sleepwalkers, in those days?]

Quite clearly, the comparison is startling; though, nevertheless, it is impossible to tell whether Ungaretti wrote the poem consciously or unconsciously as a counterpoint to Donne's lyric. A letter to Paci (*Lettere a un fenomenologo*, 57) in which he adds a further stanza to those given above seems to imply that he was unconscious of the parallel to the last; although what makes us somewhat doubtful about this is the further idea appearing in the additional lines of the merging of the lover's bodies. Donne's lines read:

> What ever dyes was not mixt equally;
> If our two loves be one, or, thou and I
> Love so alike, that none doe slacken, none can die.

There is, of course, not a hint of literalness at this stage, but the idea of the blending of two personalities in Ungaretti's lines, though memorially cast into a halo of echoes, is still cumulative evidence of literary refraction:

> Siamo lontani, in quell'alone d'echi,
> E mentre in me riemergi, nel brusío
> Mi ascolto che da un sonno ti sollevi
> Che ci previde a lungo.
> [We are afar, in that halo of echoes, / and while in me you re-emerge, in the rustling / I listen to myself since you rise from a sleep / which foresaw us long ago.]

Furthermore, the poet tells us that he found these verses on the back of an old envelope and repolished them before sending them to Paci; so that they may well have been sketched out at the same time as the rest of the lyric and the origin of the whole sequence forgotten.

On the other hand, the elegiac note shows us conclusively that Donne's words have been wholly absorbed and transformed into Ungaretti's world outlook. No further proof is needed than the fact that the person concerned is resurrected in the Italian poet's mind through the whispering of memory. Thus, whereas the English poet looked for solace from his beloved in the present and future, Ungaretti looks for it solely in a past perspective, thereby greatly modifying the impact of the entire situation. Indeed, if Donne's vision aims at justifying love's immortality by a conceit resulting from equal mixtures, the Italian poet's aim is the exact opposite: he does not justify his love through its immortality but immortality itself as being possible only through a surviving bond of love and its lingering memorial echoes.

The ninth lyric rings subtle variations on the above-mentioned concept of an immortal, if memorial, love, since it returns to the theme of time and rebirth, and both are set once again in an obsessive February landscape denoting an incipient spring. This section of the 'Ultimi cori', in fact, was once published as a separate poem,[4] and in it the poet's birthday and the cycle of nature take on the appearance of an orphic return. Likewise he now reintroduces the symbol of death, but only to wonder, as he continues his fundamental questioning, whether death too is not just another realm of illusion like life:

Mentre arrivo vicino al gran silenzio,
Segno sarà che niuna cosa muore
Se ne ritorna sempre l'apparenza?

O saprò finalmente che la morte
Regno non ha che sopra l'apparenza?

[When I draw close to the great silence, / will it be a sign that
nothing dies / if its likeness always returns? // Or shall I know at
last that death / has no dominion except over appearances?]
Though tentatively expressed, this belief in an eternal periodicity in
existence stands in contrast with his previously expressed feeling that
life is a continual process of disintegration, and it shows a distinct
recovery from the nadir of his hopes.

The next two choruses deal more optimistically with Ungaretti's
sense of love, although it is again perhaps a joy drawn memorially
from despair in so far as it commemorates his wife's death. Both lyrics
refer to a feminine absence and the delirium of desire the poet experiences at the lady's recall, in such lines as:
Le tue memori membra,
Tenebra aggiungono al mio buio solito ... ;
[Your memorable limbs, / add darkness to my accustomed
gloom.]
or else:
È nebbia, acceca vaga, la tua assenza,
È speranza che logora speranza ...
[A mist, which wayward blinds, is your absence, / it is hope
which gnaws away at hope.]
By the twelfth lyric, however, this intimate personal mourning
opens out into a more cosmic kind of gloom and, again in a letter to
Paci (*Lettere a un fenomenologo*, 60), Ungaretti tells us he is dealing
with the decadence of Europe in which the redness of a sunset is
correlative to the redness of blood. In contrast with this evocation of
a Spenglerian catastrophe, the red of the rose in the next lyric
(number 13) typifies the poet's figurations of residual love in his old
age. It also shows once more the dual thread upon which the modern
poet's life is woven, since a secret inner consolation always manages
to offset the horrors of cosmic despair:
Rosa segreta, sbocci sugli abissi
Solo ch'io trasalisca rammentando
Come improvvisa odori
Mentre si alza il lamento.

[Secret rose, you bloom over abysses / if only I shudder remembering / how unexpectedly you become fragrant / while a lamentation arises.]

The fifteenth lyric again reverts to the theme of love but now in its primitive sexual form, as in the section *Amore* of *Sentimento del tempo*. We are told that the chorus

è canto nato da esperienza sessuale. È un Adamo ed Eva: nell'atto la curiosità di conoscenza dell'uno il delirio di perdizione dell'altra. (*Lettere a un fenomenologo*, 60)

[is a song born from sexual experience. It is an Adam and Eve: in the act, the thirst for knowledge of the one and the delirium of perdition of the other.]

Later, this sense of perdition seems again to become cosmicized by the Promethean overreaching of man's sacrilegious pride, mirrored in the sixteenth and seventeenth choruses celebrating the most rash of all man's achievements so far, the launching of artificial satellites. But even this achievement, or so the poet claims, can only link our solitude from star to star. On the other hand, the type of solitude he depicts at this point still retains a touch of human scale about it: it is no more than a generalization of the solitude of the lonely old man, deprived of wife and child, raised in the nineteenth lyric virtually to a heroic level:

Veglia e sonno finiscano, si assenti

Dalla mia carne stanca,

D'un tuo ristoro, senza tregua spasimo.

[Let waking and sleep end, let there be divested / from my weary flesh, / your healing touch, unceasingly I quiver with anguish.]

As is usual with Ungaretti, this intense form of solitude can only be overcome by communion with the dead, and it is through them that he now hopes to consolidate his memories, as the shadows of evening on the literal – and of old age on the symbolic – plane foregather:

È senza fiato, sera, irrespirabile,

Se voi, miei morti, e i pochi vivi che amo,

Non mi venite in mente

Bene a portarmi quando

Per solitudine, capisco, a sera.

[It is motionless, the evening, unbreathable, / if you my dead and the few living beings I love, / do not come to mind / and bear me affection when / through solitude, I comprehend, at eventide.]

The twenty-third lyric again touches on man's wilful overreaching, his 'volere fatale' [fateful will] and tendency towards 'dismisura' [disproportion], in the modern world. The poet feels the point keenly as he flies in a jet high above the clouds between Hong Kong and Beirut. Debenedetti, in fact, interprets this lyric as a prefiguration of an orphic state of death, because the poet is suspended in the milky whiteness of the clouds, as if he were hanging there, motionless, with a sky below him as well as above.[5] Likewise, when he later returns with Sinisgalli to Egypt (again by air as symbolized by the 'nibbio' [kite] in the twenty-fourth lyric), the desert archetype reappears in all its starkness. Though now it is no longer a wasteland in which to work out the remainder of the bedouin-poet's life, but rather one on which he will finally deposit his bones; and they too, not unexpectedly, have the sparkling whiteness of an orphic residue about them:

> Mi afferri nelle grinfie azzurre il nibbio
> E, all'apice del sole,
> Mi lasci sulla sabbia
> Cadere in pasto ai corvi.
> ....
> Poi mostrerà il beduino,
> Dalla sabbia scoprendolo
> Frugando col bastone,
> Un ossame bianchissimo.

[Let the kite grip me in its blue talons / and, at the sun's zenith, / drop me on the sand / as food for crows. / / ... / / Then the bedouin will show, / by discovering them in the sand / as he rummages with his stick / a pile of pure white bones.]

After the death of his wife, therefore, Ungaretti feels that the fires of earthly passion have finally died away and even love seems nothing more than a distant mirage from the past. At this stage he takes up again the symbol of the captain; but now he is not a captain in the army, he is represented as an old sea-dog; so that in Italian the erstwhile 'agneauloup' changes into a 'lupo di mare'. In the imagery associated with him (which has a strange Montalian ring about it) the captain can himself be seen to be moving towards death and appears to perceive love beyond death as a beacon-light, offering a haven of tranquillity after the endless flux of existence:

> Balugina da un faro
> Verso cui va tranquillo

Il vecchio capitano.

[It glimmers from a light-house / towards which calmly moves /
the old captain.]

It is on this image of a residual promise beyond the grave that the
poem ends, and in it we see Ungaretti's symbolism coming full circle
as the inner spiritual coherence of the bedouin-poet is retained despite
his many metamorphoses. The views expressed remind us powerfully
of Baudelaire's poem, 'Les phares', whose aim is similarly one of
cultural conservation; for, after celebrating the manners of Rubens,
Leonardo, Rembrandt, Michelangelo, Watteau, Goya and Delacroix
in turn, the French poet likewise concludes:

Car c'est vraiment, Seigneur, le meilleur témoignage

Que nous puissions donner de notre dignité

Que cet ardent sanglot qui roule d'âge en âge

Et vient mourir au bord de votre éternité!

[Because it is truly, Lord, the finest testimony / that we can give
of our dignity / this burning sigh which rolls from age to age /
and dies away on the edge of your eternity.]

Just as Baudelaire celebrates the beacon-lights of cultural history
within the past by reference to the tastes of these widely-differing
painters, so Ungaretti celebrates the beacon-lights of personal and
social memories within the present, and indeed tries to make a symphonic pattern out of them. In the last resort, therefore, it is not the
substance of the 'Ultimi cori' which is so important as the symphonic
blending of its many spiritual inscapes. As the poet explains himself
in a note to the work (*Poesie*, 573), these themes and superimposed
archetypes when so harmonized do not count any longer as personal
experiences, they become intersubjective by being caught up in the
subtle resonances of traditional lyrical patterns. It is then, moreover,
that they communicate their maximum of humanity, so that no
true poetry can ever be regarded as inhuman. Elsewhere he observes
in the same vein that not even his own war poetry is inhuman or
shows any enmity towards his fellow-men:

Il n'y a que la prise de conscience, et le chant qui permet
d'exprimer cette prise de conscience, de la condition humaine,
de la fraternité des hommes dans la souffrance, et dans le sentiment de l'extrême précarité de leur condition. (*Propos*, 67)

[there is only self-conscious assessment, and the song which permits the expression of that assessment of the human condition,
of the brotherhood of man in his suffering, and a feeling for the
extreme precariousness of his condition.]

We must not then misunderstand Ungaretti when occasionally he talks of the Absolute as a philosophical goal. He does not mean it in the static platonic sense, but in the sense of the conservation or crystallization into imagery – normally memorial or elegiac in quality – of one's most precious personal experiences and attributes. These features square the circle of 'Becoming' and allow the poet momentarily to recapture the initial 'Being' of pre- or post-existence through the hypostasis of personal emotivity: through a phenomeno-logical suspension of man's dynamic or contingent 'essence'. The haunting spiritual desire for absolute consolidated 'Being' ingrained in every human mind thus becomes gradually transformed in his work into the secret rhythm of mankind's emotive qualities. As the poet puts it himself:

C'est ce qui est au fond de moi-même et au fond de tout homme. L'être. La chose qui est créée, qui prend une forme, n'est-ce pas, cesse d'être rien. Elle a pris sa forme. Et le secret, c'est le secret où le poète peut arriver, puiser, si Dieu l'inspire. (*Propos*, 68)
[This is what is deep within me and deep within every man: Being. The thing which is created, which takes on form, of course, ceases to be nothing. It has taken on its form. And its secret is the secret which the poet wishes to penetrate, to draw on, if God so inspires him.]

In a sense the 'secrets' in the 'Ultimi cori' may be regarded as an ontological transformation of life's contingent memories (what the Italian phenomenologists call 'fondazione' [metaphysical founding]), themselves envisaged as an intersubjective myth. Poetry, however, can only fuse together these twin qualities of objective and subjective recollection as long as it expresses them in a dynamic lyrical pattern; otherwise, poetic substance, instead of being integrated into the musical articulation of an entire composition, is crystallized or solidi-fied into so much factual detritus and tends to lose all sense of perspec-tive. This implies that for Ungaretti pure poetry is not Brémond's idea of a lyricism devoid of substance and consisting wholly of form, it is rather one in which substance is so merged with form as to become lyrically incarnate in expression and therefore unobtrusive. In the last resort he aims at such purity in the present sequence: what he hopes to represent is the *summum* of his life's experiences *as active spirit*. Even his hopes for the after-life are no longer tainted here with metaphysical speculation, but are transformed into a redimensioned sense of the potency of human affection. Consequently, in 'Per

sempre' [For ever], the last lyric of the collection, itself a touching
tribute to his dead wife, the poet looks forward to a mystically
renewed mode of human existence with her beyond the present
limits of time:

Sarai risorta, mi farà da guida
Di nuovo la tua voce,
Per sempre ti rivedo.

[You will rise again, your voice / again will act as my guide, / for
ever I shall resee you.]

At such a juncture he considers that the whole of his bodily experience
will have been transmuted into pure spiritual communion, not necessarily a communion with God but with that heavenly humanity
already prefigured in lines quoted from 'La preghiera' in *Sentimento
del tempo* (see p.114).

The next collection *Morte delle stagioni* (1967) is structurally less well
organized than its predecessor, since it is largely a reprint of *La terra
promessa* and *Il taccuino del vecchio*. Even so, it contains two new compositions, 'Apocalissi' written in early 1961 and first published in
volume form in a reprint of the *Taccuino* in 1963, and 'Proverbio',
until that time completely unpublished. These then will be the two
poems that we shall now consider. The first 'Apocalissi' provides us
with an image of the apocalyptic dawning of man's intellectual pride,
again perhaps to be associated with old age and decadence, though
this time in the race. Thereafter he is haunted by the memory of his
lost innocence and simultaneously stimulated by an irrepressible
anxiety for knowledge. He uses thought as a stepping-stone to reach
a new self-conscious 'paradise regained', thought which he constantly
annuls within himself. But, although through his mind he succeeds
in conquering matter, the more he appears to approach ultimate
truth by way of his technical ingenuity, the wider becomes his rift
with the spiritual universe. The constant fading of the primal image
is then put in an almost Reborian form of poetic argument:

La verità, per crescita di buio
Piú a volarle vicino s'alza l'uomo,
Si va facendo la frattura fonda.

[The truth, through an increase of darkness, / the more man
raises himself to fly towards it, / keeps making the fracture
deepen.]

Later, in 'Proverbio' [Proverb], this deepseated ambivalence
inherent in the human condition is momentarily resolved once more

through love, which alone now appears to be the ontological reason for song. The cosmic gratuitousness of all human singing is nevertheless emphasized in the first couplet where the poet acknowledges the desperation of his condition by writing:

S'incomincia per cantare
E si canta per finire.
[One begins by singing / and one sings at the finish.]

Although such a pose seems to imply that the bedouin-poet is merely singing to keep his courage up, and that it marks the final renunciation of his receptivity and hunger for life, this is not in fact the case. Even later we find that human love can still move Ungaretti to new heights of lyricism and his meetings with the Brazilian poetess Bruna Bianco and a Yugoslav girl called Dunja conclusively prove the point.

His relationship with Bruna Bianco forms the substance of his final volume of poetry *Dialogo* (1968) and it contains not only Ungaretti's lyrics addressed to her but also her replies. We shall, of course, be mainly concerned with Ungaretti's contributions, though it should be noted in passing that to a large extent his affection was reciprocated. Bigongiari regards the entire collection as paralleling the Dante of the *Vita nuova* [New life].[6] He points out that like Dante's spiritual awakening after his meeting with Beatrice, Ungaretti's mad and incorrigible 'new life' on the brink of death also amounts to a new awakening, involving a sacrificial offering of his heart to his love in the form of an auto-eucharistic ritual (see 'È l'ora famelica'). But even granted this ritualistic symbolism (and here we note, incidentally, that Bruna like Beatrice in Dante's dream is dressed in red when she first appears before the poet, quite apart from there being a mention of a parallel eating of the poet's heart), these love-poems are still fully comprehensible in terms of the momentary reflaring of passion, and it is in this literal sense that we prefer to interpret them. Nevertheless, the ritualistic background is probably the stimulus to some of their lyrical intensity, since the bonds of affection are deepened by subtle religious undertones, in which desire is closely linked to an almost mystical vision of spectral subsisting.

In the section *Ungà* the skein of imagery evoked by the poet's reawakened senses is presented in dramatic, baroque form, as may be seen from his description of his initial encounter with Bruna, which – according to the title of the poem – took place in Brazil on 12 September 1966:

Sei comparsa al portone

> In un vestito rosso
> Per dirmi che sei fuoco
> Che consuma e riaccende.
> [You appeared at the doorway / in a red dress / to tell me you
> are fire / which consumes and rekindles.]

Such an intense comparison is perhaps more traditionally baroque
than is usual with Ungaretti because it tends to disembody the object
of his love and make her both more and less than a distant vision of
feminine beauty. Hence she becomes virtually the flame of passion in
its very quintessence. On the other hand, other lyrics in the sequence
deal with his relationship in a more intimate way, and even in this
poem he gives us a touching description of a lovers' tryst, though
deep affection rather than overwhelming passion emerges from the
situation:

> Era di lunedí,
> Per stringerci le mani
> E parlare felici
> Non si trovò rifugio
> Che in un giardino triste
> Della città convulsa.
> [It was Monday, / to hold hands / and speak happily / we found
> no refuge / except in a sad garden / in the convulsed city.]

The poet naturally realizes that his affair with Bruna can only be a
momentary consolation; and so, although he feels overwhelmed by
it, he knows that eventually it will provoke an even more exasperat-
ing despair, as mirages of redemptive oases once did in the desert for
the bedouin-poet:

> Ma, per me, stella
> Che mai non finirai d'illuminare,
> Un tempo ti è concesso troppo breve,
> Mi elargisci una luce
> Che la disperazione in me
> Non fa che acuire.
> [But, for me, star / that will never fail to shine, / too brief a
> time has been granted to you, / you offer me a light / which in
> me can only / sharpen despair.]

Nevertheless, in 'È l'ora famelica' [It is the time of hunger], the
violence of his feelings finally overcomes his caution and the poet,
as already indicated, expresses a wish to tear out his heart and eat it,
so that he may sate his desire. Old age and its memories which hang
over him like a leaden weight of disillusionment might then be

momentarily dissipated as the emotivity of Bruna's love, entering his heart, renewed it. Indeed, she does eventually redeem him for a while, as he explains in 'Hai visto spegnersi', from the lassitude of age:

> Hai visto spegnersi negli occhi miei
> L'accumularsi di tanti ricordi,
> Ogni giorno di più distruggitori,
> E un unico ricordo
>
> Formarsi d'improvviso.
> L'anima tua l'ha chiuso nel mio cuore
> E ne sono rinato.

[You have seen extinguished in my eyes / the accumulation of so many memories, / every day more destructive, / and a single memory / / suddenly take form. / Your soul has enfolded it in my heart / and from it I am reborn.]

What is particularly noticeable in this passage is that in the immediacy of his new love the memories which he once held to be his life's consolation themselves turn corrosive, and they are replaced by the less shadowy consolations of a miracle in the present. Such an idea, however, is not really intended to run counter to his previous philosophy, but simply to emphasize the very intensity of this passionate interlude, which can seemingly modify even his deep-seated sense of anguish.

The point is later offset in 'Conchiglia' [Sea-shell], a poem written in two separate versions. Here the poet warns his beloved of the dangers of their relationship, because, if she should put the shell of his memorial darkness to her ear (and in a variant of 'Popolo' he had previously referred to a sea-shell as an 'amuleto d'amore' [an amulet of love]), she would hear the distant echoes of his anguish reverberating down the years; and she too would then become afraid as she gained some intimation of the profundity of his desolation:

> Se tu quella paura,
> Se tu la scruti bene,
> Mia timorosa amata,
> Narreresti soffrendo
> D'un amore demente
> Ormai solo evocabile
> Nell'ora degli spettri.

[If that fear / you should examine closely, / my timorous beloved, / anguish-stricken you would tell / of a demented love / now only to be evoked / in the hour of spectres.]

This feeling of desolation, moreover, would become all the more poignant, since she would be sure to pick up not only the echoes of his past but also those of his foreshortened future and approaching death. Does any comfort then remain for Ungaretti after making such a realistic assessment of his temporal condition? As a truly existential poet he tells us that he can still be partly consoled by the terrestrial pleasure of her flashing smile.

Although Leopardian echoes still operate in these poems, they tend to do so in the opposite way from those to be found in Leopardi's own lyric, 'A Silvia', since the fates of the respective protagonists are reversed. For Ungaretti the bond of affection between himself and Bruna is an eternal – yet existential – bond of fidelity which has the power to overcome the anguish of their earthly plight:

> Ma se mi guardi con pietà,
> E mi parli, si diffonde una musica,
> Dimentico che brucia la ferita.
> [But if you look at me with pity, / and speak to me, a music spreads around, / I forget that the wound burns.]

Silvia, on the other hand, is only evoked in her tremulous existentiality by Leopardi for the purpose of leading up to an imaginative definition of the hopelessness of the human condition; and, as we know, at the end of the poem she is converted into a symbol of death's inevitability:

> Tu, misera, cadesti: e con la mano
> La fredda morte ed una tomba ignuda
> Mostravi di lontano.
> [You, wretched one, fell: and with your hand / cold death and a naked tomb / you showed from afar.]

What undoubtedly saves Ungaretti from a similar form of pessimism is his sense of limited, yet eternal, hope springing from his reliance on the traditional values of mankind and associated mysteriously with the 'primal image' in his imagination. They come to the fore again here in 'Superstite infanzia', but they are so mingled with suffering at present that they too almost seem to him like a new type of alienation arising in his old age. But the poet continues to wish to live his existential tension as a man without escapism of any kind. If then his love for Bruna is to be considered as a screen in any way (and here we revert to the procedures of the *Vita nuova*), it is a screen used simply for the purpose of concealing an ever-hopeful, though deep-seated and experience-laden, form of existential stoicism.

Love's allusive and perhaps illusory consolations are, moreover, powerfully maintained by Bruna's replies, for in contrast with the hopeful desperation of his responses she raises the clarion-call of youth, assuring him that her affection will liberate him from his feeling of being out of joint with the times and so rejuvenate his shattered emotions:

Ma dall'esilio ci libererà
L'ostinato mio amore. (Poesie, 311)
[But from exile will liberate us / my persistent love.]

In short, she momentarily tips the balance away from stoicism towards further participation in life, and the bedouin-image of constant receptivity and constant rejuvenation through new experiences is again revived.

Surprising as it may seem, not even Ungaretti's love affair with Bruna marks the final stage in his emotional relations with women, though certainly his later affection for the Yugoslav girl Dunja is by no means as passionate or as all-consuming. She reminds him, in fact, of the old servant from 'Le bocche di Cattaro' who had nursed him in his childhood and who was also, we recall, a Yugoslav. In his preface to the poems addressed to Dunja he telescopes his vision of the two women, saying:

Ho ritrovato Dunja l'altro giorno, ma senza piú le grinze d'un secolo d'anni che velandoli le sciupavano gli occhi rimpiccioliti, ma con il ritorno scoperto degli occhioni notturni, scrigni di abissi di luce. Di continuo ora la vedo bellissima giovane, Dunja, nell'oasi apparire, e non potrà piú attorno a me desolarmi il deserto, dove da tanto erravo. (Poesie, 324)
[I refound Dunja the other day, no longer with the wrinkles acquired in a hundred years which troubled her shrunken eyes by veiling them, but with the open return of her large nocturnal eyes, caskets of abysmal light. I now continually see her as a lovely young woman, this Dunja, appearing in the oasis, and the desert around me can no longer distress me, in which I wandered for so long.]

Although the poet once again describes his emotion in terms of passion as he gazes on her:

Si volge verso l'est l'ultimo amore,
Mi abbuia da là il sangue
Con tenebra degli occhi della cerva,
[My last love is directed to the east, / from there my blood grows troubled / in the darkness of the eyes of the hind]

he nevertheless treats her largely as the indulgent father treats his favourite daughter. As in Arabic poetry, her youth, her lithe grace, and her affection cause him to compare her with the tenderest of animals like the hind or the foal, or, alternatively, with that most feline of all creatures, the leopard. Indeed it was probably because of the duality of her nature that Ungaretti's love for Dunja appears to him to be the most anguished of all; although his anguish, at least in part, now derives from memory rather than from immediate desire:

> L'ultimo amore piú degli altri strazia,
> Certo lo va nutrendo
> Crudele il ricordare.
> [The last love more than the others sears, / certainly it is fed / cruelly by memory.]

On the other hand, one cannot help noticing certain residual images of the Eve archetype in this poem, especially in such sybilline verses as the following:

> O, nuovissimo sogno, non saresti
> Per immutabile innocenza innata
> Pecorella d'insolita avventura?
> [O, newest of dreams, might you not be / through an innate and immutable innocence / a lamb of unusual encounter?]

Or, alternatively, in her ability to inspire insights beyond memory:

> D'oltre l'oblio rechi
> D'oltre il ricordo i lampi.
> [From beyond oblivion you bring / flashes, from beyond memory.]

In this regard the poet informs us that the nomad of the desert would immediately remind him that 'Dunja' in his language means 'universe', and the spiralling infinity of the poet's memorial universe is certainly reawakened by her beauty. Yet she does not only offer him the bonds of a sensuous slavery, she also provides a further consolation through pity. Hence in the second poem addressed to her, after a regression of thousands of years through time, her velvet eyes draw him sharply up before an immediate fulminatory emotion:

> Il velluto dello sguardo di Dunja
> Fulmineo torna presente pietà.
> [The velvet of Dunja's look / in a flash becomes present pity.]

Consequently with her, as with Bruna, the galvanizing bond of love and pity revitalizes the poet's sensibility and fills him, if not with a young lover's ecstasy, at least with a certain gentle hopefulness in his dialogue of despair with death. No doubt it was on this note that Ungaretti intended his poetry to end, because his contingent outlook on life always required him to offset the absoluteness of the past tradition and its imperturbable monuments with the fragile grace of the human form and the fluctuating emotional tensions of immediate living.

The dominant atmosphere of this last stage in Ungaretti's poetic career is accordingly characterized by the title of his penultimate collection, *Morte delle stagioni*, and its dominant symbol is undoubtedly the figure of Aeneas. For, just as Aeneas symbolically carried his father, Anchises, on his back, so Ungaretti carries on his shoulders the whole memorial burden of the Italian tradition. Indeed, this last period of his old age is deeply marked by an attempt to hallow and consolidate his imagery by blending the whole range of his personal melodies with the rich organ-music of traditional harmonies. In order to achieve his aim, the poet divests his poetic line of all decorative materials, all superfluous sensory elements, and even dematerializes his baroque imagery in an effort to combine, without distorting them, emotive and lyrical elements drawn from the past with his own personal recollections. In a sense, it is true, this period will seem somewhat more fragmentary than earlier ones, despite the unifying presence of Virgil and Leopardi and the mature existential outlook attributable to the symbol of Aeneas; but the symphonic intention nevertheless emerges frequently from the somewhat fragmentary performance, so that the constant fluctuation of emotion in the poet's chance encounters with life serves to highlight and offset the double thread of hope and despair on which his contingentist attitudes are based. The alternate waxing and waning of these two veins of inspiration give the impression that his last poems are still poems of genuine experience, of deep participation in life, rather than mere attempts at lyrical consolidation. They still represent a poetry in continual progress whose achievements are not to be assessed simply by their temporal extension but more appropriately by their sense of emotive and aesthetic depth. The symbolic complexity which results is the product of Ungaretti's unending struggle to transmute his most deeply-felt personal vicissitudes into a highly flexible and infinitely responsive word-music, and this resilient form of lyrical sensitivity, especially noticeable in the 'Ultimi cori', operates both as a continuation to, and as a commentary upon, the whole corpus of his previous work.

8. Conclusion

Despite the fact that much of the present book has been concerned with Ungaretti's lyricism, it would nevertheless be mistaken to consider him as being exclusively a poet. To adopt such an attitude would really be to diminish the relevance of his achievement which can only be described adequately within the context of his presence as a human being and literary thinker in the broadest sense of the word. As he himself observed as early as 1931:

> Je ne suis pas un 'poète' mais un 'homme' – l'espèce en est rare en effet – qui a toujours brûlé sa vie pour quelque chose de bien plus grand que l'homme et cela, en effet, c'est de la poésie. (*Saggi*, 38)
> [I am not a 'poet' but a 'man' – the species is in fact rare – who has always burned up his life for something much greater than man, and that indeed is poetry.]

We have to regard him, therefore, as a critic of life and culture as well as a major twentieth-century lyricist, because it was above all his activity as an innovator of taste and perspective which allowed him – almost without intending it – to dominate the aesthetic and poetic scene in Italy for close on fifty years.

Ungaretti would undoubtedly have been the first to admit that he grew up in the atmosphere of the late decadent age, and would also readily have acknowledged that the symbolist and other *fin de siècle* movements operated as formative backgrounds for his creative activity. But he is never himself tarred with the decadent brush, despite the fact that he seems to move freely within its poetic ethos. This is because decadentism, as Petrocchi has explained,[1] is essentially a passive submission by the artist to external circumstances, a self-imposed surrender to the moods, sensations, literary fashions and muted religious aspirations of a particular social consciousness; whereas Ungaretti's 'uomo di pena' [man of grief] is on the other hand a thorough-going active (or reactive) individual conforming to Valéry's definition of 'italianità' which the Italian poet himself reports as comprising 'Semplicità di vita – Nudità interiore – Bisogni ridotti al minimo – Gusto del reale spinto all' essenziale' (*Saggi*, 623) [Simplicity of life-style – Inner nakedness – Needs reduced to

the minimum – A taste for the real taken to the limits of the essential].
In short, Ungaretti is an individual who strips life down to its essentials
and tries to refashion the aesthetics, rather than be absorbed by the
conventions, of the society in which he lives. Yet we must also con-
cede that even he at times can be demoralized by his innate foreknowledge of life's despairing contingency.

To counteract this continual potential of despair he realized from
the beginning that his sensibility needed to be positively structured,
not passively receptive; and its vital active element gradually proved
to be an orphic process of momentary self-oblivion, an ability to
annihilate the sensory blandishments of the external world for the
purpose of re-creating it inwardly as a transfigured reality or
manifestation of the human spirit's inventiveness. From this process
he produced a new sphere of art which is characterized by what he
calls 'una conoscenza mistica dell realità' (*Saggi*, 131) [a mystical
knowledge of reality]; but for him even the adjective 'mystical'
seems to take on a special sense, one which is perhaps Leopardian in
origin and signifies 'overwhelmingly complex', or rather 'sommer-
gente' [submersive], in the Italian meaning of the word. The atmosphere it evokes represents a subtle blending of sensory and spiritual
elements, which aim at producing infinite lyrical resonances in the
sensibility; and these have the effect of causing the human mind to
become awe-stricken or mesmerized by the multiple implications of
the poetic situations which it has itself constructed. This is what we
mean when we speak of the present poet's endogenous cult of lyrical
self-surprise, as opposed to the traditional baroque poet's exogenous
cult of artful 'meraviglia' [wonder], first expressed in Marino's series
of elegantly-contrived but largely decorative conceits.

However, in all but the essential nucleus of his spiritual method on
which his aesthetic outlook is based, Ungaretti readily concedes the
primacy for his poetic impulses to the particular circumstances into
which existence has cast him, and the whole trajectory of his lyricism
follows the Petrarchan norm of recording a spiritual biography
which reflects his authentic responses to life's crucial experiences. As
he again explains,

> poesia è quella prodigiosa facoltà concessa a taluni uomini di
> usare gli oggetti del mondo esterno come immanenti specchi
> della loro vita morale. (*Saggi*, 14)
> [poetry is that prodigious faculty granted to few men to use the
> objects of the external world as immanent mirrors of their moral
> existence.]

In his case these experiences are the product of a three-fold symbiosis: the combining of his peculiar, pre-conceived attitude towards poetic creation with certain distilled, lyrical refractions from the tradition, and simultaneously with his own immediate sense-impressions. Although at first sight such a symbiosis may seem commonplace, its subtlety in Ungaretti's hands should not be underestimated, because unlike most other poets he undertakes the highly ambitious task of compelling the past tradition to coalesce and manifest itself multi-dimensionally within his melodic line. His form of representation is intended to symbolize the authentic voice of an entire culture expressed concretely – one could almost say corporeally – in all its sensory manifestations and tensions within a twentieth-century context. By such means his art is transformed into a multiple resonance-chamber, or rather a triangle of spiritual forces, held together in dynamic equilibrium by the magic of analogy and the qualitative richness – rather than the crude quantitative extension – of its imaginative texture. At all times he consciously aims at dramatizing the perennial re-emergence in the present moment of the age-old myth of man; and this myth, despite its location in a modern cultural sphere, remains touched by the time-spun hallowedness of our primitive origins and all subsequent cultural developments. It is in fact expressed not through a series of subtly-prepared machinations of the sensibility but, as his cult of variants clearly testifies, in the form of a spontaneous determination to unearth the secret inflections of our modern emotional responses and mirror them in temporally-saturated, yet open-ended, lyrical procedures.

Ungaretti's combination of a self-conscious artistry and a spontaneous understanding of the configuration of modern word-music is to be attributed to his inner sense of the artist's responsibility; and, in accepting the implications of that responsibility, he found throughout his career that he had to practise a coherent universalist, rather than a narrowly metaphysical, approach to experience. Essentially this is a multiple or multi-dimensional approach which reflects and magnifies sensory and spiritual situations for the purpose of transforming them into symbolic archetypes of the deeper truths of the human tradition. The result, as Negri has stressed,[2] is a type of mental combustion, and in this rhapsodic state of meditative insight the poet fuses the classical concept of continuity with the romantic – and later the futurist – idea of the necessary simultaneity of all lyrical tensions within the sphere of art.

The process is so deep-rooted, so authentically a reflection of the inner reaches of his sensibility, that not even his baroque cast of mind appears premeditated. Therefore, unlike Govoni's equally clear cult of baroque forms, his never seems to succumb to the rhetorical temptations of artifice. It amounts instead, as we have already stressed, to a deeply experienced form of self-surprise, in which the poet remains dumbfounded by the vigour and freshness of his own imagery. Admittedly, as Mario Diacono has pointed out (*Saggi*, XXXI), Ungaretti's poetry is not always exempt from a cult of a 'barocco esacerbato' [exacerbated baroque]; but even in his moments of baroque rage, as we have seen from 'Tu ti spezzasti' in *Il dolore*, no trace of deliberate artificiality emerges. This is because he is always conscious of the artist's need to remain faithful to the bedrock of emotive sincerity, which he senses is the only way of evoking 'una realtà mitica, una realtà che trasfiguri il linguaggio per profondità di memoria' (*Poesie*, 553) [a mythical reality, a reality which transfigures language through the profundity of memory].

Ungaretti's cult of myth also helps to provide him with a sense of tone, partly through unifying personal experiences and partly through evoking literary reminiscences. To express his vision in an integrated way he appears to combine Mallarmé's understanding of musicality as the inner articulation of the conscience with Ghil's more technical views on the subject in his concept of 'instrumentation verbale'. Although the latter inclines towards artful phonic combinations, we can never consider Ungaretti's literary refractions to be five-fingered exercises on other writers' verbal harmonies, since his 'imitations' are chiefly of lyrical modes, not of crudely plagiarized images or words. Consequently, even during his highly Petrarchan moments there always remains uppermost a touch of his own plashing, impressionistic melodiousness, as may be seen in the following lines taken from the eleventh lyric of the 'Ultimi cori':

> Da te lontano piú non odo ai rami
> I bisbigli che prodigano foglie. ...
> [From you, faraway, I no longer hear in the branches / the whispers that leaves prodigiously scatter.]

In the same way we rarely find a direct model for his peculiar baroque vision, only distant resonances of its spiritual and verbal modalities. When he seeks to express a particular baroque flavour in his verse, however, we sense that a certain verbal dexterity is always predominant, as may be seen in his evocation of a tremulous cataclysm in 'Lago Luna Alba Notte' [Lake Moon Dawn Night]:

Impallidito livore rovina ...
[A paling leadenness crumbles.]
The effect of this line depends in the first place on the repetition of the
liquid sounds 'lli' and 'li' in the first two words, which give the
reader the impression of a continuous gliding motion. This is then
reinforced in the second and third words in two ways, both of which
evoke a distinct impression of cataclysmic collapse. The first derives
from the replacement of the liquid 'l' by the more rapid – yet still
liquid – 'r' sounds; the second from the technique of the reverse
echo-syllable, by the change, that is, of 'vor' in 'livore' to 'rov' in
'rovina'. The result of this ingenious syllabic inversion is to quicken
the impression of an impending catastrophe in the reader's ear, even
though he may not realize exactly how the effect has been created.
Throughout his whole production, in fact, Ungaretti sets great store
by these phonic combinations supporting the sense, as Ossola has
recently shown; and yet they rarely amount to a gratuitous form of
word-play but aim instead to become functional and constitutive
parts of his modern Petrarchan word-music. As we have noted earlier,
the poet also makes skilful use of alliteration and assonance to convey
an impression of sound echoing sense, although again he does not
always confine the device to the context of a single line, because
alliteration may occur between lines as well. What he is particularly
adept at achieving in this area of musicality is the soft melodic flow
of wind or water, by a subtle combination of plosives and sibilants,
as indicated in the previously-quoted line from 'Silenzio in Liguria':
Scade flessuosa la pianura d'acqua ...
[Sinuously the watery plain slopes down.]
On the other hand, when the integration of sense and word-music
probes into the deeper regions of his conscience and when he endeavours to depict the baroque mode's aching spiritual void, his
poetic line reaches an absolute climax of visuo-imaginative tension;
and then even more subtle inflexions are brought into play. This may
be illustrated by the following breath-taking line of sexual frenzy from
'Giunone' [Juno]:
Diláti la tua fúria un'ácre nótte!
[Let your fury dilate an acrid night!]
Now this line is superficially a normal hendecasyllable with its main
stresses on 'fúria' and 'nótte'; but the secret of its lyrical resonance
lies in the secondary stresses where there is an assonantal use of 'a'
in 'diláti' and 'ácre'. By virtue of their extreme openness these 'a'
sounds echo as an undertone the fathomless depths of baroque

mystery, while at the same time an impression of the abysmal 'sub-merging' of the mind in instinctive urges is clearly produced on the linguistic level by the rushing 'r' sounds of 'furia' and 'acre'. By contrast, the basic idea of a sexual paroxysm is controlled or played down slightly by the halting staccato effect of the alliterative 't's' which tend to hamper its impassioned flow; and this process no doubt maintains an otherwise physiological form of expressionism within the realms of art.

Ungaretti appears to have learned to integrate his meditative sub-stance with appropriate tones and delicate phonic combinations principally through a series of careful studies of the Petrarchan tradi-tion, the baroque poets, and the decadent and symbolist movements. Yet even, for instance, when he is primarily concerned with the texture of his translations from Shakespeare, he still pays particular attention to subtle tonal effects (See Saggi, 552–3). In his essay on the 'Significato dei sonetti di Shakespeare' [The meaning of Shake-speare's sonnets] (1946/1962) he in fact associates an elegiac tone with the inner time-flow of memory and a certain thematic orientation, and such an intertwining of tone and lyrical substance always pro-vides, he asserts, an insight into the maturity of any particular language, simply because 'la lingua è il simbolo della civiltà d'un popolo' (Saggi, 83) [language is the symbol of a nation's state of civilization]. In part this explains the density of Ungaretti's own textural qualities, described in an intriguing way by Silori who wished to contrast their 'fulminatory' analogical discontinuities with their underlying tonal unity. For him Ungaretti's tonal dura-tion is 'a factor of expressive order in the broadest sense, that is to say, semantically, psychologically, and perhaps even morphologically and phonically, whereas continuity would only be a rigidly temporal concept'.[3] By creating this extremely broad and highly responsive tonal spectrum endued with a profound sense of humanity, Un-garetti was able to dilate the expressibility of language to the maxi-mum possible extent. Such dilation abolishes momentarily the limits imposed on our human purview and imparts to his verse a memorial form of 'divine illumination' or perhaps more appropriately, a perfectly balanced and perceptive sense of ethico-aesthetic insight.

In the same area of the expressibility of language the problem also arises of his connection with the hermetic school. It is, moreover, a problem which is complicated by the fact that critical definitions of the hermetic movement are often extremely diverse. Petrucciani,[4] for instance, confines it to the thirties which totally excludes the early

Ungaretti, while other critics actually regard him as the founding father of the hermetic style. Broadly speaking, he is perhaps the founder of an initial and basic form of hermeticism which puts the emphasis on involution as a means of dilating expression, whereas in the thirties the deployment of infolded imagery tended to become more of an end in itself, sometimes leading to mannerism and obscurity. Naturally, so stark a definition has to be hedged around with all sorts of qualifications, because not all of the early hermetic writers were authentic poets nor all later ones poetasters; but the corrosive trend within the movement still seems all too evident and, even with Ungaretti, the later versions of collections like *Allegria* are far more infolded than the preceding ones. Still, what always saves him from mannerism is the continual dominance of his inventiveness over mere stylistic virtuosity, whereas the reverse is often the case with some of his successors.

This again explains why in the fullness of time his apparent obscurities have been shown not to be obscurities at all but deep – though not immediately comprehensible – judgements on modern life. As he assures us himself in 'En face d'une crise de langage' [In the presence of a language crisis], authentic poetry is always based on inventiveness and is compounded of experience shorn of the obscurity of its temporal limitations:

> Quand l'art parvient à manifester la profondeur de l'homme, ou parvient à posséder l'illusion de la manifester, il est entré dans le domaine de la poésie où la durée efface ses limites. (*Saggi*, 881)
> [when art succeeds in depicting the profundity of man, or succeeds in conveying the illusion of doing so, it enters the domain of poetry in which duration abolishes its limits.]

Art must amount then, in the last resort, to an 'essai de connaissance de la profondeur humaine' (*Saggi*, 882) [an attempt at probing human profundity] and not to a superficial word-game or a speculative investigation. Indeed, he regards the deepest form of art as emerging only from a memorial dialectic between dreams and reality, in which, as we stated earlier, perfect insight inheres in

> un linguaggio poetico dove, nella ricerca del vero che è il sacro, la memoria s'abolisca nel sogno e dal sogno rifluisca agli oggetti, e viceversa, incessantemente (*Fedra di Jean Racine*, 11)
> [a poetic language in which, in the search for the truth which is sacred, memory annihilates itself in the dream and from the dream flows back to objects and vice versa, incessantly.]

To put the point into final perspective we can consider the Ungarettian dream as the poet's attempt to range over the vast sounding-board of traditional values. His acts of regression to a dream-like state and his subsequent returns to reality aim at infusing into present sensations a series of orphically-inspired resonances from the past to provide his sense-impressions with the necessary historical and aesthetic perspective. Indeed, the 'eternal return' to the past which such a dialectic implies is not a characteristic which is confined to the individual poet in Ungaretti's view, it can be extended to the unfolding of cultural history as a whole. What he is probably asserting is that art has tended to achieve its aims from the dawn of history right down to the present day by operating as a filter for atavistic tastes and resonances. As he puts it himself:

La poesia è scoperta della condizione umana nella sua essenza, quella d'essere un uomo d'oggi, ma anche un uomo favoloso, come un uomo dei tempi della cacciata dall'Eden: nel suo gesto d'uomo, il vero poeta sa che è prefigurato il gesto degli avi ignoti, nel seguito di secoli impossibile a risalire, oltre le origini del suo buio. (*Poesie*, 505)

[Poetry is the discovery of the human condition in its essence, that of being a man of today, but also a man of fable, a man, as it were, of the time of the Fall from Eden: in his gestures as a man, the true poet knows that the gestures of his unknown ancestors are adumbrated, in a chain of centuries which it is impossible to reascend, beyond the origins of his own darkness.]

In short, he considers it each poet's sacred duty to body forth globally in his melodic line the mysteries implicit in human history and to make every absence buried in the past a presence, because it is only through such pious recollections that the artist can reassert the continuity of the cultural tradition within the passing moment. Indeed, unless he does so reassert it, he fails to function as an artist at all, since he is unable to impose the evaluative, tonal symmetries of the humanly-consolidated past on to what is, realistically speaking, only the chance-experiences of time manifesting themselves as our current human activities.

The lineaments of Ungaretti's literary presence are accordingly to be understood in their deepest sense as a reaffirmation of the solidarity and the underlying unity of the cultural tradition, after its disruption by the futurists: a group of writers who advocated among other things the burning of libraries and the destruction of museums. In this respect his critical self-consciousness and appreciation of the importance of the past mark him off from most, if not all, of his

immediate contemporaries. As we have indicated, he does not claim
the views he puts forward in respect to the cultural process to be
wholly of his own making: they are simply the logical consequences
drawn by him from the lyrical practices of his major Petrarchan predecessors. Where then does his own originality lie? To explain this
we have to consider his critical view on Petrarch's originality with
respect to Dante. On that subject he notes:

> Come è già diversa, poco dopo, l'idea del Petrarca; parla di
> posteri e di antichi, d'un regno temporale dell'uomo, ma è idea
> già nauseata del presente, già lamentosa del passato e del futuro
> come di due paradisi perduti. (*Saggi*, 259)
>
> [How different, a little later, is the conception of Petrarch; he
> speaks of posterity and the ancients, of the temporal realm of
> man, but it is a conception nauseated by the present, already
> regretful of the past and the future as two lost paradises].

Now from this attitude we deduce that, although Petrarch replaces
Dante's conception of an objective eternity with one of human
'durata', he in turn limits his own purview by abolishing the present.
He too is alienated, in other words, from contemporary life and
forced, in the modern poet's eyes, to adopt a dissociated, dualistic
approach to experience. Ungaretti's own originality with respect to
the fourteenth-century poet must necessarily lie, therefore, in the
reintegration of the present into Petrarchist poetry. He actually
achieves this by upturning the idealistic aspirations of the symbolist
image (i.e. Mallarmé's ideal rose-image in 'l'absente de tous bouquets'
[the absent from all bouquets]) and by replacing it with an immanent,
ethical realism implicit in the hermetic analogy. So, instead of remaining a 'correspondance' in the Baudelairian sense, that is to say, a
metaphysical probe seeking to fuse the real with the ideal, his particular form of analogy becomes an authentic recollective or meditative
transfiguration of everyday experience. Even though Ungaretti's
immediate sensations then are equally swathed in memorial associations, his own view of the present, in contrast with the normal
Petrarchist's 'degraded' view of it, amounts to a type of immediacy
which has almost been fully 'redeemed'; and its redemption is brought
about not by applying memory simply as a balm to imagery, but by
using it as a way of intimately resuturing the present and the past.
Petrarch's aesthetico-moral devaluation of the current ethos of his
times is in this way partially rectified by Ungaretti, although he too
still suffers to some extent from the dissociative void left by the latter's
attitudes. This void is, in the last resort, symbolized for him by the

yawning chasm of spiritual unease which he detects in Michelangelo and the baroque Petrarchists and which he claims is also endemic in the modern lyrical outlook.

One is naturally led to speculate on whether his rehabilitation of the present through the memory will make the Ungarettian *Lebenswelt* capable of supporting a comprehensive – non-relativistic – modern mythology to replace the absoluteness of the ancient one. After all, he himself acknowledges that one of his major literary aims was to recondition language and restore to it its sense of eternity, of religious awe. Might not then his interest in the broad spectrum of St John Perse's lyricism be a pointer in this direction? Could his desire for the restoration of an overall mythology be instrumental in producing a renewed 'epic' form, which is precisely what the French poet struggled all his life to perfect? This is, in fact, not the case. If we look at his commentary on the latter's work, it is not its 'epic' framework which appears to have interested Ungaretti so much as its conforming to the modalities of his own reconditioned cultural universe. Hence he asserts:

> La poesia si manifesta ..., ci conferma l'opera di Perse, quando negli oggetti ogni memoria sembra abolirsi e vi rifluisca di colpo, come per miracolo; quando cioè il vocabolo è reso atto a passare di continuo dal distacco del sogno all'infinito dei grovigli e degli impegni della memoria. (*Saggi*, 652)
>
> [poetry manifests itself ..., as Perse's work confirms for us, when all memories appear to be annihilated in objects and suddenly flow back to them, as if by a miracle; when, that is, the word is made capable of passing continually from the detachment of the dream to the infinite complexities and obligations of memory.]

On the other hand, if we wish to perceive an incipient return to a Dantesque form of 'epic' in the hermetic movement, we have only to look to the work of Luzi and Bigongiari, to mention but two significant second-generation hermetics. In contrast with Ungaretti's (and, incidentally, with Campana's) *subjective* orphism, Luzi's in *La barca* [The boat](1935) initiates what will later be the progressive development of an *objective* orphic myth: one which evolves away from the purely inner world of the individual spirit towards a balanced assessment of the external world in a broadly social setting. This indeed may be the true direction the later hermetics were destined to take, for the earlier ones, including Ungaretti, tend to lack a strong and distinctive social conscience despite their essentialized realism.

It would, therefore, in our view be a misunderstanding of Ungaretti's artistic manner if it were to be suggested that he supported the
creation of an objective mythology of this sort. He would regard
such a *modus operandi* as putting the clock back to pre-Leopardian,
even to pre-Petrarchan times, because he was convinced that once
the relativity of existence had been discovered by Petrarch all objective myths of the ancient discursive or sociological type had become
outmoded and therapeutically ineffective. In his opinion even Petrarch
ultimately came to realize the profound revolution he had initiated,
although its deeper implications were perhaps only fully worked out
later by Leopardi. Consequently, the fourteenth-century poet sought
his new lyrical dimension within the meditative sphere of the human
spirit itself rather than in external effects, and strove to make a myth
of the poet's very thought processes. After this revolution Ungaretti
considered that the only way the artist could overcome his metaphysical sense of relativity was by continuing to move away from
objective or abstract modes of thought and creating a wider range of
fresh, subjective feelings within a sphere of ethical realism. These
indeed represent our modern standards of value, our new mythology,
whether they are expressed in an aesthetic or a moral key. Hence the
expressive absolute for him no longer subsumes eternal truth but
rather judgements or ethical meditations on life crystallized into an
appropriate aesthetic form.

From this we deduce that Ungaretti considers that immanentism
and inwardness of reflection will remain the lot of the lyricist for the
foreseeable future whether he intends it or not. So, while his own
emblems and analogies often move towards a re-creation in a modern
sense of former mythical archetypes, he believes that these must be
internalized, made relevant to the age, and above all compatible with
Petrarchan meditative attitudes before they can have any real impact
on our modern sensibilities. However, the fresh inner spiritual design
which he offers us is by no means less grandiose and all-embracing
than an objective or 'epic' one, and it tends in the fullness of time to
border on a fully-developed philosophy of art. This explains why in
the last analysis his inventiveness cannot be confined to his actual
poetic output, but is a manifestation – as he undoubtedly intended it
to be – of his entire life as a man.

CHAPTER ONE: Ungaretti's Life
1. *Ungaretti*, dirigé par P. Sanavio, 249.
2. See G. Palermo, 'Due articoli "egiziani" di Ungaretti e una poesia dispersa di Pea', in *Italianistica* (1973) 3, 557–68.
3. See 'Lo stile di Bergson', in *Vita d' un uomo: Saggi e interventi* (1974) 87.
4. In *Le gant de crin* (1927): 'Le poète est un four à brûler le réel'.

CHAPTER TWO: Personal Aesthetics
1. See F. Montanari, 'Poesia e durata', in *Studium* Anno LX (1964) 477–83.
2. Marcel Raymond, *De Baudelaire au surréalisme*, 351. See also Ezra Pound, 'Vorticism', in *Fortnightly Review* (1914) 96.
3. In 'Tradition and the individual talent', now in T. S. Eliot, *Selected Essays* (Faber & Faber, London 1963) 15.
4. L. Rebay, *Le origini della poesia di G. Ungaretti* (1962) 70–103.

CHAPTER THREE: *Allegria*
1. This poem appears in additional French poems (1914–19) published by E. Falqui in 1947 under the title of *Derniers jours 1919*, a volume which also contains *La guerre* (See *Tutte le poesie*, 363).
2. See E. Palmieri's article 'Civiltà d'oriente' in the *Corriere adriatico* (15 April 1933).
3. In *Scènes et doctrines du nationalisme* (1945) vol. 1, 93. First edition 1902.

CHAPTER FOUR: *Sentimento del tempo*
1. Ofelia d'Alba was the daughter of the poet Auro d'Alba. She was apparently extremely beautiful and died young. This information was kindly provided by Prof. Piero Bigongiari.
2. In 'Sulla genesi del "Sentimento del tempo"', in *Letteratura* (1958) 35–6, 163: 'È ricerca che riporta il poeta verso una realtà che sia umana e che nello stesso tempo divenga astrazione temporale, sublime innocenza ...'

CHAPTER FIVE: *Il dolore*
1. See G. Cambon, *Giuseppe Ungaretti* (1967) and T. O'Neill, 'Ungaretti tra Leopardi e Góngora: Appunti per una lettura di "Tu ti spezzasti"', in *Rivista di letterature moderne e comparate* XXVII (1974) 1, 50–64. Cambon has recently enlarged his work and published it in Italian under the title of *La poesia di Ungaretti*.
2. G. Marzot, *Il decadentismo italiano* (1970) 224.
3. See *Il simbolo*, Vol. IV, 152.
4. In *Letteratura* (1958) 35–6, 319.
5. U. Marvardi, 'Carattere della poesia d'oggi e Giuseppe Ungaretti', in *Responsabilità del sapere* (1947), fasc. 3, 97.
6. F. Piemontese, 'Il sentimento religioso nella poesia di Ungaretti', in *Studium* (1949) 5, 230.
7. See first version in *Parallelo* (1943) 1, under the title of 'Poeti d'oltreoceano, vi dico'. This text is now included in *Tutte le poesie*, 780–2.
8. G. Bàrberi Squarotti, *Il codice di Babele* (1972) 80–1.

CHAPTER SIX: *La terra promessa*
1. See *Pensées* (Nelson, Paris 1946) 70: 'Car, enfin, qu'est-ce que l'homme

dans la nature? Un néant à l'égard de l'infini, un tout à l'égard du néant, un milieu entre rien et tout.'

2. Ibid., 124.

3. See L. Piccioni, 'Le origini della "Terra promessa"', in *La terra promessa* (1954) 49–81. See also *Tutte le poesie*, 427–64.

4. In *Saggi e interventi*, 472. The whole argument seems to be taken from Schopenhauer who wrote: 'If I contemplate a tree aesthetically, i.e. with artistic eyes, and thus recognize, not it, but its Idea, it becomes at once of no consequence whether it is this tree or its predecessor which flourished a thousand years ago and whether the contemplator is this individual or any other who lived anywhere and at any time; the particular thing and the knowing individual are abolished with the principle of sufficient reason, and there remains nothing but the Idea and the pure subject of knowing ... (*The World as Will and Idea*, trans. by R. B. Haldane and J. Kemp, 3 vols., Routledge & Kegan Paul, London, 1883, see vol. I, 271.) The importance of Schopenhauer's aesthetics on the symbolists, and therefore on Ungaretti, is not to be underestimated.

5. See M. Hanne, 'Ungaretti's "La Terra Promessa" and the "Aeneid"', in *Italica* (1973) I, 3–25.

6. See V. Poschl, *The Art of Virgil*; especially the second chapter dealing with the major figures.

7. In *Life of a Man* (1958) trs. by Allen Mandelbaum.

CHAPTER SEVEN: The final collections

1. See P. Bigongiari, 'Sugli autografi del "Monologhetto"', now in G. Ungaretti, *Tutte le poesie*, 465–93.

2. G. Spagnoletti, *Tre poeti italiani del Novecento* (1956) 60.

3. C. Ossola, *Giuseppe Ungaretti* (1975) 391–3.

4. Choruses 10 to 13 followed by 9 were published in *Paragone* (1958), no. 98, under the title of 'Compleanno' and in a sense can be said to form a complete unit in their own right. They nevertheless merge symphonically into the wider lyrical texture of the definitive sequence of poems, as an integral part of a greater whole.

5. G. Debenedetti, 'L'infinito dal jet', in *Rinascita* (1970) 24, 14–16.

6. See 'La luce figurata dell'ultimo Ungaretti', in *L'Approdo letterario* (1972) no. 57, 31–49.

CHAPTER EIGHT: Conclusion

1. G. Petrocchi, 'Irrequietudine religiosa del decadentismo italiano', in *Humanitas* (1946) 2, 1157.

2. R. Negri, *Leopardi nella poesia italiana* (Le Monnier, Florence 1970) 115.

3. L. Silori, 'La difficile scoperta di Leopardi', in *Letteratura* (1958) 35–6, 225.

4. M. Petrucciani, *La poetica dell'ermetismo italiano* (Loescher, Turin 1955).

a) Ungaretti's works
POETRY

Il porto sepolto (Stabilimento Tipografico Friulano, Udine 1916)
La guerre (Établissements Lux, Paris 1919)
Allegria di naufragi (Vallecchi, Florence 1919)
Il porto sepolto (Stamperia Apuana, La Spezia 1923)
L'Allegria (Preda, Milan 1931)
Sentimento del tempo. Con un saggio di Alfredo Gargiulo (Novissima, Rome 1933)
L'Allegria (Novissima, Rome 1936)
Sentimento del tempo. Con un saggio di Alfredo Gargiulo (Novissima, Rome 1936)
Vita d' un uomo: L'Allegria (Mondadori, Milan 1942)
Vita d' un uomo: Sentimento del tempo. Con un saggio di Alfredo Gargiulo, (Mondadori, Milan 1943)
Frammenti per la terra promessa. Con una litografia originale di Pericle Fazzini (Concilium Lithographicum, Rome 1945)
Vita d' un uomo: Poesie disperse. Con l'apparato critico delle varianti di tutte le poesie e uno studio di Giuseppe De Robertis (Mondadori, Milan 1945)
Derniers jours 1919. A cura di Enrico Falqui (Garzanti, Milan 1947)
Vita d' un uomo: Il dolore (*1937–1946*) (Mondadori, Milan 1947)
La terra promessa. Frammenti. Con l'apparato critico delle varianti e uno studio di Leone Piccioni (Mondadori, Milan 1950)
Gridasti: Soffoco ... . Con cinque disegni di Léo Maillet (Fiumara, Milan 1951)
Un grido e paesaggi. Con uno studio di Piero Bigongiari e cinque disegni di Giorgio Morandi (Schwarz, Milan 1952)
Vita d' un uomo: La terra promessa. Frammenti. Con l'apparato critico delle varianti e uno studio di Leone Piccioni (Mondadori, Milan 1954)
Vita d' un uomo: Un grido e paesaggi. Con uno studio di Piero Bigongiari (Mondadori, Milan 1954)
Il taccuino del vecchio. Con testimonianze di amici stranieri del poeta raccolte a cura di Leone Piccioni, e uno scritto introduttivo di Jean Paulhan (Mondadori, Milan 1960)
Vita d' un uomo: Il taccuino del vecchio (Mondadori, Milan 1961)
75° compleanno: Il taccuino del vecchio, Apocalissi (Le Noci, Milan 1963)
Apocalissi e sedici traduzioni (Bucciarelli, Ancona 1965)
Ungaretti: Poesie. A cura di Elio Filippo Accrocca (Nuova Accademia, Milan 1964)
Il Carso non è piú un inferno. A cura di Vanni Scheiwiller, per festeggiare i 50 anni del primo libro di Ungaretti *Il Porto Sepolto* (1916) e la liberazione di Gorizia, 9 agosto 1916 (Scheiwiller, Milan 1966)
Morte delle stagioni: La terra promessa, Il taccuino del vecchio, Apocalissi. A cura di Leone Piccioni, con il Commento dell'autore alla *Canzone* (Fógola, Turin 1967)
Dialogo (Bruna Bianco – Giuseppe Ungaretti). Con una combustione di Burri e una nota di Leone Piccioni (Fógola, Turin 1968)

Allegria di Ungaretti. A cura di Annalisa Cima, con tre poesie inedite, una prosa rara e dodici fotografie di Ugo Mulas (Scheiwiller, Milan 1969)

Il dolore, con 36 xilografie di Pasquale Santoro (Rome 1969)

Croazia segreta, con la traduzione di Drago Invanišević, uno studio critico di Leone Piccioni e quattro acqueforti di Piero Dorazio (Grafica Romero, Rome 1969)

Tutte le poesie (Mondadori, Milan 1969). All refs from 6th ed., 1972.

L'impietrito e il velluto, grande foglio con due acqueforti di Piero Dorazio (Grafico Romero, Rome 1970)

PROSE

'Sete di Cristo' in *Il Simbolo*, vol.IV, Pro civitate christiana (Assisi 1947) 149–58

Il povero nella città (Edizioni della Meridiana, Milan 1949)

'Sentimento di Dio' in *Il problema di Dio*, a cura di G. Savio e T.Gregory, ed. 'Universale di Roma', (Rome 1949) 327–40

Il deserto e dopo. Prose di viaggio e saggi (Mondadori, Milan 1961)

Viaggetto in Etruria, con una acquaforte di Bruno Caruso (ALUT, Rome 1965)

Innocence et mémoire (Gallimard, Paris 1969). Appearing in the text as *Innocence*.

Propos improvisés (Gallimard, Paris 1972). With J. Amrouche

Lettere a un fenomenologo (All'Insegna del pesce d'oro, Milan 1972)

Vita d' un uomo: Saggi e interventi (Mondadori, Milan 1974). Appearing in the text as *Saggi*. For a virtually complete bibliography of Ungaretti's critical writings, see this volume, 1025–51

TRANSLATIONS

Traduzioni: Saint-John Perse, William Blake, Góngora, Essenin, Jean Paulhan, Affrica (Novissima, Rome 1936)

XXII Sonetti di Shakespeare scelti e tradotti da Giuseppe Ungaretti (Documento, Rome 1944)

Vita d' un uomo: 40 sonetti di Shakespeare tradotti (Mondadori, Milan 1946)

L'Après-midi et le Monologue d'un Faune di Mallarmé, tradotti da Giuseppe Ungaretti con litografie originali di Carlo Carrà (Il Balcone, Milan 1947)

Vita d' un uomo: Da Góngora e da Mallarmé (Mondadori, Milan 1948)

Vita d' un uomo: Fedra di Jean Racine (Mondadori, Milan 1950)

Finestra del caos, di Murilo Mendes (Scheiwiller, Milan 1961)

Vita d' un uomo: Visioni di William Blake, con un Discorsetto del traduttore e una appendice a cura di Mario Diacono (Mondadori, Milan 1965)

Saint-John Perse: Anabase, seguita dalle traduzioni di T.S.Eliot e Giuseppe Ungaretti, illustrata da Berrocal (Le Rame, Verona 1967)

Cinque poesie di Vinicius de Moraes, con una notizia sull'autore e quattro acqueforti di Piero Dorazio (Grafica Romero, Rome 1969)

TRANSLATIONS of Ungaretti into English

Life of a Man, a version with introduction by Allen Mandelbaum, Hamilton, London; New Directions, New York; Scheiwiller, Milan, 1958. Enlarged and reprinted as *Selected Poems of Giuseppe Ungaretti*, translated and edited by Allen Mandelbaum (Cornell University Press 1975)

Giuseppe Ungaretti Selected Poems, edited and translated by P. Creagh
(Penguin Books 1969)
Agenda, Giuseppe Ungaretti Special Issue, edited by Andrew Wylie
(London 1970). Contains selected translations of poetry and prose.

b) Select bibliography of criticism
This section contains all the books referred to in the text, together with
a number of others dealing specifically with Ungaretti's works:
MONOGRAPHS
G. CAMBON, *Giuseppe Ungaretti* (Columbia University Press, New
York/London 1967)
— *La poesia di Ungaretti* (Einaudi, Turin 1976)
G. CAVALLI, *Ungaretti* (Fabbri, Milan 1958)
I. GUTIA, *Linguaggio di Ungaretti* (Le Monnier, Florence 1959)
G. LUTI, *Invito alla lettura di Ungaretti* (Mursia, Milan 1974)
C. OSSOLA, *Giuseppe Ungaretti* (Mursia, Milan 1975)
L. PICCIONI, *Vita di un poeta Giuseppe Ungaretti* (Rizzoli, Milan 1970)
F. PORTINARI, *Giuseppe Ungaretti* (Borla, Turin 1967)
L. REBAY, *Le origini della poesia di Giuseppe Ungaretti* (Edizioni di
Storia e di Letteratura, Rome 1962)
GENERAL CRITICISM
L. ANCESCHI, *Le poetiche del Novecento in Italia* (Paravia, Turin 1972[4])
— *Barocco e Novecento* (Rusconi e Paolazzi, Milan 1960)
S. ANTONIELLI, *Aspetti e figure del Novecento* (Guanda, Parma 1955)
M. APOLLONIO, *Ermetismo* (Cedam, Padua 1945)
G. BACHELARD, *La poétique de l'espace* (Presses universitaires de France,
Paris 1957)
G. BÀRBERI SQUAROTTI, *La cultura e la poesia italiana del dopoguerra*
(Cappelli, Bologna 1968)
— *Il codice di Babele* (Rizzoli, Milan 1972)
M. BARRÈS, *Scènes et doctrines du nationalisme* (Plon, Paris 1945), vol. I.
P. BIGONGIARI, 'Sugli autografi del Monologhetto' in G. Ungaretti,
Un grido e paesaggi (Mondadori, Milan 1954)
—'Per un'analisi della lirica Sentimento del tempo', in *Letteratura*,
Anno V (1958) 35–6, 168–73
— *Poesia italiana del Novecento* (Fabbri, Milan 1960). Reprints various
articles on Ungaretti including the above.
— 'La luce figurata dell'ultimo Ungaretti' in *L'Approdo letterario*, Anno
XVIII (1972) no. 57, 31–49
W. BINNI, *La poetica del decadentismo italiano* (Sansoni, Florence 1963)
C. BO, *Otto studi* (Vallecchi, Florence 1939)
H. BRÉMOND, *La poésie pure, avec un débat sur la poésie de R. de Souza*
(Grasset, Paris 1926)
G. CAMBON, 'Ungaretti's poetry from evocation to invocation' in
Italian Quarterly. vol 5. (1961–2), nos. 21–2, 97–105
F. CAMON, *Il mestiere di poeta* (Lerici, Milan 1965). Contains an
interview with Ungaretti.
D. CAMPANA, *Canti orfici* (Ravagli, Marradi 1914; see also Vallecchi,
Florence 1952[4])

V. CARDARELLI, *Poesie* (Mondadori, Milan 1948)

— *Opere complete* (Mondadori, Milan 1962)

J. CARY, *Three modern Italian poets* (New York University Press, New York 1969)

G. CONTINI, *Esercizi di lettura* (Parenti, Florence 1939)

G. DEBENEDETTI, 'L'infinito dal jet', in *Rinascita* (1970) 24, 14–16

G. DE ROBERTIS, 'Sulla formazione della poesia di Ungaretti', in G. Ungaretti, *Poesie disperse* (Mondadori, Milan 1945)

— *Scrittori del Novecento* (Le Monnier, Florence 1946)

G. DI PINO, 'La presenza del Petrarca nella poesia italiana del Novecento', in *Italianistica* (1974) 2, 243–59

F. FLORA, *La poesia ermetica* (Laterza, Bari 1936)

— *Orfismo della parola* (Cappelli, Rocca Casciano 1953)

G. FOLENA AND OTHERS, *Ricerche sulla lingua poetica contemporanea*, Quaderni del circolo filologico padovano (Liviana, Padua 1966)

A. FRATTINI, *Poeti italiani del Novecento*, Accademia di studi 'Cielo d'Alcamo', Alcamo 1952

— *Da Tommaseo a Ungaretti* (Cappelli, Rocca San Casciano 1959)

H. FRIEDRICH, *La lirica moderna* (Garzanti, Milan 1961)

G. GENOT, *Sémantique du discontinu dans L'Allegria d'Ungaretti* (Klincksieck, Paris 1972)

F. GIANNESSI, *Gli ermetici* (La Scuola, Brescia 1951)

M. HAMBURGER, *The truth of poetry* (Penguin Books 1972)

M. HANNE, 'Ungaretti's La terra promessa and the Aeneid' in *Italica*, vol. L (1973) 1, 3–25

E. HUSSERL, *Ideas, pure phenomenology* (Allen & Unwin, London 1931)

F. J. JONES, 'Sulle varianti di Ungaretti' in *Cenobio*, Anno IX (1960) 1, 3–21

— *La poesia italiana contemporanea* (*da Gozzano a Quasimodo*) (D'Anna, Florence 1975)

O. MACRÍ, *Caratteri e figure della poesia italiana contemporanea* (Vallecchi, Florence 1956)

— *Realtà del simbolo* (Vallecchi, Florence 1968)

G. MARINO, *Opere* (Rizzoli, Milan 1967)

G. MARONE (see entry under Shimoi)

U. MARVARDI, 'Carattere della poesia d'oggi e Giuseppe Ungaretti', in *Responsabilità del sapere* (1947) fasc. 3, 77–97

G. MARZOT, *Il decadentismo italiano* (Cappelli, Bologna 1970)

B. MERRY, 'Semantica: "E chi sarà quel lepido"', in *L'Approdo letterario*, Anno XVIII (1972) 57, 133–6

F. MONTANARI, 'Poesia e durata', in *Studium* Anno LX (1964) 7–8, 477–83

A. NOFERI, *Le poetiche critiche novecentesche* (Le Monnier, Florence 1970)

R. NEGRI, *Leopardi nella poesia italiana* (Le Monnier, Florence 1970)

T. O'NEILL, 'Ungaretti and Foscolo: a question of taste' in *Italian quarterly* XII (1968) 73–89

— 'The problem of formalism in Ungaretti's Poetry', in *Italian quarterly* XIV (1970) no. 54, 59–73

— 'Ungaretti tra Leopardi e Góngora: appunti per una lettura di "Tu ti *spezzasti*"', in *Rivista di Letterature moderne e comparate* XXVII (1974) 1, 56–64

E.PACI, *Ungaretti e l'esperienza della poesia*, in *Letteratura*, Anno V (1958) 35–6, 83–93, now reproduced in G. Ungaretti, *Lettere a un fenomenologo*, ed. cit., 1972

G.PALERMO, 'Due articoli "egiziani" di Ungaretti e una poesia dispersa di Pea' in *Italianistica* (1973) 3, 557–68

R.PALMIERI, 'Civiltà d'oriente', in *Corriere adriatico* (1933) 15 April

B.PASCAL, *Pensées* (Nelson, Paris 1946)

E.PEA, *Vita in Egitto* (Mondadori, Milan 1949)

G.PETROCCHI, 'Irrequietudine religiosa del decadentismo italiano' in *Humanitas* (1946) 2, 1156–63

M.PETRUCCIANI, *La poetica dell'ermetismo italiano* (Loescher, Turin 1955)

— *Poesia pura e poesia esistenziale* (Loescher, Turin 1957)

L.PICCIONI, *Sui contemporanei* (Fabbri, Milan, n.d.)

F.PIEMONTESE, 'Il sentimento religioso nella poesia di Ungaretti' in *Studium*, Anno LV (1949) 5, 217–31

V.POSCHL, *The Art of Virgil* (University of Michigan Press, Ann Arbor 1962)

E.POUND, 'Vorticism' in *Fortnightly Review* (1914) 96

G.POZZI, *La poesia italiana del Novecento* (Einaudi, Turin 1965)

S.RAMAT, *L'ermetismo* (La Nuova Italia, Florence 1969)

— *Storia della poesia italiana del Novecento* (Mursia, Milan 1976)

M.RAYMOND, *De Baudelaire au surréalisme* (Correa, Paris 1933)

P.REVERDY, *Le gant de crin* (Plon, Paris 1927)

S.F.ROMANO, *Poetica dell'ermetismo* (Sansoni, Florence 1942)

P.SANAVIO, *Ungaretti* (Editions de *L'Herne*, Paris, n.d.)

A.SCHOPENHAUER, *The World as Will and Idea*, trans. by R.B. Haldane and J.Kemp, 3 vols. (Routledge & Kegan Paul, London 1883)

A.SERONI, *Ragioni critiche* (Vallecchi, Florence 1944)

E.SEWELL, *The Orphic Voice* (Yale University Press, New Haven 1960)

M.SHIMOI & G.MARONE, *Poesie giapponesi* (Ricciardi, Naples 1917)

L.SILORI, 'La difficile scoperta di Leopardi', in *Letteratura*, Anno V (1958) 35–6, 224–9

G.SINGH, 'The poetry of Giuseppe Ungaretti', in *Italian Studies* XXVIII (1973) 64–82

S.SOLMI, *Scrittori negli anni* (Il Saggiatore, Milan 1963)

G.SPAGNOLETTI, *Tre poeti italiani del Novecento* (ed.ERI, Turin 1956)

— *Poesia italiana contemporanea* (Guanda, Parma 1959) (Anthology)

N.TEDESCO, *La condizione crepuscolare* (La Nuova Italia, Florence 1970)

A.VALENTINI, *Semantica dei poeti* (Bulzoni, Rome 1970) (Ungaretti and Montale).

SPECIAL NUMBERS of reviews dedicated to Ungaretti

Letteratura, Anno V (1958), Nos.35–6, containing articles by A.Bonsanti, Libero de Libero, C.Pavolini, G.Ferrata, L.Piccioni, E.Paci, U. Marvardi, A.Schiaffini, G.Bàrberi Squarotti, O.Macrì, M.Gugliel-

minetti, A. Bocelli, U. Apollonio, G. Cavalli, P. Bigongiari, E. Cecchi,
G. De Robertis, A. Romanò, O. Navarro, E. Sanguineti, E. Falqui,
A. Guidi, L. Silori, L. Rogoni, L. Anceschi, G. Mariani, together with
many other shorter contributions including 'testimonianze'.

Galleria, special number in 1968 dedicated to Ungaretti's 8oth birthday. It
includes articles by Alberti, Palazzeschi, Accrocca, Anceschi, Arnao,
Assunto, Barbieri, Barlozzini, Berenice, Benari, Bigiaretti, Bigongiari,
Bocelli, Brignetti, Calvino, Ciccaglione, De Mandiargues, Guillevic,
Heurgon-Desjardins, Lucchese, Marianni, Marniti, Mauro, Mazzullo,
Petrucciani, Piccioni, Serra, Silori, Sinisgalli, Tognelli, Tundo,
Turoldo, Zàccaro. (edited by O. Sobrero.)

L'Approdo letterario, Anno XVIII (1972), 57. Contains articles by Luzi, Bo,
Debenedetti, Bigongiari, G. Quiriconi, Contini, Seroni, Rossi, A.
Rizzardi, Falqui, Cambon, B. Merry, and also an interview between
Ungaretti and J. Amrouche.

Forum italicum, VI, (1972), no. 2. Contains articles by Bàrberi Squarotti,
Bigongiari, Cambon, Caproni, Cary, Durán, Picon, Ramat, Rebay,
Guillén, Bergin.

See also special issue of *Agenda* listed under Ungaretti's poetic works, and
L'Herne listed under *P. Sanavio*.